TH

Please return o
is payable
one week f
elepho
during
794

1

3

Feminist Perspectives on The Past and Present Advisory Editorial Board

The *Real* Facts of Life:
Feminism and The Politics of Sexuality c 1850–1940

Margaret Jackson

Taylor & Francis
Publishers since 1798

UK   Taylor & Francis Ltd, 4 John St., London WC1N 2ET
USA   Taylor & Francis Inc., 1900 Frost Road, Suite 101, Bristol, PA 19007

First published 1994

A Catalogue Record for this book is available from the British Library

ISBN 0 7484 0099 0
ISBN 0 7484 0100 8 pbk

Library of Congress Cataloging-in-Publication Data are available on request

Series cover design by Amanda Barragry, additional artwork by Hybert • Design & Type. Illustration by Judy Stevens.

Typeset in 10/12 pt Times
by Graphicraft Typesetters Ltd., Hong Kong

Printed in Great Britain by Burgess Science Press, Basingstoke on paper which has a specified pH value on final paper manufacture of not less than 7.5 and is therefore 'acid free'.

For Joyce, with love

Acknowledgments

The roots of this book go back a very long way, and I would like to acknowledge first and foremost my friends in the Patriarchy Study Group,
without whom I would probably never even have begun. For a couple of
years in the late '70s and early '80s we met about every six weeks in each
others' houses in different parts of the country to engage in intensive discussion about sexuality and male power. It was those meetings which provided
the stimulus for my research, enabled me to develop some of my ideas, and
gave me the confidence to begin writing. Since that time I have received from
many other groups and individuals, directly or indirectly, a mixture of support, encouragement, criticism, friendship, love and practical help, which has
sustained me through the difficult times and enabled me to complete what
often seemed an impossible task.

I would like to thank in particular Rosemary Auchmuty, Joyce
Cunningham, David Doughan and the Fawcett Library, Ian Hextall, Sheila
Jeffreys, Pat Mahony, Maureen McNeil and Janice Raymond. I am also very
grateful to all those women at feminist workshops and conferences and on
Women's Studies courses, who have provided so many opportunities over the
years to discuss my work, and who have given me much valuable feedback.

Contents

Introduction

Feminism, Sexuality and Male Power
The Political *versus* the Natural

The research on which this book is based grew out of my involvement in the Women's Liberation Movement in the 1970s and 1980s, and especially in the Patriarchy Study Group. The group's main concern was to explore precisely how patriarchy worked to oppress women. We found ourselves continually returning to the centrality of sexuality, and in particular the construction of male sexuality and its function in the social control of women. I began my research by examining the role of sexologists, from Havelock Ellis to Kinsey and Masters and Johnson, in constructing common-sense notions about what is 'natural' in sexual behaviour, particularly in relation to the biological basis of male sexuality. It soon became clear that much of this 'objective' science of sexuality did little more than reinforce the well-known myth that the male sexual urge or drive is essentially aggressive and difficult or impossible to control. This patriarchal myth, now commonly believed to be a scientific 'fact', continues to legitimate the institution of prostitution and is still frequently used to excuse the whole gamut of male sexual violence, from minor forms of sexual harassment to sexual abuse of children and rape. It also became clear that sexologists did not develop their ideas in a political vacuum: that by the early twentieth century, when sexology began to be established as a science, feminists had for many years been engaged in a struggle to change male sexuality, by waging campaigns against male sexual violence and abuse of women and children, by challenging the institutions of marriage and prostitution, and by asserting in theory and in practice the right to female sexual autonomy. Despite the excellent research published by some feminists into these important and fascinating aspects of feminist history, there were still huge gaps in our knowledge, and I felt impelled to try to fill some of them. I wanted to know when and why sexuality became an important political issue for nineteenth-century feminists; to trace the history of the campaigns against the double standard of sexual morality; to discover more about feminists' ideas and theories about sexuality; and to understand why they were so divided in their views about sexual freedom and its relationship to

1

women's emancipation. This book is the product of my exploration of those questions, and of the relationship between what feminists were saying about sexuality and what the scientific 'experts' were saying about sexuality in the late nineteenth and early twentieth centuries.[1]

During the last twenty years feminist research into the history of sexuality has made important contributions to the theoretical understanding of the relationship between sexuality and male power. Most feminists agree that the construction of sexuality plays a crucial role in structuring or maintaining male power, though there is considerable disagreement about the centrality of sexuality, and about the processes by which it is constructed. Many of these political disagreements stem from different fundamental assumptions about the structure of male power as well as its relationship to sexuality, and I believe it is important for a writer to make her assumptions explicit at the outset, so that the reader knows where she is coming from. The fundamental assumptions on which this book is based are as follows: that sexuality is, and probably always has been (though in different ways at different times) a critical area of struggle between the sexes; that the process by which sexuality is constructed is to a large extent the outcome of such struggles; that female sexual autonomy is a *sine qua non* of women's liberation; and that the history of feminist struggles for sexual autonomy, which includes the history of male resistance, is of vital political importance to our continuing struggles. It is also crucial to make a clear distinction between the concept of female sexual autonomy, which is defined in terms of the right of women to define and control their own sexuality, and has its origins in feminism, and the concept of sexual 'liberation', which many feminists have criticized or rejected as male-defined. Much of the impetus of the radical feminism of the early 1970s stemmed from a realization that the 'sexual revolution', with which the concept of sexual liberation has been closely identified, was, from the point of view of women, no revolution at all. It was perceived as an ideology which legitimated male sexual values and practices, and functioned to make women's bodies ever more accessible to male sexual demands. One of my purposes in doing this research was to tease out some of the political and historical origins of the ideology of sexual 'liberation', and to differentiate it more clearly from the feminist concept of female sexual autonomy.[2]

My main aim in writing this book is to make a contribution towards understanding the history of the struggle for female sexual autonomy, a struggle which I have conceptualized in terms of a struggle between 'the political' and 'the natural'. My central argument is that the challenge to the specifically *sexual* basis of male power was central to Victorian and Edwardian feminism; and that, as an integral part of the broader struggle for women's social, economic and political independence, it posed a significant threat to the patriarchal social structure. More specifically, it posed a threat to the structure of hetero-relations which many feminists believe to constitute the sexual-economic basis of male power. 'Hetero-relations' have been defined by Janice Raymond as 'the wide range of affective, social, political and economic relations that are ordained between men and women by men'. She uses it in conjunction with the term 'hetero-reality', which she defines as 'the world view that woman exists always in relation to man'. Hetero-relations and hetero-reality as concepts have always been central to radical and revolutionary feminist theory and practice, though they have often been expressed in different terms and forms. My own definition of hetero-relations is adapted from Raymond: the totality of the sexual-political-economic relations between the sexes, by means of which male power is structured.[3]

The struggle for female sexual autonomy was conceptualized by nineteenth- and early-twentieth-century feminists in terms of the emancipation of women from 'sex slavery'. I have traced the progress of this struggle from the organized campaigns of the Victorian and Edwardian Women's Movement around marriage, spinsterhood, and the sexual double standard, up to the end of World War I and women's partial enfranchisement. The evidence suggests that by the end of the Edwardian era, feminists had made a significant advance, in theory and in practice, towards the goal of female sexual autonomy. A key factor in this process was the struggle to *politicize* sexuality: feminists succeeded in exposing the sexual exploitation and coercion of women in heterosexual relationships, inside and outside marriage, and in developing an analysis of male sexuality as a social construct and a weapon of male power. This entailed challenging the patriarchal model of sexuality, according to which men's imperious and aggressive sexual 'needs' were defined as 'natural'. Feminists argued that they were not natural but *political*, and demanded that men change. By the turn of the century, when the possibility of economic independence was becoming a reality for increasing numbers of women, feminists had also made significant progress towards the development of a feminist model of sexuality, which was potentially revolutionary in its implications, both for individual heterosexual relationships and for the structure of hetero-relations.

In the early twentieth century, however, the ideology of sexual 'liberation' began to gain ground, and after World War I, feminism, and especially the form of feminism which challenged the male sexual exploitation and control of women, went into decline. I argue that a key factor in this process was the intervention of sexology, which reinforced the patriarchal model of sexuality by endowing it with scientific legitimation, and subverted the further development of the feminist model of sexuality. What feminists had argued was *political*, sexologists redefined as *natural*, and asserted could not be changed. The construction of the sexological model of sexuality eroticized male dominance and female submission and redefined them as 'laws of nature', which protected them from feminist challenge. The sexological model, which was heavily promoted and popularized by means of the marriage manuals of the inter-war period, was essentially the patriarchal model, repackaged in scientific form. It substituted a male-defined concept of sexual 'liberation' for women's liberation, paving the way for the 'sexual revolution'. It undermined the struggle for female sexual autonomy and exacerbated tensions and divisions within the Women's Movement, thus making a significant contribution towards its decline.

Chapter 1 traces the process of politicizing sexuality within the Victorian and Edwardian Women's Movement, a development which was an integral part of the feminist challenge to the institution of marriage, and of the assertion of spinsterhood as a valid and positive choice. Feminist spinsters explicitly rejected the 'hetero-relational imperative' which is fundamental to male power: the myth that woman only exists in relation to man, and *for* man. They also rejected the underlying assumption that a woman without a man is sexually incomplete. The challenge to the double standard of sexual morality also grew out of the critique of marriage as a form of institutionalized sexual slavery, and developed over a period of more than fifty years into a series of campaigns against the whole range of male sexual exploitation and violence. In Chapter 2 there is a detailed analysis of these campaigns during the phase of militant feminism, including World War I. The aims of the campaigns were to break the conspiracy of silence and expose what feminists called 'the *real* facts of life' about female sexual slavery, and to force men to stop using sexuality as a weapon of male power. Chapters 3 and 4 examine in depth the feminist ideas and debates about sexuality in the late nineteenth and early twentieth centuries. Chapter 3 focuses exclusively on Elizabeth Blackwell, whose significance as a feminist sexual theorist, and the first woman to analyze sexuality from both a feminist and a scientific perspective, has been almost entirely ignored. I argue that her radical redefinition of 'the natural' provided a theoretical basis, both for the challenge to the patriarchal model of sexuality, and also for the construction of a feminist model of sexuality, based on the concept of female sexual autonomy. In Chapter 4 I explore further developments of this model at the turn of the century, as well as the tensions and divisions between feminists around sexuality which sharpened during the phase of militant feminism. In Chapter 5 I analyze the sexological model of sexuality which emerged around the same time, arguing that it gave scientific legitimation to the patriarchal model and undermined the construction of a feminist model of sexuality. The main focus of the chapter is Havelock Ellis, who, as the 'founding father' of sexology, was a key figure in reasserting patriarchal definitions of the 'natural', and eroticizing male dominance and female submission by means of the 'art of love'. Chapter 6 is devoted to a reassessment of the role of Marie Stopes in promoting her own, idiosyncratic version of the sexological model. I analyze the contradictions inherent in her prescriptions for overcoming marital sexual disharmony, explaining these in terms of her attempt to 'marry' the feminist and scientific models of sexuality. Chapter 7 examines the popularization of the sexological model by means of marriage manuals during the inter-war period, and explores the anti-feminist implications of the 'facts of life' which the new sex 'experts' purveyed.

Notes

1   Some of the work of the Patriarchy Study Group, including my own research into
Havelock Ellis, Kinsey, and Masters and Johnson, was published in *The Sexuality
Papers* (Coveney *et al.*, 1984).

2   'The right of all women to define their own sexuality' was originally included as
part of the sixth demand of the Women's Liberation Movement, which now demands an end to discrimination against lesbians. After considerable and heated
debate at the British National Women's Liberation Conference in Birmingham
in 1978, it was decided that 'the right of all women to define their own sexuality'
should become a statement of principle preceding all the other demands. See
Feminist Anthology Collective (1981, pp. 172–4). For critiques of the 'sexual
revolution' and the concept of sexual 'liberation' see Coveney *et al.* (1984) and
Rhodes and McNeill (1985).

3   Raymond (1986), esp. pp. 3–7. See also Myron and Bunch (1975); Shulman (1980);
Rich (1981); Coveney *et al.* (1984); Jeffreys (1985).

Chapter 1

Sex, Class and Hetero-Relations
Feminism and the Politicization of Sexuality in Victorian and Edwardian England

The process of politicizing sexuality is as old as feminism itself, though it has been given varying degrees of emphasis at different times and by different individuals and groups of feminists. In histories of British feminism there has been a tendency to regard the campaigns against the Contagious Diseases Acts in the late nineteenth century as marking the beginning of the process, but the political and intellectual roots of these campaigns go back much further, before the development of an organized Women's Movement. Issues such as prostitution, spinsterhood, celibacy, the double standard of sexual morality, and critiques of male sexual behaviour have been recurrent themes in feminist writing since at least the seventeenth century. The first British feminist to articulate an analysis of female sexual slavery as an integral part of a general analysis of women's oppression was Mary Wollstonecraft, and there is a strong continuity between her ideas and those of Victorian and Edwardian feminists. Wollstonecraft's feminist rationalism, and specifically her insistence that sexual passion could and should be tempered by reason, laid the groundwork for the campaigns around marriage, prostitution and the sexual double standard which began during the second half of the nineteenth century and continued right up to and beyond World War I.

A Vindication of the Rights of Woman, which was first published in 1792, was as far as we know the first theoretical statement of the link between sexuality and women's oppression. In it Wollstonecraft described marriage as 'legal prostitution', arguing that wife and prostitute were both equally oppressed, since both were forced by social and economic necessity to earn their keep by selling their bodies. She also argued that it was male passion, or sensuality, which was responsible for the political subordination of women: 'All the causes of female weakness, as well as depravity . . . branch out of one grand cause, want of chastity in man'. She frequently described women as 'slaves of casual lust', forced to be 'slaves to their persons', sometimes comparing women directly with African slaves. She also made it clear that she saw male behaviour as socially constructed, a product of tyranny rather than nature, just as she saw women's many faults and weaknesses as a result of oppression. She advocated passionless friendship between husband and wife, after a brief period of passion which she believed would naturally die if not artificially stimulated. She believed that sexual passion, or appetite, could be transformed into love and affection, which alone could lay the foundations for a reasonable and virtuous relationship between the sexes. She did not believe that passion was in itself a bad thing, but that the sexuality of both sexes could be rationally controlled and that women's emancipation *required* that men cease to be sensualists. As long as men were sensualists, she thought, women would be their slaves.[1]

As we shall see it was this feminist rationalism, rather than sexual puritanism or prudery, which underpinned the demands of Victorian and Edwardian feminists for chastity, purity, and an end to the double moral standard. It is important to be clear that there was a crucial distinction between puritanical and feminist demands for chastity. Puritanical demands for chastity were based on the assumption that sexuality is a natural or animal instinct which must be controlled in the interests of the 'social order'; in other words in the interests of the maintenance of patriarchy, class, and other forms of social inequality. Feminists' demands for chastity, in contrast, stemmed from the belief that sexuality was socially constructed and that male sexuality was a political weapon used to maintain male power. For feminists, the struggle for equality entailed challenging patriarchal definitions of what was natural in male sexual behaviour and heterosexual relations. To Wollstonecraft, as to later feminists, male sensuality was a means of enslaving women and, far from being natural, a violation of nature's laws.

The notion that passion should be tempered by reason was also a major theme in the Utopian Socialist movement of the early nineteenth century, particularly within Owenite Socialism, where there is clear evidence of a struggle between feminists and others around marriage and sexuality. Anna Wheeler, for instance, argued that woman's love had 'fixed and perpetuated the degradation of her sex' and that the 'invigorating influence of a co-operating reason' needed to be brought to bear in sexual relationships. Most of the men, and some of the women, espoused a libertarian sexual philosophy, underpinned by a male-defined concept of sexuality as a compulsive urge or instinct which must have an outlet. It was only the institution of marriage which they saw as oppressive; sexuality itself, freed from the constraints of marriage, was assumed to be a natural phenomenon, and therefore outside the realm of the political. The feminists within the Owenite movement challenged this male-centred form of sexual radicalism by arguing that only when all other sources of sexual inequality had been eliminated would greater sexual freedom be possible without greater sexual exploitation of women. Despite male protestations about 'natural laws' they not only questioned the masculine concept of sexual liberation but dared to critique male sexual behaviour. They pointed out the differences between women's sexual feelings and needs and those of men, emphasizing the importance of affection and respect as against the 'animal propensities' of the men. This suggests that they were beginning to challenge the patriarchal model of sexuality and to redefine sexuality in a more woman-centred way.[2]

It is clear then that long before the development of an organized Women's Movement some women (and probably many more than we actually know about) recognized that heterosexual relations were power relations. Although it was not until the late nineteenth century that feminists directly confronted the sexual double standard and the patriarchal model of sexuality, feminists within the early Women's Movement did not ignore issues of sexuality. The institution of marriage was for them a critical area of debate and struggle and provided a context in which they were able to continue to articulate their concerns about male sexuality, and to explore the relationship between sexuality and male power.

Marriage and the Sexual Economics of Male Power

Feminist ideas about sexuality are inextricably linked to feminist struggles around marriage, which has always been seen as the pivotal institution of male power. As the Women's Movement gained momentum from the mid nineteenth century onwards, the institution of marriage became a central focus of feminist criticism and challenge. Most historians have viewed the significance of their campaigns primarily in terms of the legal reforms that were achieved, such as the Married Women's Property Acts. What women gained however needs to be measured not simply in terms of reforms but also in terms of consciousness-raising and theorizing the relationship between marriage, sexuality, and male power. Most feminists viewed marriage as a form of institutionalized female sexual slavery, the legalized equivalent of prostitution. In all the key feminist texts of the period which dealt with the issue, the marriage relation was conceptualized in terms of a power relation: women were forced to earn their living by selling their bodies to men. Although most feminists sought to reform marriage rather than abolish it, the challenge to marriage represented an attack on the sexual-economic basis of male power. Coupled with the campaigns for women's economic independence, for equal access to education, and for women's suffrage, it threatened the system of hetero-relations through which male power is constituted.

When an organized women's movement emerged in the 1850s a protracted campaign for the legal reform of marriage was immediately launched. Barbara Bodichon, the main instigator of the first Married Women's Property Bill of 1856, simultaneously launched a campaign for women's economic independence, which incorporated a critique of marriage as an institution. She attacked the assumption that woman was only made for man, and that marriage was her one true vocation, insisting that the practice among men of exchanging women and forcing women into economic dependence on them was prostitution, and was degrading to women: 'Fathers have no right to cast the burden of the support of their daughters on other men . . . It lowers the dignity of women; and tends to prostitution, whether legal or on the streets'.[3] This first attempt at feminist reform of the institution of marriage was frustrated by the Matrimonial Causes Act of 1857. Although this legislation gave wives very limited rights in respect of their property and earnings, its anti-feminist implications in terms of sexuality and male power were quite profound. It represented in effect the encoding into statute law of the double standard of sexual morality. Under the provisions of the Act a husband could divorce his wife for adultery alone, but a wife needed to have additional grounds such as cruelty or desertion. The fundamental assumption underlying the Act was that marital infidelity on the part of husbands could not in itself constitute grounds for divorce because it was *natural* and therefore to be expected; in women, however, such behaviour was unnatural and unacceptable and therefore *could* constitute grounds for divorce. Elizabeth Blackwell commented in 1902 that the Act had a very bad effect in terms of legitimizing the double standard and encouraging the myth that men were physiologically incapable of controlling their sexual impulses: 'In our own country the unjust condonation of adultery, by law, in 1857, against the strenuous opposition of far-seeing statesmen, has educated more than one generation in a false and degrading idea of physiology'.[4]

One of the unintended consequences of the Act of 1857 was that the newly-established divorce courts highlighted the issue of wife-battering, stimulating the development of a feminist analysis of the politics of male violence. Frances Power Cobbe, a spinster and member of the Married Women's Property Committee, publicized cases in which men who brutally assaulted or murdered their wives for trivial acts of 'disobedience' or 'nagging' received only light sentences or even escaped scot-free; while women who had done no more than defend themselves from their husbands' brutality received harsh sentences. She argued that violence against women was not the aberrant behaviour of a few isolated males but an extension of a system of laws and practices, encoded by men, which decreed that whatever women had was available to them as of right. She maintained that the relationship between husband and wife was that of master and slave, that marriage was a structure created by men for men, to give them absolute power over women; and that they exercised control in two ways – by purse or stick.[5]

There was little pressure from feminists for easier divorce. This seems to have been partly for religious reasons, and partly because they were aware that until women were able to be economically independent of men, divorce would almost invariably make them even more vulnerable. The issue of free love was also avoided for similar reasons. During the 1880s and 1890s however there was a revival of the ideology of free love, and some individual feminists were prepared to debate the issue publicly. A few even dared to flout conventional morality and enter into free unions with men because they believed that it would enable them to have greater control over their own lives and bodies. They were careful however to make a clear distinction between the *feminist* concept of free love, which was based on rejection of the notion of women as the sexual property of their husbands, and the male-defined libertarian concept, which they associated with sexual irresponsibility or 'excess'. John Stuart Mill, whose writings were strongly influenced by Harriet Taylor and much quoted by feminists, declared: 'Among the barbarisms which law and morals have not yet ceased to sanction, the most disgusting surely is, that any human being should be permitted to consider himself as having a *right* to the person of another'. He considered that wives, being 'but personal body-servants of a despot', were in some respects less privileged than the female slave, who in Christian countries had at least in theory the right and the moral obligation to refuse her master 'the last familiarity'. Not so the wife:

> however brutal a tyrant she may be chained to – though she may know that he hates her – though it may be his daily pleasure to torture her, and though she may feel it impossible not to loathe him – he can claim from her and enforce the lowest degradation of a human being, that of being made the instrument of an animal function contrary to her inclinations.

Harriet Taylor and Mill attempted their own private reform of marriage by making a written declaration that Mill disclaimed and repudiated 'all pretensions to have acquired any rights whatever by virtue of such marriage', and that Harriet 'retains in all respects whatever the same absolute freedom of action and disposal of herself and of all that does or may at any time belong to her, as if no such marriage had taken place'.[6]

Those feminists who chose 'free love' as a strategy for overcoming the institutionalized sexual slavery inherent in marriage made it clear that control over their own bodies was paramount and that the concept of 'conjugal rights' was the most abhorrent aspect of marriage. Annie Besant, for instance, declared:

> A married woman loses control over her own body; it belongs to her owner, not to herself; no force, no violence, on the husband's part in conjugal relations is regarded as possible by the law; she may be suffering, ill, it matters not; force or constraint is recognised by the law as rape, in all cases save that of marriage; the law 'holds it to be a felony to force even a concubine or harlot' . . . but no rape can be committed by a husband on a wife; the consent given in marriage is held to cover the life . . .

Elizabeth Wolstenholme also insisted that sexual coercion of the wife by the husband was rape, and that 'Only with the full recognition of the wife's continuing right of physical inviolability will the institution be accepted by either party in the near future'. Most leading feminists publicly disapproved of what they regarded as 'irregular' lifestyles and the movement as a whole, being concerned to maintain an image of respectability, distanced itself publicly from advocates of 'free love'. When Elizabeth Wolstenholme became pregnant as a result of her relationship with Ben Elmy she yielded to pressure and married him, though both took the name Wolstenholme Elmy as a gesture against patriarchal marriage. What women said in public, however, was not necessarily the same as what they said in private. Henrietta Muller, for instance, told Maria Sharpe privately that she was against marriage, but at the Men and Women's Club, of which they were both members, she argued only for legal reform. She believed that only in the future, *after* women were free, would alternatives to marriage be possible. The name originally proposed for the Club, which was founded in 1885, was the 'Wollstonecraft Club', but the women members objected because of the possibly damaging association with Wollstonecraft's 'irregular' lifestyle. They were concerned to avoid being branded 'free lovers' and opposed the membership of Eleanor Marx because of her free union with Edward Aveling. Women in the Club expressed their abhorrence at men's conjugal rights, but 'they were also resolute that *for the present*, given women's vulnerability and disadvantage, *reformed* legal marriage was infinitely preferable to a non-marital relationship'. They also made it clear that marriage reform required, first and foremost, the reform of the man, especially his sexual behaviour, and that once economically independent, women would refuse marriage, unless men reformed.[7]

As feminist activism and radicalism became stronger and more visible, so the analysis of the relationship between the institution of marriage and the sexual-economic basis of male power gained in depth and clarity. By the turn of the century a class analysis of women's position was being articulated, though not in the narrow economic sense in which that term is normally used. Women's class position in relation to men was seen by many feminists as deriving ultimately from their sex. There were two aspects to this: first, women *as* a sex were subordinate to men; and second, men had organized society in such a way that women's *sexuality* – their 'power of sex attraction' – was virtually their sole means of livelihood. Thus for women the heterosexual relation was a power relation, both in the economic sense, and in the sense of being compulsory. It was this understanding of how male power is constituted which underpinned the concept of women as a class.

One of the best examples of this trend in feminist theory was Charlotte Perkins Gilman, an American feminist who was recognized on both sides of the Atlantic as a major feminist theorist. Gilman argued that the relationship between the sexes was primarily an economic one, and that the basis of that relation was 'sex attraction'. She regarded marrage as the most degraded relationship in the animal kingdom:

We are the only animal species in which the female depends on the male for food, the only animal species in which the sex relation is

> also an economic relation. With us an entire sex lives in a relation of economic dependence on the other sex.

She believed that through marriage men had appropriated women's resources, allowing women to retain and to sell only themselves – their bodies, their labour, their emotional resources. As a result women were 'over-sexed', in the sense that their sexual characteristics had been unnaturally exaggerated, like the cow who has been bred as a milking-machine. They were not even allowed to trade openly; any woman who openly classified marriage as a market and sought to make a mercenary match was condemned, and those who realistically sold their wares as prostitutes were made outcasts. Women who did not secure a livelihood through marriage – 'old maids' – were despised because they had no value; because there were no buyers for their sex attraction they were failures, and figures of fun and ridicule. Women in general, therefore, were compelled to marry, regardless of their true wishes and regardless of the way men treated them: 'The fear exhibited that women generally, once fully independent will not marry, is proof of how well it has been known that only dependence forced them to marriage as it was'.[8]

Hetero-relations as the basis of male power was also the theme explored by Cicely Hamilton in *Marriage as a Trade*. Hamilton was a playwright and a member of the Actresses' Franchise League, and supported the militant wing of the suffrage movement. Her ideas provided a major stimulus to the militant feminist campaign against the double standard of sexual morality. Like Gilman, Hamilton argued that marriage was both a sexual and an economic relation. She defined woman's relationship to marriage as 'the exchange of her person for the means of subsistence', arguing that while marriage was voluntary for men, for women it was practically compulsory: 'In sexual matters it would appear that the whole trend and tendency of man's relations to woman has been to make refusal impossible and to cut off every avenue of escape from the gratification of his desire'. She argued that man's motive in concentrating all woman's energy on the trade of marriage was to deny it any other outlet, and that his persistent refusal to allow women new spheres of activity was rooted in the knowledge that 'economic independence would bring with it the power of refusal'.

Because all her energy had to be concentrated on the trade of marriage, Hamilton considered that contemporary woman was largely a 'manufactured product', the result of the unnatural, 'hothouse' forcing of two of her faculties to the obliteration of all others. These two faculties were motherhood and, above all, sex: 'Sex is only one of the ingredients of the natural woman – an ingredient which has assumed undue and exaggerated proportions in her life owing to the fact that it has for many generations furnished her with the means of livelihood'. Woman was forced to cultivate only 'those narrow and peculiar qualities of mind and body' which would fulfil the demand 'that she should enkindle and satisfy the desire of the male, who would thereupon admit her to such share of the property he possessed or earned as should seem good to him'. Hamilton observed that all women were perceived by men as having 'a definite and necessary physical relation to man', without which they were defined as 'incomplete ... for all practical purposes non-existent'. In addition to the economic pressures which forced most women to marry there was another compelling social pressure: 'a fear of spinsterhood with its accompaniments, scorn and confession of failure in your trade'. How many children, she wondered, were born each year merely because their mothers were afraid of being called old maids?

Despite the man-made divisions between women, Hamilton argued that fundamentally they were all in the same position in relation to men, and hence members of one class. As a consequence many of their attributes and characteristics were 'not really the attributes and characteristics of their sex, but of their class – a class persistently set apart for the duties of sexual attraction, house-ordering and the bearing of children'. Any woman who had realized this would no longer despise the prostitute, for she would remember that she too had been brought up to believe that 'nothing counted in her but the one capacity – the power of awaking desire', and that it alone must be her means of livelihood. There was, in any case, no essential difference between marriage and its 'unlegalised equivalent'. Hamilton observed that there were already signs that women were becoming conscious of themselves as a class, and conscious of a new power – the power of organization. The experience of working together – in the mill, in the factory, in the office, as well as in political organizations, was breaking down the age-old isolation of women, so that 'In short, for the first time in her history she is becoming actively class-conscious'.[9]

Another key text of the Edwardian period was Olive Schreiner's *Woman and Labour*. Essentially this was a demand for the right of women to be economically independent of men, and although it was critical of marriage as an institution, it offered a very different analysis from those of Gilman and Hamilton. Schreiner viewed the struggle between the sexes as a consequence of the general upheaval in society, the conflict between old and new ideals 'in which the determining element is not sex, but the point of evolution which the race or the individual has reached'.[10] She emphasized that she did not blame men as a sex for women's oppression, and argued that if women became economically independent, both patriarchal marriage and prostitution would cease to exist, and the relations between the sexes, inside and outside marriage, would blossom and flourish. Hamilton and Schreiner represented different strands in feminist thinking about the relationship between sexuality and women's oppression. For Schreiner, the primary cause of women's oppression was economic, and sexuality and hetero-relations were secondary issues; whereas for Hamilton, hetero-relations were absolutely intrinsic to male power – its basis was both sexual and economic. The conflict between the sexes was seen by Hamilton, not as a consequence of women's economic subordination, but as inherent in it. While Schreiner saw women's emancipation in terms of an evolutionary change toward economic independence and greater cooperation between the sexes, Hamilton saw it much more in terms of a fundamental power struggle between opposing classes.

The explanation for these differences lies to a large extent in the different political roots of Hamilton and Schreiner. Schreiner distanced herself from direct involvement in the Women's Movement. Her political and intellectual roots lay in the Men and Women's Club, a small, rather elitist mixed group which was heavily dominated by Karl Pearson's brand of social and biological Darwinism. She also had a close personal relationship with Pearson, and with Havelock Ellis, the 'founding father' of sexology, with whom she had many discussions about sexuality.[11] Hamilton, in contrast, was an active member of one of the leading militant suffrage organizations, and was directly involved in feminist politics. She was also a spinster and, as we shall see in the following section, saw spinsterhood both as a positive choice for women, and as a means of resisting female sexual slavery. *Marriage as a Trade* represented, in my view, a significant advance in the theorization of the link between marriage and the sexual-economic basis of male power, and pointed towards the possibility of a far more revolutionary change in the relations between the sexes than *Woman and Labour*.

Although most feminists were united in their condemnation of institutionalized female sexual slavery, only a small minority believed that the abolition of the legal bond of marriage would in itself bring about a radical change in hetero-relations. Most feminists actively supported campaigns which were aimed both at reforming the institution itself and at securing economic independence for all women, so that no woman should be forced into marriage – or prostitution – by economic necessity. By the end of the nineteenth century significant gains had been made: the married woman was at last recognized in law as a person in her own right and entitled to retain ownership of her property and income, and a degree of economic independence was becoming more of a reality, though still mainly for middle-class women.[12] The struggle against conjugal rights and, more generally, for female sexual autonomy, inside and outside marriage, intensified, and will be explored in subsequent chapters.

The Silent Strike: Spinsterhood and the Power of Refusal

For some feminists marriage reform was simply not radical enough. There was, throughout the Victorian and Edwardian periods, a growing and increasingly vocal proportion of women who chose to challenge the system of hetero-relations by resisting marriage and advocating spinsterhood. Feminist spinsters asserted that spinsterhood was a positive choice for women, both as a form of resistance to female sexual slavery, and as valid and fulfilling in its own right. They explicitly rejected, not only the patriarchal doctrine that woman's primary vocation was marriage and motherhood, but the hetero-relational imperative, with its underlying assumption that a woman without a man was sexually incomplete. Towards the end of the nineteenth century, as more and more middle-class women became economically independent of men, more and more feminists made it clear that their decision to remain single was a political decision.

The growing imbalance in the sex ratio during the Victorian period is generally acknowledged as one of the most significant reasons for the development of the Women's Movement.[13] In 1850 the *Westminster Review* claimed in alarmist tones that there were 500,000 'surplus women', and bemoaned the apparently increasing unpopularity of marriage, especially among women. The census of 1851 noted that for the age group 40 to 45, a quarter of the women were unmarried. Frances Power Cobbe claimed in 1862 that the proportion of spinsters was 30 per cent, and that one in four was certain never to marry. She also pointed out wryly that roughly 25 per cent of men were bachelors; but that very little concern was expressed about *them*! Contemporary research showed that most of the 'redundant' women were from the middle class. In 1892, Clara Collet, a social investigator, reported that in the richer suburbs unmarried women aged 35 to 45 outnumbered unmarried men by over three to one, and only a third of these were domestic servants. The fact that there was considerable demand for domestic servants also meant that working-class spinsters were not perceived as a problem.[14]

The economic position of the middle-class Victorian spinster, who was virtually excluded from the world of paid employment and dependent upon the unpredictable generosity of male relatives, was for all but a privileged few extremely precarious. Bessie Rayner Parkes, while acknowledging the theoretical foundations of feminism, considered that it was the economic position of the single woman which constituted the material basis of the emergence of the Women's Movement: 'except for the material need which exerted a constant pressure over a large and educated class, the "woman's movement" could never have become in England a subject of popular comment, and to a certain extent of popular sympathy'. It was thus not surprising that many spinsters were in the forefront of campaigns for women's education and women's employment rights, and that their efforts were directed in particular towards achieving economic independence for women. Although some of the most prominent feminists, for example Josephine Butler and Millicent Fawcett, were married, it is probably fair to say that spinsters constituted the backbone of the Victorian Women's Movement.[15]

Twentieth-century discussions of the 'plight' of the spinster are usually based on the tacit assumption that, in addition to economic deprivation, she must have suffered acutely from loneliness, sexual frustration and the denial of her maternal instincts. The possibility that the spinster actively chose and enjoyed her single (and usually child-free) state has, until recently, rarely been considered.[16] Yet Victorian spinsters were in the forefront of the attack on the institution of marriage and explicitly rejected the heterosexist belief that a woman without a man was 'incomplete'. Frances Power Cobbe, for instance, asserted that the belief that marriage should be the chief aim of a woman's life was 'disgraceful and abominable', and suggested that celibacy for women might be preferable to marriage and male domination, especially in view of the prevalence of male violence against wives that the divorce court was currently bringing to light. Cobbe's reasons for advocating spinsterhood were not, however, purely negative: she painted an extremely attractive picture of the spinster's life:

> The 'old maid' of 1861 is an exceedingly cheery personage, running about untrammelled by husband or children . . . in the power of devoting her *whole* time and energies to some benevolent task, she is enabled to effect perhaps some greater good than would otherwise have been possible. . . . And further, if a woman have but strength to make up her mind to a single life, she is enabled by nature to be far more independently happy therein than a man in the same position. . . . If she have no sister, she has yet inherited the blessed power of a woman to make true and tender friendships, such as not one man's heart in a hundred can even imagine; and while he smiles scornfully at the idea of a friendship meaning anything beyond acquaintance at a club or the intimacy of a barrack, she enjoys one of the purest of pleasures and the most unselfish of all affection.[17]

In Victorian Britain 'celibate' simply meant unmarried, and this is still its dictionary definition. Given the religious and moral prohibitions on sexual relationships outside marriage, celibacy would also have implied sexual abstinence, though it did not acquire this specific connotation until well into the twentieth century, when it became possible to speak of a person as being unmarried but not necessarily celibate. This description probably applied to a number of Victorian spinsters, and it would certainly be incorrect to assume that they were not involved in sexual relationships, though it may of course have been true of some. Middle-class feminists were very concerned with respectability, and few of those who had sexual relationships with men were sufficiently daring to admit it openly. It is even more difficult to know how many were engaged in sexual relationships with other women. Most people do not leave evidence of their sexual activities for historians to find, and the historical invisibility of lesbians has been made especially acute by the anti-lesbianism of those such as heirs and biographers who have destroyed letters, diaries, or other potentially significant material. Nevertheless there is growing evidence that many women during this period were involved in 'passionate friendships' with other women, some of whom were spinsters, and some married. Frances Power Cobbe, for instance, had a long-term relationship with the sculptor Mary Lloyd, and wrote in her autobiography: 'Of a friendship like this . . . I shall not be expected to say more'. We also know, with varying degrees of certainty, that many other feminists were probably what we would regard today as lesbians: examples include Emily Faithfull, who campaigned for women's employment rights and founded the Victoria Press;

Edith Simcox, writer, lecturer and trade union organizer; Sophia Jex-Blake, who fought for women to be admitted to the medical profession; Ethel Smyth, musician and composer, who worked closely with the Pankhursts; Margaret Haig, later Lady Rhondda, suffragette and editor of *Time and Tide*; Eleanor Rathbone, constitutional suffragist and, from 1929, Member of Parliament; and many, many more.[18]

There were also many strong, independent women who were only peripherally or not at all involved with the Women's Movement, and whose relationships with women could be described as 'passionate', 'romantic', or 'lesbian'. The question of the distinction between 'passionate friendship' and lesbianism is an extremely complex one, not least because of the difficulties in defining the word 'lesbian' in a historical context. Even lesbian feminist historians disagree about this. Some follow Adrienne Rich's concept of the lesbian continuum, which ranges from those who may be in relationships with men but have emotional ties to other women, to those with a full emotional, sexual, and political commitment to women. Some argue that this is too broad and desexualizes lesbianism, which should only apply to those who have explicitly sexual feelings for women which are expressed through genital contact. Others argue that lesbianism should be defined not only in sexual but in political terms: that lesbians are women who make their love for women central to their existence and refuse to organize their lives around men as patriarchy demands. Ann Ferguson has defined a lesbian as 'a woman who has sexual and erotic-emotional ties primarily with women' or who 'sees herself as centrally involved with a community of such women', but adds that she should also be 'self-identified' as a lesbian. A major problem with this latter criterion is the difficulty of obtaining evidence. As Lis Whitelaw argues in her biography of Cicely Hamilton, there is nothing in the surviving material in which Hamilton explicitly defines herself as a lesbian, 'but in every other way she fulfils Ferguson's criteria, especially in terms of the community within which she chose to live her life'.[19]

As the Lesbian History Group has pointed out, 'lesbian experience varies not only from era to era but from individual to individual according to both the prevailing theories of lesbianism and each woman's acceptance or rejection of them.'[20] This implies that there can never be a fixed or absolute definition of what it means to be a lesbian. When we add to this the problem that the dominant patriarchal definition of lesbianism in the nineteenth and twentieth centuries has been that of sexual perversion, with all the adverse consequences of this, such as withholding, distortion, or destruction of evidence, whether by others or by self-censorship, it is clear that it is very difficult indeed to estimate how many Victorian and Edwardian spinsters were lesbians. Nevertheless it is extremely important to challenge the heterosexist assumption that spinsters who were not involved in sexual relationships with men must have been sexually frustrated. Such an assumption not only denies the existence of lesbians but also equates celibacy in the sense of sexual abstinence with sexual frustration. It is significant that according to the prevailing patriarchal model of sexuality there is no way of describing celibacy in positive terms: it can only be described in terms of a lack of sexual activity, with the implication of deprivation or abnormality.

Regardless of whether Victorian and Edwardian spinsters were, or were perceived as, lesbians, they were certainly perceived by most men as a threat. Spinsterhood was seen as so threatening by some male commentators that extreme solutions were proposed, from female emigration – named by Cobbe more precisely as 'deportation' or 'transportation' – to polygyny and even female infanticide! Cobbe thought the reason why spinsterhood was such a threat was obvious: if, as a result of increasing educational and employment opportunities, marriage were to become for women a matter of real choice, it was possible that more and more women might reject their 'one true vocation'. She insisted that instead of forcing women to marry through economic necessity or 'dinning into their ears from childhood that marriage is their one vocation and concern in life' feminists would act on the reverse principle:

> We shall make single life so free and happy that they shall not have one temptation to change it save the one temptation which *ought* to determine them – namely, love ... it is only on the standing-ground of a happy and independent celibacy that a woman can really make a free choice in marriage.[21]

By the turn of the century there were already definite signs that the threat to male power posed by the spinster was beginning to materialize. Feminist agitation had led to the expansion of higher education for women and the opening up of some of the professions. Changes in the capitalist economy had also led to other changes in the occupational structure, such as the expansion in white-collar occupations, which provided greater opportunities for the employment of women. The possibility, albeit still very limited, of economic independence which such changes offered, meant that more and more women, particularly from the middle classes, were in a position to exercise what Cicely Hamilton called their 'power of refusal'. Hamilton, who, as we have already seen, cited the fear of spinsterhood as one of the social pressures impelling women towards marriage, was able to write in 1909:

> I suppose that in the recent history of woman nothing is more striking than the enormous improvement that has taken place in the social position of the spinster.... By sheer force of self-assertion we have lifted ourselves from the dust where we once crawled as worms and no women; we no longer wither on the virgin thorn – we flourish on it....

In the course of a public debate with G.K. Chesterton at Queen's Hall in 1911 she asked: 'Do you suppose that forty or fifty years ago a woman would have dared to stand up on a platform and say, without the slightest shame, that she was over thirty and unmarried?' Answering her own question she declared: 'She could not do it. That is past'.[22]

Hamilton believed that the spinster was 'by her very existence . . . altering the male conception of her sex', and that she was steadily destroying the prestige of marriage, which had 'hitherto been an important factor in the eagerness of women for matrimony'. Once it had gone, some other way would have to be found to induce women to marry:

> once it makes absolutely no difference to the esteem in which a woman is held, whether she is called Mrs or whether she is called Miss, a new inducement will have to be found, at any rate for the woman who is not obliged to look upon marriage as a means of providing her with bread and butter.

She scorned the way that men and marriage glorified 'certain qualities and certain episodes and experiences of life at the expense of all the others'. She was especially scathing in her dismissal of the notion that the celibate spinster was 'incomplete' or 'unnatural' because she had not experienced hetero-sexual intercourse:

> If we are more or less politely incredulous when we are informed that we are leading an unnatural existence, it is not because we have no passions, but because life to us means a great deal more than one of its possible episodes.

Celibacy, she insisted, was preferable to 'squalid faith in the essential glory of animalism', though nowadays to speak in praise of celibacy was 'tantamount . . . to high treason'. Her arguments reveal the growing conflict between the feminist analysis of sexuality and the sexological-medical model which was already becoming influential. She contrasted the feminist insistence on the possibility of sexual self-control with the sexological assertion that control was a biological impossibility:

> one is half inclined to suspect that the modern dislike of the celibate has its root in the natural annoyance of an over-sexed and mentally lax generation at receiving ocular demonstration of the fact that the animal passions can be kept under control. It saves such a lot of trouble to assume at once that they cannot be kept under control; so, in place of the priest we have the medical man, whose business it is to make pathological excuses for original sin.

It was not surprising, continued Hamilton, that man had consistently adopted an uncompromising and even brutal attitude towards the spinster, of which witch-burnings were only the most extreme example. According to the male conception of sexuality, to be chaste was to be inhuman; but the 'active and somewhat savage dislike' he had always entertained for the spinster suggested that it must have originated 'in the consciousness that the perpetual virgin was a witness, however reluctantly, to the unpalatable fact that sexual intercourse was not for every woman an absolute necessity'.[23]

It is well known that there was a large proportion of spinsters among the suffragettes, especially in the Women's Social and Political Union, 63 per cent of whose members in 1913 were spinsters – and many of the rest, like Emmeline Pankhurst herself, were widowed. It is also known that the rate of marriage reached an all-time low in 1911. The Registrar General's statistics show that although the proportion of women to men in that year was no greater than in 1901, 1911 represented a peak for the number of women in each age group from 25 upwards who remained single. Sheila Jeffreys' analysis of feminist statements at that time also strongly suggests that some women were not only deliberately choosing to remain single but were articulating their decision loudly and explicitly in political terms. They believed, like Hamilton, that the position of all women could only be improved in a society where there was a large class of celibate women.[24]

Lucy Re-Bartlett, for instance, pointing out that very few women were taking advantage of the special schemes enabling single women to emigrate to the colonies, commented that this hardly indicated a burning desire to marry. She also suggested that women's increasing awareness of problems such as the sexual abuse of children and the traffic in women were a major cause of their refusal to marry. This constituted more than a revolt against marriage: it was a protest against against all forms of 'sex-slavery' – a strike:

> In the hearts of many women today is rising a cry somewhat like this . . . *I will know no man, and bear no child until this apathy is broken through – these wrongs be righted!* . . . It is the 'silent strike' and it is going on all over the world.

Scoffing at the notion of 'incompleteness' promulgated by 'those who wanted to be scientific', she described the new independent woman as a 'warrior maid', who was no longer prepared to assimilate the old doctrine of women's subordination and was determined to be mistress of herself. She praised the wonderful solidarity which she saw springing up between women 'of the new type' all over the world, and maintained that a period of withdrawal from men was necessary, in order that the 'old relations' between the sexes might be set aside and 'new and nobler ones established'.[25]

Further ammunition against marriage came in 1913 from Christabel Pankhurst, whose series of articles in *The Suffragette* on the subject of venereal disease, subsequently reprinted as a book entitled *The Great Scourge and How to End It*, were based on the same understanding of the sexual economics of marriage and male power as Charlotte Perkins Gilman and Cicely Hamilton:

The system under which a married woman must derive her livelihood from her husband – must eat out of his hand, as it were – is a great bulwark of sex-subjection, and is a great reinforcement to prostitution. People are led to reason thus: a woman who is a wife is one who has made a permanent sex-bargain for her maintenance; the woman who is not married must therefore make a temporary bargain of the same kind.[26]

Pankhurst, too, called for the conspiracy of silence surrounding venereal disease to be broken, so that women could no longer be kept in ignorance of one of the most dangerous occupational hazards of marriage. She publicized quantities of medical evidence, culled from authoritative sources, which apparently showed that the majority of men, either before or during marriage, contracted venereal disease from prostitutes, often transmitting it to their wives. What particularly enraged feminists about VD was that husbands, usually in collusion with their doctors, deliberately concealed the real nature of their illness from their wives. Pankhurst was determined to make women aware that the poor health from which so many married women suffered – women 'who "have never been well since they married" ' – was directly attributable to this cause. 'Never again', she wrote, 'must young women enter into marriage blindfolded'. Pankhurst believed that once women's eyes had been opened to the true nature of marriage and its real, physical dangers, they would no longer be prepared to tolerate it. She declared: 'There can be no mating between the spiritually developed women of this new day and men who in thought and conduct with regard to sex matters are their inferiors'. This statement is usually cited as an example of her extremism and her puritanical attitude towards sex, rather than as a rational response to the current state of hetero-relations as she perceived them. Viewed in its full political context her statement made it quite explicit that resistance to marriage was for some women a rational political response to female sexual slavery and male sexual behaviour, and an attack on the central institution of male power.[27]

Many modern commentators on militant feminism and spinsterhood have not only failed to comprehend its political significance, in terms of the challenge to the structure of hetero-relations, but have viewed it through the twin lenses of heterosexism and hetero-reality. Even some feminists have assumed that in rejecting marriage and heterosexual relationships the feminist spinsters were *de facto* rejecting any possibility of sexual relationship, of motherhood, even of affection. Jane Lewis, for instance, in her comments on Cicely Hamilton, observes that she 'probably underestimated the difficulties and costs that might be involved for other women forced to choose between love and work'. She is critical of what she sees as Hamilton's 'insistence on equality on male terms', because 'it might well necessitate the rejection of sexuality and children'. She also considers that 'it may well be that the early feminist movement underestimated the need women have for love and affection'. It appears to be inconceivable to Lewis that love, affection, sexuality, and motherhood may be experienced outside of relationships with men, and that relationships between women, whether sexual or not, might be far more fulfilling than heterosexual relationships. As I have already pointed out, some Victorian and Edwardian feminists were undoubtedly lesbians, some 'passionate friends'; some single women adopted children, some advocated or practised single motherhood, and for all we know some may even have practised self-insemination – there is no technical reason why they should not have done so! Above all, it should not be assumed that in advocating spinsterhood they were being negative, or asking women to make sacrifices. For them, spinsterhood was extremely positive, and preferable by far to being enslaved in marriage or heterosexuality.[28]

The growing achievements of the Women's Movement and the development of militant feminism during the Edwardian period led to an intensification of hatred of the spinster. 'The antis', as feminists referred to those who opposed women's suffrage, were only too well aware of the link between feminism, women's independence and spinsterhood, and anti-feminist statements and tracts almost invariably included vitriolic attacks on the spinster, depicting her as 'sexually embittered', 'dissatisfied', 'frustrated', or in a condition of 'retarded development'. This was often combined with a deliberate attempt to undermine female solidarity by using 'divide and rule' tactics. The biologist Walter Heape, for example, who regarded spinsters as the 'waste-products of our population', argued that there were 'two classes of women', the wife-mother and the spinster, each with 'quite different aims in life', and that concessions to the latter would prejudice the interests of the former. Even those men who professed support for women's rights joined in the attack, an example being Walter Gallichan, who was married to a feminist and was to become one of the leading popularizers of sexology during the inter-war period:

> Among the great army of sex, the regiment of aggressively man-hating women is full of strength, and signs of the times show that it is being steadily recruited. On its banner is emblazoned, 'Woe to Man'; and its call to arms is shrill and loud. These are the women who are 'independent of men', a motley host, pathetic in their defiance of the first principle of Nature, but of no serious account in the biological or social sense.[29]

The use of such stereotypes as a weapon to discredit feminism and divide women is not surprising to feminists today, as it is still an all too familiar tactic. It is disturbing however to see the same stereotype and the same kind of vitriolic attack emanating from the pens of other feminists, and it makes one pause to wonder whether the tactic of divide and rule was in fact succeeding. Mrs Gasquoigne-Hartley, a self-defined feminist who was married to Walter Gallichan and sometimes wrote or lectured under the name of Mrs Walter Gallichan, wrote an extremely anti-spinster book in which she insisted that the true feminist motto should be 'Free *with* Man!'. She also gave a lecture in Caxton Hall in which she argued that 'woman's highest good and happiness could be gained by merging herself – whole-heartedly, ungrudgingly – in man, and that the assertion of individuality was not of supreme importance to woman'. Her views did not however go unchallenged: members of the Women's Freedom League attended the lecture, many of whom were spinsters and contributed, no doubt forcefully, to the ensuing discussion. According to the brief and somewhat terse report in *The Vote*, many members of the WFL were not in agreement with Mrs Gallichan: they considered that 'women had occasionally found men very trying, and some of them, at any rate, could quite easily live without men'.[30]

Those feminists who did express anti-spinster sentiments tended to be closely linked with the socialist movement, and to believe, like Olive Schreiner, that the key to women's emancipation was economic independence. Schreiner also made derogatory references to 'old maids and man-haters', and declared emphatically in the final chapter of *Woman and Labour* that male and female were two halves of one whole, and that the human female was 'bound organically' to the males of her society. She devoted many pages to reassuring men that no amount of freedom could in any way diminish woman's need of the physical and mental comradeship of man; that the attraction between the sexes was 'ineradicable'; that the most fierce ascetic religious enthusiasm through the ages had 'never been able to extirpate nor seriously to weaken for one moment the master dominance of this emotion'.[31] Nevertheless it is clear that spinsters were a significant political force within the Women's Movement. They challenged, not only in words but in their lives, the hetero-relational imperative, and the assumption that a woman without a man is sexually incomplete. They were, in a very real sense, the embodiment of female sexual autonomy. They threatened to undermine, not only the institution of marriage, but the structure of hetero-relations which is so fundamental to male power. The hostility and vehemence of male responses to feminist spinsterhood suggests that many men were only too conscious of the nature of the threat that feminist spinsters posed. The hostility of the responses of some feminists is harder to explain, and is an issue to which I shall return in later chapters.

The Politicization of Sexuality: Feminist Campaigns against the Double Standard

The debates about marriage and spinsterhood were integrally related to the campaigns against the double standard of sexual morality, and many of the most active and militant feminists, single and married, were deeply involved in those campaigns. Most histories of the last wave of feminism mention the double standard only in passing, and either use it as an opportunity to sneer at the 'prudery' of middle-class Victorian spinsters or distort and dismiss it as evidence of their demand for 'equal sexual repression'.[32] Yet opposition to the double standard is as old as feminism itself, and within less than ten years of the emergence of an organized women's movement there began the first of a series of campaigns which were to be sustained for over sixty years. For much of this time the campaigns against the double standard were, for tactical reasons, organized separately from those around education, employment, and women's suffrage. Millicent Fawcett, for example, the leader of the non-militant suffragists, felt that the issues of the vote and the double standard should be kept separate, lest the inevitably sensational nature of the latter damage the former. But this did not mean that she considered the double standard to be less important than, or unrelated to, the broader question of women's emancipation. Like many other feminists she was involved in the campaign against the double standard and the struggle for the vote at the same time, though many with less time and energy at their disposal had to choose to concentrate only on one.

All the campaigns had the same political aim: to emancipate women from 'sex slavery'. This entailed breaking the conspiracy of silence which served to keep women in ignorance of what feminists referred to as 'the *real* facts of life'. 'Sex slavery' included all forms of what we would refer to today as the sexual abuse and exploitation of women by men, inside and outside marriage. It covered the state regulation of prostitution, including compulsory medical control of prostitutes; the international traffic in women and children; pimping, procuring, and sexual solicitation of women by men; the sexual abuse of girls, inside and outside the home; sexual harassment of women by men, in public places, in the workplace, and by sending obscene letters; rape, including marital rape and wife abuse, and the transmission of sexual diseases to wives without their knowledge; and all other forms of male violence and sexual coercion of women and children, from 'indecent assault' to murder. The demand for an equal, or single, moral standard was in essence a demand for an end to the use of male sexuality as a weapon of male power, and a means of maintaining both the oppression of women in general, and their sexual subjection in particular. It represented an attempt by feminists to politicize sexuality explicitly and directly: to show that sexuality, just like the other areas of women's lives, was under the control of men, and thus a political matter. The strategies which feminists used included confronting men directly, attempting to change the laws, institutions, and customs which protected them, and using every possible means to make women aware of what men were doing and how they were able to get away with it. Knowledge and publicity were seen as crucial weapons in the struggle to empower women to challenge men's sexual control. To this end there was a great outpouring of journals, books, pamphlets, leaflets, newssheets, and other organs of propaganda, all designed to promote awareness and solidarity among women and to provide ammunition for the struggle.

The first and best-known of the feminist campaigns against the double standard of sexual morality was the agitation against the Contagious Diseases

Acts of the 1860s. The Acts were aimed at controlling the spread of venereal diseases in the armed forces by means of the compulsory medical examination of women suspected of working as prostitutes in garrison towns and ports. Josephine Butler's courageous and inspired leadership of the campaign to repeal the Acts is legendary. It drew feminists in large numbers into the campaign to repeal the Acts, and for the first time gave large numbers of women the experience of raising their consciousness about sexuality and its relationship to their oppression. Butler was secretary of the Ladies' National Association for the Repeal of the Contagious Diseases Acts. Established in 1869, this was one of the first examples in modern times of a separate women's political organization. Feminists opposed the Acts on the grounds that the examinations, and the subsequent nine months' confinement in a VD hospital if found to be infected, constituted an infringement of women's civil rights. However, the long struggle for repeal (the Acts were eventually repealed in 1886), and the experience of working in a women-only organization, gave them the opportunity to develop a much broader analysis, not only of prostitution and the double standard of sexual morality, but of the patriarchal model of sexuality which legitimated it.[33]

The fundamental feminist principle which underpinned the campaign was the assertion of a woman's right to control her own body. Butler and her supporters condemned the enforced medical examination of prostitutes as 'instrumental rape' by the 'steel penis', and insisted that all women had the right to walk the streets without fear of molestation. Unlike the majority of social purity crusaders who later came to dominate the movement, Butler never judged or interfered with a woman who freely chose a life of prostitution. She always made it clear that her interest lay only in attacking *organized* prostitution. She declared the state regulation of prostitution to be a form of legalized slavery, and denounced the CD Acts as the institutional embodiment of the double standard of sexual morality. This was made blatantly obvious by the Royal Commission on the CD Acts (1871) which asserted that 'with one sex the offence is committed as a matter of gain, with the other it is an irregular indulgence of a natural impulse'.[34]

Butler countered that prostitution was 'not a question of natural vice nearly so much as one of political and social economy'. She shared with the feminists whose writings on marriage and spinsterhood have already been discussed, a similar analysis of the sexual-economic basis of male power. She understood the relationship between male sexual control over women's bodies and the male-controlled legal, economic, political, and ideological structures. She also understood how all these combined to drive women to sell their bodies as a means of economic survival, either in marriage or in prostitution.[35] She was very clear about where the ultimate responsibility for this state of affairs lay – with men:

'It is men, men, only men from the first to the last, that we have to do with! To please a man I did wrong at first, then I was flung about from man to man. Men police lay hands on us. By men we are examined, handled, doctored, and messed on with. In the hospital it is a man again who makes prayers and reads the bible to us. We are had up before magistrates who are men, and we never get out of the hands of men until we die'.[36]

As Judith Walkowitz has pointed out, for Butler, prostitution 'served as a paradigm for the female condition'; it was an expression of 'the archetypal relationship between men and women'. This first direct campaign against the double standard challenged that relationship by challenging the ideology of male sexuality on which it was based: the assumption that the male sexual urge is natural and must be satisfied, and the corollary that men have the right of sexual access to women's bodies. The refutation of the patriarchal notion that prostitution is necessary and inevitable, because of the nature of male sexuality, became a recurrent theme in feminist writing from the 1870s. Annie Besant, who condemned the CD Acts as 'the legalisation of female slavery', expressed it thus: 'It is urged that "man's physical wants must be satisfied, and therefore prostitution is a necessity". Why therefore? It might as well be argued, man's hunger must be appeased, and therefore theft of food is a necessity.'[37]

The CD Acts were suspended in 1883, and finally repealed in 1886, but this was by no means the end of the feminist campaign. By the early 1880s it had broadened to include the international traffic in women and children and, following W.T. Stead's sensational disclosures in the *Pall Mall Gazette* in 1885 (regarding the procuring of young girls) there was tremendous pressure to raise the age of consent. The public furore aroused by this issue gave rise to a proliferation of 'social purity' organizations which aimed to eliminate prostitution and the sexual abuse of children. Most of these organizations were inspired by a mixture of commitment to civil liberties and Christian evangelism and moralism. The membership included men, who were expected to work out ways of strengthening their powers of self-control and helping other men to do the same, in order to bring an end to the demand for prostitution and the consequent abuse of women. Some of the organizations (a few of which excluded men) were also strongly influenced by feminist principles, an aspect which has been undervalued and misunderstood by most historians, who have tended to interpret the movement for social purity either as simply repressive, puritanical, and 'anti-sex', or as a form of 'moral panic'.[38]

A reassessment of feminist involvement in the social purity movement has been made by Sheila Jeffreys, who argues that feminist ideas and action significantly shaped its direction and concerns. Her research has helped to clarify the differences between the feminists and the more conservative, reactionary elements, who wished to eliminate 'vice' by 'protective' – which usually meant restrictive – measures against women. In contrast, the distinctive contribution of feminists within social purity was to challenge the assumption (still prevalent today) that prostitution and other forms of male sexual abuse and exploitation of women were a necessary and inevitable consequence of men's allegedly uncontrollable sexual urges:

> Feminists within social purity saw prostitution as the sacrifice of women for men. They fought the assumption that prostitution was necessary because of the particular biological nature of male sexuality, and stated that the male sexual urge was a social and not a biological phenomenon. They were particularly outraged at the way in which the exercise of male sexuality created a division of women into the 'pure' and the 'fallen' and prevented the unity of the 'sisterhood of women'. They insisted that men were responsible for prostitution and that the way to end such abuse of women was to curb the demand for prostitutes by enjoining chastity upon men, rather than by punishing the supply.[39]

The fact that both feminists and conservatives shared a common sexual vocabulary has tended to obscure their political differences and to fuel accusations that the feminists not only were 'prudes' but undermined their own cause by making alliances with the equivalent of today's 'moral majority'. Words like 'chastity', 'purity', 'the social evil', 'vice', 'continence', 'sexual excess', 'lust', and so on can certainly give this impression to the late-twentieth-century reader. We should remember however that this period was characterized by religious revivalism and that most feminists still subscribed, in a fairly uncritical way, to Christian beliefs and values. As Jeffreys points out, they used this vocabulary because it was the only one available to them. Furthermore, the use of words like 'purity' and 'chastity' in the nineteenth and early twentieth centuries did not necessarily imply a repressive or puritanical code of morality. As I pointed out in the introduction to this chapter, Mary Wollstonecraft and the early-nineteenth-century feminists, who also used this vocabulary, were not sexual puritans but rationalists, who believed in the power of reason and the ability of human beings to exercise rational control over their sexual passions. This is very different from repressing them. The feminists who campaigned for an equal moral standard, including those feminists who worked within the social purity organizations, shared essentially the same belief. There is also a sense in which they deliberately appropriated this language as a way of shaming men – especially those in positions of moral authority – out of their hypocrisy.

One of the most strongly and openly feminist organizations within the movement for social purity was the Moral Reform Union, which was particularly noted for activities such as exposing and prosecuting men suspected of sexual abuse, and promoted the idea of legislation against male soliciting and 'persecution by immoral men', or what feminists today would call sexual harassment. An important aspect of the work of the MRU was the provision of moral education literature. They published and sold pamphlets by many feminists, including Josephine Butler, Elizabeth Wolstenholme Elmy, and Elizabeth Blackwell, a founder member of the MRU, whose writings are particularly significant for their challenge to the ideology of male sexuality which legitimated the double standard. Blackwell, who was the first woman to qualify as a doctor, firmly believed that the ideology of male sexual 'needs' which was used to legitimate prostitution and the CD Acts was 'an audacious insult to the nature of men, a slander upon their human constitution'. She condemned as a 'perversion of the truth' the assertion that 'men are not capable of self-control, that they are so inevitably dominated by overwhelming physical instincts, that they can neither resist nor control the animal nature, and that they would destroy their mental or physical health by the practice of self-control'.

Unlike some other women doctors, such as Elizabeth Garrett Anderson, she was uncompromising in her refusal to contemplate the use of compulsory medical examinations in order to control the spread of venereal diseases. She maintained that 'the right of an adult over his or her own body is a natural fundamental right', insisting that 'this natural right of sovereignty over our own bodies' should never be given up. Blackwell felt it her duty as a physician to acquaint women with certain facts which she considered 'essential to the intelligent comprehension of the relations of the sexes'. She wanted in particular to correct the 'false theories of human nature' which legitimated the double standard and were enshrined in the divorce laws, in the CD Acts, and in the institution of prostitution, which she called the 'trade in women'. The most fundamental error which Blackwell felt compelled to challenge was the assumption that the sexual instinct in men was much stronger than in women and much more difficult to control:

> The radical physiological error, which underlies ordinary thought and action in relation to the evils of sex, is the very grave error that men are much more powerfully swayed by this instinct of sex, than are women. From this radical error are drawn the false deductions that men are less able to resist that instinct; that they are more injured by abstinence from its satisfaction; and that they require a license in action which forbids the laying down of the same moral law for men and women.[40]

She went on to argue that 'the passion of sex is as strong a natural force in woman as in man', and that all legislation concerning the relations of the sexes should be based on a recognition of this equality.

Blackwell also produced another pamphlet in which she analyzed the sexual economics of prostitution. Most feminists rejected economistic theories of prostitution, which purported to explain it simply in terms of poverty, or the 'laws' of supply and demand. They argued that not only did men create the demand, they also created the supply, by creating the economic conditions which produced the supply. Thus both demand and supply were man-made, as opposed to natural. This argument was developed in depth by Blackwell. She maintained that the understandable horror at the effects of sexual abuse on children, which had resulted in the recent raising of the age of consent, had diverted attention from the real causes of such crimes. These were to be sought in the relations of the sexes, in particular in the trade in women and the ideology which legitimated it. She argued that the trade in women was a modern phase of slavery which was destroying the freedom, and therefore the necessary conditions of growth, in one half of the human race: 'It is into the last possible phase of limitless competition in buying and selling, that our nineteenth century has entered, by permitting one-half of the race to become the merchandise of the other half'. She dismissed as 'sophistry' and 'specious hypocrisy' the defence that women, unlike slaves, 'consented' to be purchased. Freedom of contract, she asserted, could only take place between equals, so that neither party was compelled by pressure of circumstances or fear of want to accept conditions which were unjust or unwise. 'There is no freedom if both parties are not free. Any insistence upon consent to a bargain ignorantly or forcibly made is fraud'.[41]

Applying what she called 'the principles of political economy' to the trade in women, Blackwell compared the relations between the sexes in prostitution to the relations between capital and labour in the economy. She argued that the people primarily responsible for the trade in women, the people with power, were men, and that as long as the female body remained an article of merchandise women could never achieve economic or political equality or justice. But she also blamed 'the man or woman who excuses and sanctions the purchase of women, by upholding a double standard of morality for the sexes'. She was extremely critical of the advice and teachings offered to women regarding their relationships with the opposite sex: 'All assert their knowledge of "Nature and Instinct", of "Science and History", or "the tragical plea of material necessity", to justify opinions founded on misunderstood data'. It was the responsibility of women to 'unmask with a relentless justice' those 'cultivated intellects' who upheld the double standard. Women must spread the truth which they were now learning: 'the necessity that every man should be chaste. This is the truth so long unrecognised, but at last discovered as the solution of the great social problem. Without male chastity, female chastity is impossible'.[42]

Some organizations within the movement for social purity were very far from being feminist and aimed to eliminate prostitution by means of restrictive legislation against women. This led to many clashes between feminists and anti-feminists, and after 1900 a new wave of organizations sprang up in which feminism played little or no part.[43] During the early years of the twentieth century most of the feminist energy was channelled into the suffrage campaign, though many suffragists, like Millicent Fawcett, continued to campaign separately around sexuality within organizations such as the National Vigilance Association. Founded as a direct result of the indignation aroused by W.T. Stead's revelations concerning the procuring and abduction of young girls for prostitution, the NVA played a leading role in the campaign to raise the age of consent. The Criminal Law Amendment Act of 1885 raised the age of consent for sexual intercourse from 13 to 16, but left it at 13 for indecent assault. Many feminists joined the NVA, which was a mixed organization, in order to work for further legislation to protect children from sexual abuse and to close the many loopholes in the Act of 1885, particularly the clause which enabled men to defend themselves on the grounds that they had 'reasonable cause to believe' that the girl was over the age of 16. They also campaigned against many other forms of sexual exploitation and harassment of women, and provided solicitors to conduct prosecutions in cases of rape, sexual assault, indecent exposure, and sexual harassment in the street, and against senders of obscene letters. They also campaigned for soliciting by men to be made an offence, and were particularly concerned to protect girls from sexual abuse by men in positions of authority and trust. They campaigned strongly for legislation against incest; this was eventually achieved in 1908, and meant that, for the first time in history, young women were offered legal recourse against male sexual abuse and violence within their own families.

The political aims of these feminists were much broader and more fundamental than the achievement of protective legislation *per se*. What they wanted was to break the 'conspiracy of silence' which prevented open discussion about the sexual abuse of girls, protected the perpetrators, and obscured both the realities and the understanding of the relationship between sexuality and male power. Millicent Fawcett, in an article entitled 'Speech or Silence?', attacked both the double standard and the conspiracy of silence which prevented 'the terrible facts of life' from being known, arguing that open discussion of such issues was intolerable to those who benefited from the existing social arrangements. She also made explicit the connection between sexuality and the political and economic aspects of women's oppression: 'Deep down at the bottom of the questions that have been raised by the recent agitation is the economical and political subjection of women'. Countering anti-feminist protestations that legislation was an inappropriate weapon to use against sexual immorality, she argued:

> We are told *ad nauseam* 'that we cannot make men moral by Act of Parliament'. The Criminal Law Amendment Bill was an attempt, not to make men moral by Act of Parliament, but to protect the young from becoming victims of their immorality.[44]

The campaign to gain further legislation against the sexual abuse of children continued throughout the first two decades of the twentieth century, including World War I, with Bill after Bill being presented to Parliament and defeated, until eventually limited success was achieved with the passing of the Criminal Law Amendment Bill of 1922.[45] Although some feminists continued to work within social purity organizations during this period, most preferred to work within suffrage societies. Militant feminists in particular decided to integrate the campaign against the double standard into the struggle for the vote, and this phase of the campaign will be discussed in the next chapter.

Notes

1   Wollstonecraft's thoughts on sexuality and male power are discussed in greater detail in Jackson (1990). See also Brody (1983). Because of Wollstonecraft's 'irregular' sexual relationships with Imlay and Godwin, and the scandal which they aroused, the early Women's Movement distanced itself from her for some time. It was not until the late nineteenth century that she was 'rehabilitated', and even then it was her views on women's education and motherhood which feminists such as Millicent Fawcett chose to emphasize. For examples of feminism before Wollstonecraft see Spender (1982).
2   For a more detailed analysis of the significance of feminist ideas within Owenite Socialism see Jackson (1990). The evidence may be found in Barbara Taylor's thoroughly researched *Eve and the New Jerusalem* (1983), although my interpretation differs from hers.
3   Bodichon (1857) p. 11. The collections of primary sources on all aspects of Victorian and Edwardian feminism which were found most useful in the preparation of this section were: Bauer and Ritt (1979); Hellerstein, Hume, and Offen (1981); Jeffreys (1987); Murray (1984); Riemer and Fout (1983); Rossi (1970; 1974). General secondary sources on the Women's Movement and changes in the position of women during this period include: Banks (1981); Dyhouse (1989); Forster (1984); Jalland (1986); Kamm (1966); Levine (1989); Lewis (1984); Rover (1970); Spender (1982; 1983); Strachey (1978 [1928]).
4   Blackwell (1902), vol. 2, p. 69.
5   Cobbe (1868).
6   Mill (1848), p. 372 (emphasis in original); Mill (1974 [1869]), p. 69; Murray (1984), p. 124. On Mill's ideal of marriage see Susan Mendus' article in Mendus and Rendall (1989). Mendus argues that Mill believed in the *suppression* of sexuality, but I consider that the evidence does not support this argument, which seems to me to be based partly on an uncritical acceptance of a Freudian interpretation of Mill's writings, and partly on the assumption that the only possible cure for sexual slavery in the nineteenth century was abstinence (Mendus, 1989, p. 189).
7   Besant (1882), p. 13; Wolstenholme Elmy (1897), p. 48; Bland (1986), p. 128.
8   Gilman (1966 [1899]), pp. 5, 91.
9   Hamilton (1981 [1909]), pp. 35–6; p. 26; p. 136; p. 44; pp. 130–1; p. 129. There are strong similarities between Hamilton's concept of women as a class and the concept of 'sex-class' held by contemporary radical and revolutionary feminists. There have been some objections to this way of theorizing male power, especially by socialist feminists and Marxists, who believe that the concept 'class' should only be used in the strict Marxist sense, and that it is therefore incorrect to conceptualize the relation between women and men as a class relation. It seems wrong to me that Marxists should claim a monopoly over the meaning of a particular word and in my view the radical feminist concept of women and men as opposing classes is perfectly valid.
10 Schreiner (1978 [1911]), pp. 259–60.
11 For an account of the Men and Women's Club and its influence on Schreiner, as well as her relationship with Pearson, see First and Scott (1980). For an analysis

of the Club's discussions on sexuality see Chapter 4; see also Bland (1986) and Walkowitz (1986). Havelock Ellis' model of sexuality is discussed in Chapter 5. For an account of his relationship with Schreiner, see Grosskurth (1980), ch. 5.

12 For a survey of these and other changes in the position of women during this period see Lewis (1984). On the significance of the Married Women's Property Acts of 1870 and 1882, see Holcombe (1977).

13 See, for example, Bauer and Ritt (1979), ch. 3, from whom these figures are taken.

14 Cobbe (1862); Collet (1902).

15 Parkes (1865), p. 55; for detailed evidence and argument concerning the role of spinsters in the nineteenth-century Women's Movement see especially Jeffreys (1985). Philippa Levine (1989) has challenged this interpretation and has asserted the 'substantial' role of married women. However, the figures which she cites still show that spinsters were in the majority.

16 In the late nineteenth and early twentieth centuries there was an increasing trend for middle-class and upper-class single women to adopt orphaned or abandoned children, especially girls. Sometimes they brought them up as daughters, but sometimes their status was more akin to that of companion or 'special' domestic servant. Elizabeth Blackwell is one example of this kind of single mother, who did not see why, in rejecting marriage, she should also deny her maternal instincts (see Chapter 3). Other spinsters questioned the concept of maternal instincts. Cicely Hamilton, for instance, pointed out that woman's sense of maternity was not dependent on the accidents of marriage and childbirth, and that the concept of motherhood as a physical and instinctive process was essentially male (Hamilton, 1981 [1909], p. 143).

17 Cobbe (1862), pp. 228–35, emphasis in original.

18 See especially Mohin and Wilson (1983); Jeffreys (1984; 1985, ch. 6), and Lesbian History Group (1989). See also, with emphasis on the American context, Smith-Rosenberg (1975); Faderman (1981).

19 Whitelaw (1990), p. 110. See also Rich (1981); Ferguson (1981); and Lesbian History Group (1989), especially introduction and ch. 1.

20 Lesbian History Group (1989), p. 14.

21 Cobbe (1862b), p. 597, emphasis in original; see Bauer and Ritt (1979), p. 54.

22 Hamilton (1981 [1909]), pp. 133–4; *The Vote*, 15 April 1911.

23 Hamilton, *op. cit.*, p. 135; p. 141; pp. 144–5; p. 36.

24 Rosen (1974); Lewis (1984); Jeffreys (1985).

25 Re-Bartlett (1912), p. 25, emphasis in original.

26 Pankhurst (1913), p. 113; also published in a slightly different edition as *Plain Facts about a Great Evil*.

27 Pankhurst (1913), p. 98.

28 See Jane Lewis' introduction to Hamilton's *Marriage as a Trade* (1981, p. 13). On the adoption of children by single women see above, note 16. Christabel and her widowed mother Emmeline Pankhurst also adopted a child. Olive Schreiner believed that every woman should be allowed to have at least one child, irrespective of whether she was married, and some contributors to *The Freewoman* advocated single motherhood outside of heterosexual relationships.

29 Heape (1913), p. 6; Gallichan (1909), p. 49.

30 *The Vote*, 10 August 1913.

31 Schreiner (1978 [1911]), p. 228.

32 See, for example, Mitchell (1977) and Banks (1981).

33 There have been numerous accounts of Butler and the campaigns against the CD Acts, of which the most recent comprehensive feminist study is Walkowitz (1980). Other useful, and often neglected, feminist sources include Neilans (1936); Rover (1970); Strachey (1978) [1928]; and Uglow (1983). For selected primary sources

see Murray (1984); Riemer and Fout (1983); and, of course, Butler herself, a select bibliography of whose writings may be found in Uglow (1983).

34 Uglow (1983), p. 153; this view was asserted by William Acton, a doctor and contemporary 'expert' on prostitution, whose views on sexuality were challenged by Elizabeth Blackwell (see Chapter 3).

35 Most commentators take care to note that Butler herself was happily married, which seems to me to be intended to imply that she was not a 'man-hater', and therefore to be taken seriously. One wonders to what extent certain historical interpretations of Butler's work would change, were it to be revealed that she was not, after all, happily married?

36 These were the words of a woman confined in a Lock Hospital, whose story Butler publicized in *The Shield*, 9 May 1870; reprinted in Horowitz (1984).

37 Walkowitz (1980), p. 128; Besant (1876), p. 93.

38 See, for example, Bristow (1977); Gorham (1978); Mort (1987); Walkowitz (1982); Weeks (1981).

39 Jeffreys (1985), pp. 7–8. This book is a very important source on feminism and social purity, especially on the campaigns to raise the age of consent, which are extensively documented in chs. 3 and 4.

40 Blackwell (1881), p. 5; (1891), p. 2.

41 Blackwell (1902), pp. 154–6; *The Purchase of Women* was reprinted in 1902 in a collection of Blackwell's essays. It was also reprinted as a separate pamphlet in 1916, with a foreword by Millicent Fawcett.

42 Blackwell (1902), pp. 171–2.

43 One result of this development was that the term 'white slavery' began to take on racist overtones. This did not go unchallenged by feminists. See, for example, Nina Boyle's pamphlet on *The Traffic in Women* (1912), which is discussed in Chapter 2.

44 Fawcett (1885), pp. 4–5; this article was originally published in *The Contemporary Review* in September 1885, and subsequently reprinted as a pamphlet by the NVA. Available in Fawcett Library.

45 See Jeffreys (1985).

Chapter 2

'The *Real* Facts of Life'
Militant Feminism and the Double Standard of Sexual Morality

Feminism entered its militant phase in October 1905, when Christabel Pankhurst and Annie Kenney deliberately caused a disturbance in order to get themselves arrested. Their purpose was to generate greater publicity for the cause of women's suffrage by doing something 'newsworthy'. This marked a turning point in the tactics of the Women's Social and Political Union (WSPU) and by early 1906 a new word was beginning to come into general currency: 'suffragette'. This word has come to stand for all the women who campaigned for the vote, but at the time it was used specifically to distinguish the new militants from the 'suffragists' who continued to seek the vote by constitutional means. By 1907 differences within the WSPU had resulted in a split and the formation of the Women's Freedom League (WFL), led by Charlotte Despard. The WSPU and the WFL were the two leading militant feminist organizations, and both published weekly newspapers which were widely distributed. To historians the feminist newspapers are an important source of evidence on the issue of the vote and how it was won. As a source of feminist ideas and action around issues of sexuality, however, they have been virtually ignored.[1]

There were three militant feminist newspapers: *Votes for Women*, initially the organ of the WSPU, superseded in 1912 by *The Suffragette*; and *The Vote*, the organ of the WFL.[2] They provide valuable evidence not only of the development of the suffragettes' campaign against the double standard, but of how they conceptualized the relationship between sexuality and male power. They provide further clarification of what was distinctive about the feminist challenge to the double standard, as opposed to the 'social purity' approach. Although militant action officially ceased with the outbreak of war, the struggle for the vote and the campaigns around sexuality were maintained and even intensified by the WFL and other suffragettes who disagreed with the Pankhursts' decision to redirect their energies towards patriotism and the war effort. This analysis therefore includes the activities of the WFL during the period 1914 to 1918 and concludes with the end of the war and the partial enfranchisement of women.

Initially the suffragettes seem to have tacitly adopted the same policy in relation to sexuality as Millicent Fawcett, who believed that because of its unavoidably sensational nature, it should be kept separate from the struggle for the vote. Once the suffragettes had embarked upon militancy, however, they automatically lost their 'respectability', and publicity was grist to their mill, so they had nothing to lose, and much to gain, by tackling sexual issues as well. As militancy intensified, and more and more violence was used against them by male opponents of women's suffrage, the WSPU and the WFL began to make explicit the link between the campaign for votes for women and the campaign for an equal moral standard. By 1912 they had begun to produce quantities of evidence and propaganda in the attempt to demonstrate that the demand for an equal moral standard was integrally related to the struggle for the vote. This should be seen as much more than political ammunition; it was also a reflection of the increasingly sophisticated analysis of the relationship between sexuality and male power which feminists were developing. Many of the tactics they used in their campaigns were also in direct continuity with those of Josephine Butler and feminists who had struggled within the 'social purity' movement.

'How Men Protect Women': Male Violence and Sexual Abuse of Women and Children

The feminist newspapers were established in order to report and promote the struggle for the vote. Soon, however, they began to concern themselves with the much broader question of women's subordination to men, and to challenge male power in all its forms. The slogan 'Votes for Women' came to stand, not merely for a specific legal reform, but for a means of empowering women in the wider struggle for equality. *The Vote*, the organ of the WFL, was the first to take up the issue of male violence, including sexual violence, against women and children. Early in 1910 it carried a column headed 'Brutality', which expressed anger and indignation at the judicial system for refusing to take wife-battering seriously, and suggested a parallel between racial and sexual subordination:

> A man recently tried to excuse the conduct of certain white men when dealing with coloured races. He said that an unconquerable and inexplicable aversion, arising from the fact that these were subject races – and dark at that – caused the white man to lose control over his passions and be guilty of abominable and unspeakable cruelties. Perhaps it is the same feeling that they are dealing with a subject race that makes instances of brutality to women on the part of so-called working men so common that they cause laughter in court and serve as amusement for the magistrate and his officers.

Later the same year *The Vote* published a report expressing concern at the exclusion of women from the courts in cases involving sexual offences, and protesting at the exposure of young girls 'to the infamy and shame of being judged by a man alone in the presence of evil gloating male loungers'. Suffragettes had always protested against the male bias of the judiciary in dealing with their own cases, but now they began to take note of the bias against women in general, as expressed in particular in the outrageously low sentences given to men convicted of rape, murder, battering, and sexual assault. They reported the case of a man who killed his wife, just after she had been awarded custody of their daughter; the man was found not guilty of murder and given one month's imprisonment for carrying an offensive weapon.[3]

By the beginning of 1912 this concern and indignation had begun to be channelled into a specific campaign. In February 1912 *The Vote* introduced a new regular column, ironically entitled 'How Men Protect Women'. The writer expressed her outrage at the number of sexual assaults on little girls and the insignificant sentences – three or four months' imprisonment was the norm. The purpose of the column was to publicize details of cases and sentences and to compare the relatively light sentences for men convicted of violence against women and children, with the much heavier sentences given to women convicted of petty offences. The comparisons included the following:

Girl Thief

Three years' penal servitude for girl of twenty-two caught walking out of house of which she had found the door open, with stolen watch and chain.

Lighter Offences?

Husband, at Glasgow, threw tongs at his wife and killed the sick baby in her arms. Excuse, that he had come in and found no supper. Sentence, four months' hard labour. . . .

Readers were urged to keep watch on the courts and to monitor sentencing and other unjust procedures. A week later the column reported 'salutary' sentences on two men convicted of the sexual abuse of young girls, and claimed that 'these sentences show that the steady agitation kept up by Suffrage societies is not without its effect'. It was also claimed that in the Isle of Man, where women were already enfranchised, sentences were much harsher, reflecting the greater political power of women. In July 1913 the title of the column was changed to 'The Protected Sex' and it was announced that the journal now had its own correspondent whose job was to watch the courts and report on cases of male violence against women and sexual assualts on children. The correspondent was Edith Watson who, together with Nina Boyle, the head of the political and militant department of the WFL, remained in the forefront of this campaign until 1918.[4]

'How Men Protect Women' was also the title of a talk given by Nina Boyle in March 1912, in which she pointed out that 'protection' had invariably meant a deprivation of liberty and personal rights, and argued that the view that a woman had no right to her own person was enshrined in social conventions all over the world and in all ages, citing such examples as the persecution of witches, the *droit de seigneur*, and the mobbing of suffragettes – a reference to the increasing violence used by the police and other men against suffragette demonstrations. On one particular occasion, 18 November 1910 – afterwards known as 'Black Friday' – large numbers of suffragettes had been severely beaten up and some also sexually assaulted by police and male bystanders. This event marked a turning point in the militant tactics of the Women's Social and Political Union, which immediately stepped up its campaign of destruction of property. It probably also made suffragettes much more aware of male violence and sexual aggression against women and increased their determination to take up the issue. Nina Boyle analyzed the cases reported during her term of office with the WFL and showed that the overwhelming majority of crimes of violence was committed by men on women, alleging that 'no crime was so lightly punished in "civilised" countries as violence on the persons of women'.[5]

On 1 April 1912 the WFL organized a meeting to discuss the formation of a 'Watch Committee' to monitor cases of injustice in the courts. This was supported by seven other suffrage societies, some of whom set up their own 'police court rotas'. In August 1912 *Votes For Women*, the organ of the WSPU, began its own regular column headed 'Comparison of Punishments' in which it compared a sentence of six months for white slave trafficking with six months for a suffragette who broke a window. Although the column was discontinued when *The Suffragette* was inaugurated in October 1912, the WSPU never missed an opportunity of pointedly comparing the harsh sentences given to suffragettes – whose offences were always against property, never against the person – with the token sentences given to men convicted of sexual offences against women and children. Under the independent editorship of Emmeline and Frederick Pethick-Lawrence, *Votes For Women* continued the 'Comparison of Punishments' column, and the feature was later expanded to include a comment section in which the political implications of sentencing were explicitly addressed. It was pointed out, for example, that sentences for sexual offences against boys were much heavier than for those against girls. Why, asked the writer, is a boy so much more valuable than a girl? – and why should men have the exclusive right to fix the scale of punishments?[6]

The '*Real* Facts of Life': Shoving Mrs Grundy Aside

The year 1912 saw a resurgence of feminist campaigning around prostitution, the age of consent, and 'white slavery'. Some militant feminists, such as Alison

Neilans of the WFL, had been campaigning separately around these issues
for many years, but it was not until about 1910 that they began to be reported
in the suffragette newspapers. Again, it was the WFL which began the campaign, though its role has been ignored by most historians, who have chosen
to focus exclusively on Christabel Pankhurst's more sensational pronounce-
ments. Early in 1910 *The Vote* carried an advertisement for a book called *The
White Slaves of England* (author unknown), and publicized the speeches of
Alice Abadam who frequently addressed suffrage meetings on the subject of
prostitution. Abadam argued that one of the main causes of prostitution was
the starvation wages which so many women were paid. She related an incident where a manager had justified a reduction in the wages of his women
workers with the words: 'if they complain, simply tell them they can supple-
ment their earnings on the street'. She also claimed that when the House of
Lords had debated the Bill to raise the age of consent, one member had
warned: 'Take care, my Lords, lest in passing this measure you interfere with
the advantages of your sons'. She argued that the reason that no government
had ever made a real effort to deal with the sexual exploitation and abuse of
women was that 'they were responsible to a one-sex electorate'.[7]

The monitoring of the courts heightened feminist consciousness, not
merely about the double standard of sentencing, but about the double standard of sexual morality which was enshrined in the legal system. Despite the
usual practice of excluding women from the courts in cases involving sexual
offences (a practice against which feminists always protested vociferously),
they were still able to find ways of discovering and publicizing the details of
such cases, which invariably revealed the double standard of sexual morality
on which the law was based. In cases of soliciting it was always the women
who were punished, never the men; in cases of rape and sexual assault, including of children, the victims would be blamed for tempting or luring the
'innocent' male, and even when a conviction was obtained the sentence was
often nominal, on the grounds that the offender had merely succumbed to a
momentary temptation to which 'any otherwise decent man' might have given
way. The feminist newspapers now began to go further than merely reporting
such cases. Articles began to appear asserting women's right to know what
they called 'the *real* facts of life', namely the realities of male sexual abuse
and exploitation of women:

> We thinking women of England are sick of cant and humbug and are
> determined to face the truth, having no doubt but that knowledge
> will prevent, and light cure, the prevalence of the 'fallen man', who
> is the necessary prelude and accompaniment of every 'fallen woman'.

In November 1911 *Votes For Women* also took up the issue by publicizing the
work of Sister Henriette Arendt, former police assistant in Stuttgart, Germany, who had helped to expose the international traffic in women and children under the age of consent. The reviewer of Arendt's books, K. Douglas

Smith, argued that such phenomena would not disappear until women were able to participate in the making of legislation:

> it is an undeniable fact that the laws of European countries are not of women's making, and they have had no share in the framing of them. It is a man's world, and he permits these things to exist, nay even to flourish . . . throwing the burden entirely on to the woman's shoulders. Finally, it must never be forgotten that the cause of this traffic existing at all is that the demand creates the supply, and that it is a *man's demand*.[8]

Ever since the raising of the age of consent in 1885 from 13 to 16, feminists within the 'social purity' organizations had been continuing to campaign to close loopholes in the Act of 1885, and for further measures to prevent the sexual abuse and exploitation of women. One such measure which feminists had long demanded was that soliciting by men should be made illegal. In 1907, as a result of pressure from several organizations, including the National Vigilance Association and the Jewish Association for the Protection of Women and Girls, a White Slave Traffic Bill had been drafted, which included a clause on male soliciting. The government had refused to sponsor it and when it finally came before the House of Commons in 1912 it was repeatedly blocked by a leading anti-suffragist, Sir Frederick Banbury. In April 1912 W.T. Stead, who together with Josephine Butler had been influential in getting Parliament to raise the age of consent in 1885, went down in the *Titanic*. His death gave further impetus to the movement to amend the Criminal Law Amendment Act of 1885. Many meetings were arranged in commemoration of Stead's work, and were clearly intended to rouse public opinion, not only on the issue of the continuing international traffic in women and children, but also on the outrageous treatment of the White Slave Traffic Bill in Parliament. Speakers laid great emphasis on the parallel between the present struggle and that of Josephine Butler and her contemporaries, drawing attention to the male bias in legislation and the need for women to have the vote in order to bring an end to the traffic in women:

> speaker after speaker harked back to the need for the woman's vote in trying to cure this canker in our social system. The men who are engaged in fighting the evil are a small minority; only the women, who feel the whole question with a passionate intensity, can supply the necessary voting power which would force the Government to take action.

The WSPU also suggested that there was a connection between the strength of feeling on the issue and the militancy of recent years:

> Year by year a holocaust of women are sacrificed in what may be ironically termed 'the cause of purity', but, at last, women are in open revolt, primarily against the idea that they exist before all things for the satisfaction and pleasures of man. Militancy has shown the nation that women are very alive to their political disabilities and consequent injustices, and that they are jealous for the care and honour of womanhood. . . .

They argued that the political disability of women was the prime cause, not only of the long delay in passing the Bill, but of the traffic itself, since it could not exist in a society where women had equal status with men. At the same time they were far from naive about the significance of such legislation and made it clear that they did not believe that the Bill would, in itself, eradicate the problem of sex slavery:

> The Bill, if passed, will do something. But Votes for Women will do more; for only when women have come into their own, only when they have the same power to protect themselves as men have, will it be impossible any longer for the souls and the bodies of women to be made a lucrative branch of modern commerce.

Unable to obtain official data on the extent of trafficking in Britain they used data from other countries, especially in Europe and America, to show that it was organized by business syndicates and that women and girls were usually procured by trickery and prevented by force from leaving, so that they were indeed kept in a condition of slavery.[9]

Reports of the debates on the passage of the Bill in Parliament demonstrated the fundamental conflict of interest between women and men on the issue. They highlighted the usual male defence of the double standard in terms of the necessity of prostitution because of the nature of male sexuality:

> Reading the discussion upon the Bill, the conclusion is irresistible that the existence of vice of a certain kind is accepted by the representatives of men as part of the necessary order of things, a permanent factor not only to be taken into account, but even to be admitted on certain terms, and one that certainly must not be dealt with over harshly. . . . In more senses than one 'It's the way men look at women that drives women on the streets'.

Support for this legislation came from a large number of women's organizations and 'social purity' organizations, but the enormous publicity given to it by militant feminists, whose newspapers were widely distributed and sold on the streets of London and other large cities, was probably significant in bringing pressure to bear on the government, through women in the Liberal Party, to adopt the Bill. Feminists did not, however, rejoice at its passing, which was only achieved at the cost of a number of amendments which effectively rendered it worthless from the feminist viewpoint. Although it increased the power of the police and magistrates in dealing with pimps and procurers, the clause on male soliciting had to be completely dropped, apparently because MPs feared that it would be used by suffragettes as a weapon against anti-suffrage MPs! Nevertheless, the time spent on the Bill was not regarded as wasted, because it served to make women more aware of the issue of sex slavery and its political significance. It also resulted in closer liaison between suffragettes and feminists in social purity organizations such as the Association of Moral and Social Hygiene, and the formation of the Criminal Law Amendment Committee. This included militant and non-militant feminists such as Millicent Fawcett, Emily Davies, Alison Neilans, and Maude Royden. The committee circulated a leaflet urging that a national campaign be organized in order to raise the age of consent to 18, to repeal the 'reasonable cause to believe' clause, and to maintain the pressure for male soliciting to be made an offence. The committee was supported by most of the suffrage societies as well as many other women's organizations, and suffrage journals carried regular progress reports of its activities.[10]

Throughout the remainder of 1912 and the whole of 1913, the militant feminists' campaign against the double standard continued to gain momentum, broadening out to include the relationship between prostitution and sweated labour, the state regulation of prostitution in India and other countries in the British Empire, and the problem of venereal disease. During the same period there was an escalation in militancy, with more and more attacks on property, culminating in the arson campaign. There was also an escalation in violent attacks on suffragettes by male anti-suffragists. In September 1912 there was another particularly nasty incident, this time in Wales. Suffragettes were at a meeting, heckling Lloyd George, who two weeks earlier had encouraged his audience to beat up suffragette disrupters. Some men seem to have taken him at his word, for a number of suffragettes were assaulted and stripped almost naked. Emmeline Pankhurst referred to this incident a month later when she addressed a meeting at the Albert Hall. This speech marked the official launch of the WSPU's campaign for an equal moral standard:

> Why are we militant? The day after the outrages in Wales I met some of the women who had exposed themselves to the indecent violence of that mob...those women suffered from assaults of a kind which it was impossible to print in a decent newspaper...one woman said 'All the time I thought of the women, who, day by day, and year by year, are suffering through the White Slave Traffic, and I said to myself "I will bear this, and even worse than this, to help win power to put an end to that abominable slavery". '

Pankhurst drew on her experience as a Poor Law Guardian to explain why she now saw the campaign for an equal moral standard as integral to the struggle for the vote:

> Until by law we can establish an equal moral code for men and women, women will be fair game for the vicious section of the population, inside Parliament as well as out of it. . . . When I began this militant campaign I was a Poor Law Guardian, and it was my duty to go through a workhouse infirmary, and I shall never forget seeing a little girl of thirteen lying in bed playing with a doll. . . . I was told she was on the eve of becoming a mother, and she was infected with a loathsome disease, and on the point of bringing, no doubt, a diseased child into the world. Was not that enough to make me a Militant Suffragette? . . .
>
> We women Suffragists have a great mission – the greatest mission the world has ever known. It is to free half the human race, and through that freedom to save the rest.[11]

Anti-suffragists commonly alleged that the suffrage movement was a movement of rich women, and irrelevant to working-class women. Flora Drummond of the WSPU (nicknamed 'The General' because of her role in marshalling suffragette demonstrations) countered by arguing that there was a close relationship between the sweating of women workers and organized prostitution. She maintained that there were three questions which, above all others, fired suffragettes' indignation and determination to get the vote:

1 The sweating of women workers. The starvation of women is undermining the health of the mothers of the race, and is driving thousands to a life of shame.
2 The White Slave Traffic. Even under the new Bill which is now being carried a man can get less punishment for trapping an innocent girl and forcing her to a life of shame than for stealing a loaf of bread.
3 The outrages committed upon little girls, some of them only babies. This is a growing evil, which working-class mothers are determined to stamp out, and to do this they must have the vote.[12]

Edith Watson and other members of the WFL's 'Watch Committee', who continued to monitor the courts, protesting vociferously whenever they were excluded, concentrated particularly on cases of sexual abuse of children and procuring. Nina Boyle wrote a widely-sold pamphlet entitled *The Traffic in Women* in which she produced evidence from all over the world to show that it was a hugely profitable enterprise organized mainly by business syndicates. Aware of the racist implications of the term 'white slavery' she also emphasized that it was not a question of white women only, but involved women of all colours. She drew attention to the connection between organized prostitution and the opposition to women's suffrage, showing how vice trusts and traffickers all over the world were actively involved in trying to prevent the enfranchisement of women, because they feared that it would put them out of business. This was a theme which both the WSPU and the WFL began to pursue with considerable vigour during 1913. They claimed that the increasing violence towards both suffragettes and suffragists was orchestrated by white slave traffickers, who were becoming alarmed by the campaign against them and determined to 'stop the Women's Movement'. Emmeline Pankhurst also accused the press of encouraging the persecution of suffragettes and 'rousing that element from which the White Slaver is drawn, from which the brute who lives on the immoral earnings of his child is drawn'.[13]

On 3 April, 1913, at one of her many appearances on trial at the Old Bailey, Emmeline Pankhurst initiated a new tactic. She delivered a tirade against men of wealth and status, including judges, accusing them of regularly using prostitutes and sexually abusing girls. She claimed to have evidence that:

> there is in this country, in this very city of London, a regulated traffic, not only in women of full age, but in little children; that they are being purchased, entrapped, and trained to minister to the vicious pleasures of persons who ought to know better in their station of life.

This tactic was to be used on many subsequent occasions when suffragettes were on trial. On 14 July, for instance, Grace Roe asked at the Old Bailey: 'I want to know why you raid a wholesome place like Lincoln's Inn House [WSPU headquarters] instead of raiding the brothels around Bond Street', whereupon the judge ordered her removal from court. Shortly after her mother's Old Bailey speech Christabel Pankhurst wrote an editorial article, subsequently reprinted and sold as a pamphlet, in which she claimed:

> White Slavery exists because thousands upon thousands of ordinary men want it to exist, and are willing to pay to keep it going. These men, in order to distract the attention of the other women who are not white Slaves, are very willing to make scapegoats of a few of the Slave Traders, but all the time they rely upon there being enough traders to maintain the supply of women slaves. By force, by trickery, or by starvation enough women will, they believe, be drawn into the Slavery of vice.

She indicted the government for complicity in the sexual exploitation of women, accusing them of driving women on to the streets by setting inadequate wages for government contracts. She also accused them of being, in effect, 'procurers of women', by sanctioning the use of 'regulated' brothels by soldiers in India. But she made it clear that the ultimate responsibility for the double standard lay not merely with the Government, but with men, with whom the remedy lay: 'Men have a simple remedy for this state of things. They can alter their way of life'.[14]

Opponents of the campaign against the double standard attempted to undermine it by calling the militant feminists 'Mrs Grundys', an insult equivalent to today's 'prude'. In an article in *The Vote* entitled 'Hell and Mrs Grundy', Gertrude Colmore turned the tables on the anti-feminists and praised the Women's Movement for bringing the traffic in women to light. The real 'Mrs Grundys', she insisted, were those (mainly men) who sought to maintain the conspiracy of silence about sex slavery and prevent the facts from being exposed.

> She [Mrs Grundy] sits on the throne of British respectability and mention, by spoken or written word, of the existence of hell is forbidden by her ancient and inviolable law. . . . It is women who have shoved Mrs Grundy aside; it is the Woman's Movement that has compelled authorities to investigate and report upon this hell.

She criticized 'Mrs Grundy' for blaming only the 'middlemen', the procurers, pointing out that, as in the case of the trade in fur and feathers, if the demand ceased, so would the supply. *The Vote* proved that its deeds were as good as its words by expressing unequivocal support for a teacher in Derbyshire who was threatened with the sack for talking to the older girls about the 'facts of life'.[15]

Judith Walkowitz has claimed that the 'obsession with male vice again side-tracked early twentieth century feminists into another crusade against white slavery (1912), while obscuring the economic basis of prostitution'. This evidence shows that nothing could be further from the truth. It is clear that militant feminists were attempting to demonstrate that the question of sex slavery could not be separated from the broader question of women's subordination, including their economic position; that it was central to male power and therefore central to women's emancipation. Far from identifying with 'Mrs Grundy', their clear intention was to expose what they saw as the *real* facts of life. By making the links between women's economic position, the exploitation of their sexuality, and their subordination as a sex, they highlighted, rather than obscured, the economic basis of prostitution. Underpinning the campaigns and the slogans was an analysis of the sexual economics of male power in which heterosexual relations were seen as power relations. This analysis was also reflected in the famous series of articles on venereal disease written by Christabel Pankhurst at the height of the campaign in 1913.

'Votes for Women, Chastity for Men!'

Militant feminists began to address the problem of venereal disease in the spring of 1913. Public agitation around this issue had in fact been started almost five years earlier by suffragists such as Millicent Fawcett, leader of the

National Union of Women's Suffrage Societies. In 1910 Dr Louisa Martindale, at the request of the NUWSS, published what Helena Swanwick referred to as 'a courageous little book' entitled *Under the Surface*. It was essentially a statement of facts about VD and prostitution, framed by an analysis of the political economy of prostitution, and an argument for the enfranchisement of women: 'My one object', she wrote, 'has been to prove to those who do not yet believe it, that the existence of Prostitution in our land, is due to the fact that women are not treated as, or believed to be, the equals of men'. Although she explained prostitution primarily in terms of women's economic dependence on men and lack of political power, she also argued that male power, male sexuality, and the socialization of girls into submission were crucial causal factors:

> When we study the life of a so-called common prostitute we find that in the first place she was seduced; then, ashamed to return to her home she finds herself alone without credentials or testimonials and unable to find employment. It is then that she is forced to go on the streets.
>
> With reference to this preliminary seduction, we have to remember that, from her earliest days, she has been imbued with the belief in the superior knowledge of the other sex. She has been taught to be affectionate and charming, and above all to be unselfish. She has been taught to regard her future husband as master, and one she must obey. . . . She has been trained from her earliest years in the very qualities which make her an easy prey to the professional seducer or procurer.

If a young girl fell into the hands of a scoundrel, she argued, it was hardly surprising that there was little chance of her successfully resisting him. In her profession she had met hundreds of them and had been struck by their helplessness and the 'physical paralysis' that crept over them. It was men who had not only made it possible, but had *demanded* that a whole class of women should be set aside for their momentary pleasure. They had deliberately trained a whole class of women to minister to men's alleged sexual needs: 'Even further', she continued, 'it is these men who have instilled into their womenfolk the idea that sexual indulgence is a necessity to their health – one of the greatest fallacies that ever existed'.[16]

Swanwick wrote that the publication of the book 'was the occasion of a furious onslaught on the National Union in the House of Commons by a Member, who held the book to be injurious to morals'. In fact, he demanded that the Home Secretary ban it. In Swanwick's words: 'This proved a great advertisement: the book was sent to every Member of both Houses of Parliament, and its candour and moderation were widely acknowledged'. In 1913 the International Medical Congress in London recommended the appointment of a Royal Commission on Venereal Diseases, on which Millicent Fawcett was invited to sit. She refused, but wrote to the Prime Minister urging that the connection between sweated labour and prostitution should be included in the terms of its investigation. The militant feminists were impatient. They did not want to await the publication of the Royal Commission's report, which did not appear in its final form until 1916. They decided to expose the facts about VD in the same way that they had exposed the realities of the trade in women and children. Emmeline Pankhurst fired the first shot in her Old Bailey speech of 3 April, 1913:

> the horrible evils which are ravaging our civilization will never be removed until women get the vote. They know that the very fount of life is being poisoned . . . that because of the unequal standard of morals, even mothers and children are destroyed by one of the vilest diseases that ravage humanity.

The Vote published a full-page article describing the horrific effects of the diseases, especially on children and babies, many of whom had been raped. The article also cited statistics from the Society for the Prevention of Cruelty to Children, which suggested that sexual abuse of children inside as well as outside the home was widespread. 'Only when women have the vote', concluded the article, 'will such horrors be grappled with and the age of consent raised'.[17]

This was the context in which Christabel Pankhurst produced her series of editorial articles on prostitution and venereal disease, subsequently published as a book entitled *Plain Facts about a Great Evil: The Great Scourge and How to End It*. Written over several months, the articles represented the high point of the militant feminists' campaign for an equal moral standard. It gathered together into an integrated whole all the ideas and arguments about the sexual exploitation and abuse of women that militant feminists had been developing in recent years. Viewed in its entirety, it reflected an analysis of the relationship between sexuality and male power which had its roots in over a century of feminist thinking and struggle. It was, in essence, a critique of the sexual-political-economic relations which constituted male power over women.[18] The immediate purpose of the articles was to provide more ammunition for the campaign against the double standard, by exposing the facts about VD. Several articles were devoted to detailed descriptions of the symptoms and the damage they caused, both short-term and long-term, especially to women and children. Pankhurst cited numerous medical authorities who estimated that 75 to 80 per cent of men contracted one or other form of VD, either before marriage or after it. Pankhurst thought it was vital to alert women to the risk of infection by their husbands and the conspiracy between husbands and doctors to conceal the real nature of their own and their husbands' illnesses. She emphasized that there was no cure, that the absence of symptoms did not necessarily mean the absence of disease, and the dangerous side effects of treatment with the recently invented drug,

Salvarsan. She also attacked the other time-honoured remedy, which was still widely advocated, namely the state regulation of prostitution, and warned that women would never accept its reintroduction, albeit under the apparently innocuous label of 'notification of disease':

> Against any such system women will fight to the very death. No woman-slavery of that kind can be tolerated at this time of day. If men venture to re-establish in this country a system according to which certain women will be segregated, controlled, and medically examined for the purposes of vice, that will mean the establishment of a sex war.[19]

Pankhurst's basic argument was that the ultimate cause of sexual disease was the subjection of women, specifically the assumption 'that women are created primarily for the sex gratification of men ... the doctrine that woman is sex and beyond that nothing'. As a consequence of this doctrine 'the relation between man and woman has centred in the physical', and had become that of 'master and slave'. She argued that men had divided women into two main classes, wives and prostitutes, all other females being regarded as superfluous. Both wives and prostitutes were 'sex-slaves', kept in subjection by man-made laws and through economic dependence:

> This desire to keep women in economic subjection to themselves – to have women, as it were, at their mercy – is at the root of men's opposition to the industrial and professional employment of women.
> If a woman can earn an adequate living by the work of her hand or brain, then it will be much the harder to compel her to earn a living by selling her sex.

She asserted that the real reason for opposition to women's suffrage was that 'those who want to have women as slaves obviously do not want women to become voters'. Men were determined to continue the sexual exploitation of women, and well aware of the threat to this posed by the Women's Movement:

> Under all the excuses and arguments against votes for women, sexual vice is found to be lurking.
> The opposition argues thus; if women are to become politically free they will become spiritually strong and economically independent, and thus they will not any longer give or sell themselves to be the playthings of men. That, in a nutshell, is the case against votes for women.

She felt that raising the issue of sexual disease and showing its relationship to the subjection of women would appeal to and unite all women, inspiring them with the renewed anger and energy which the suffrage campaign badly needed.[20]

Since the ultimate cause of VD was sex slavery, ultimately the only cure was to end sex slavery. The slogan 'Votes for Women, Chastity for Men!' encapsulated the two elements Christabel thought necessary to achieve this: the exercise by men of sexual self-control, and the political power of women. 'Out of the present impasse in sex matters', she wrote, 'there is only one way – chastity for men, guaranteed and confirmed by the greater independence that the vote will give to women'. She explained that by chastity for men, she meant the observance by men of the same moral standard they set for women. She refuted the 'ridiculous and wicked theory advanced by many men and some doctors' that men were biologically incapable of this, and that prostitution was necessary and inevitable, again citing medical authorities in support of her views. She insisted that male sexual incontinence was a 'violation of Nature's laws'; chastity was, for both sexes, natural and healthy, and men were just as capable as women of exercising control over their sexuality.

Pankhurst's idea of sexual self-control was based, not on repression or coercion, but on rationality and education. To those men who insisted that prostitution would always be necessary she replied: 'We think better of men than this, provided that the necesary work of education and reform is done amongst them'. 'The true cure for prostitution', she maintained, 'consists in this – the strengthening of women, and the education of men'. She did not, of course, believe that the vote would in and of itself end the sexual slavery of women, rather that it would empower women to bring about the changes in their social and economic position that would render prostitution unnecessary:

> When women have political power, equal with that of men, they will not tolerate the exploitation of their sisters. . . . Nor will they themselves submit to exploitation. They will secure such economic independence and prosperity as shall save them from the danger of being driven to live by the sale of their sex.

She believed that the vote, which she saw as symbolizing the recognition of the freedom and human equality of women, would at least make it possible for women to change the man-made laws which encouraged the sexual exploitation of women and protected the perpetrators, such as the unequal divorce laws, the leniency of sentences for men convicted of the sexual abuse of girls, and the 'reasonable cause to believe' clause which let so many abusers off the hook. The demand for votes for women meant 'a revolt against wrongs of many kinds', she wrote, but most of all 'it is a revolt against the evil system under which women are regarded as sub-human and as the sex-slaves of men'.[21]

As Christabel was writing *The Great Scourge*, there occurred a *cause célèbre* which fuelled feminists' anger and also provided them with more useful propaganda. In July 1913 the 'Piccadilly Flat Case', which was reported in all the newspapers and aroused wide public concern, resulted in questions being asked in Parliament. The case involved the procuring of young girls, barely over the age of consent, to work in an illicit brothel run by a woman called Queenie Gerald. The brothel was patronized by upper-class men, including, it was alleged, MPs and judges; not only did they escape punishment, but the Government and the judiciary conspired to conceal their identity. Feminists demanded that their names be revealed, and Keir Hardie was persuaded to take up the case in the House of Commons. Emmeline Pankhurst publicly alleged that the WSPU's offices had been raided in order to seize evidence which suffragettes could have used to expose the role of the Government in the affair, claiming that 'the people who are most against us in the House of Commons are the men who want things hushed up'. Christabel Pankhurst declared: 'In the Piccadilly Flat Case, with its foul revelations and its still fouler concealments, is summed up the whole case against Votes for Women'. It was an illustration, she argued, of the 'Anti-Suffragist theory of life and the position of women', because it reflected the belief 'that women are of value only because of their sex functions, which ... are to be used at the orders and in the service of men'. Pointing out that those who were anti-suffrage were also anti-spinster, she suggested that men's fear and horror of 'superfluous women' (i.e. those who were neither wives nor prostitutes) might have something to do with the fact that they appeared to have no need of men, and therefore constituted a threat to the system of sex slavery. 'As he does not hesitate to tell her', she wrote, 'the Anti-Suffragist is of opinion that apart from her sex activity the world would get on quite well without her. He does not realise that the same thing might at least as truly be said of men by women'.[22]

This analysis of *The Great Scourge* suggests that, viewed in its full political context, the slogan 'Votes for Women, Chastity for Men!' should be seen, not as a puritanical demand for equal sexual repression, but as a political demand for female sexual autonomy. To demand an equal moral standard was a rational, political response to a system of male power which institutionalized female sexual slavery in its laws and in its practices, and justified it in terms of men's biological 'needs'. 'Chastity for Men!' was a distillation of a message which may be decoded as follows: 'Men's sexual needs are essentially no different from women's. We are all, as rational human beings, equally capable of exercising control over our own sexuality. The sexual exploitation of women by men is political, not natural, and it can, and must, be brought to an end'. In conjunction with the assertion of spinsterhood as the ultimate representation of female sexual autonomy, this was a powerful challenge to the sexual-economic basis of male power.

'Justice' and Women Police

Meanwhile Edith Watson and Nina Boyle of the WFL were intensifying their campaign against the injustices to women perpetrated by the courts in cases of male violence and sexual abuse, particularly of children. Even small children would be forbidden the company of their mothers when they faced the onslaught of counsel, who frequently implied that they were already sexually experienced and had 'seduced' the innocent male. Edith Watson's 'Protected Sex' column now often filled a whole page and Nina Boyle produced special features entitled 'Justice' in which she publicly named and challenged lawyers, magistrates and judges for operating a double standard against women. For several months during 1913, this 'New Crusade' against the courts was a front-page issue, and included a specific campaign against a certain Mr Mead, a London magistrate with a particularly bad reputation for his treatment of women.

As a result of the campaign, Mrs Parrott, a working-class women whose 14-year-old daughter Violet had been raped and made pregnant by a policeman who was a lodger in her house, contacted the WFL and asked for their support in securing the conviction of Wetherall, the policeman concerned. The Public Prosecutor refused to prosecute the man on the grounds that Violet had no 'corroborative evidence', and also because of Wetherall's allegation – also uncorroborated – that she had willingly had sexual intercourse with other men. The Wetherall case became a scandal of even greater proportions than the Piccadilly Flat Case, and the campaign was considered sufficiently important for special headquarters to be set up in a shop in Homerton, East London, where the Parrott family lived. *The Vote* reported that many women were calling in to obtain information and offer support. A special pamphlet was produced which sold in thousands and was distributed to all MPs, peers, bishops, judges, and barristers, as well as to the press and police. It emphasized that the case exemplified the bias of the legal system against the working classes as well as against women, arguing that if it had been the Home Secretary's daughter who had been abused, the outcome would probably have been very different. The wide publicity generated an enormous amount of public support: numerous petitions and protests were delivered to the Home Secretary, and there was a picket of Scotland Yard and the Department of Public Prosecutions, as a result of which four women were sent to Holloway prison for refusing to recognize the court or pay their fines. Despite all this effort, the campaign was unsuccessful in terms of securing justice, though it did succeed in bringing the issues involved to wide public attention.[23]

The WFL's crusade for legal justice and an equal moral standard led to a campaign for women police. Ever since feminists had begun campaigning around prostitution and the sexual abuse of girls there had been suggestions that a special service of women police assistants, or matrons, be established, so that the victims of male violence and sexual assault could be sympathetically dealt with and protected from further abuse by the male police force. These suggestions gradually developed into demands, both for women doctors and matrons to attend to the medical and emotional aspects of such cases, and for women police, with the same powers as the men. The first suffragette to voice such a demand was Nina Boyle. Throughout 1912 and 1913 she campaigned strongly for women-only police vans and women officers to accompany women prisoners to and from the courts and the prisons, in order to prevent the sexual harassment of the prisoners, who included not only suffragettes but women involved in the cases which Edith Watson and others had been monitoring in the courts. Suffragettes also made repeated demands for women police to support and protect women and children in court, particularly in cases of sexual abuse, when women were excluded. There was also a growing demand for women police to protect suffragettes from harassment at Speakers' Corner.[24]

During 1914 the pressure for women police increased, from both militant and non-militant suffrage societies as well as social purity organizations, and deputations to the Home Office and obstruction protests were organized. When war was declared and the Government put out a call for volunteer Special Constables Nina Boyle seized the opportunity to establish a force of Women Volunteer Police. She argued that 'if we now equip every district in the country with a body of women able and willing to do this class of work it will be very difficult for the authorities to refuse to employ women in such a capacity after the war'. On 28 August 1914 *The Vote* reported that the first two women had been enrolled at Sandgate in Kent, and from then on there was a steady stream of volunteers. In November the WVP amalgamated with another group of volunteers organized by Margaret Damer Dawson of the Criminal Law Amendment Committee, to form the Women Police Volunteer Corps. Despite the reluctance of the Commissioner of Police they were given permission to train and patrol in London on a voluntary basis. Their role was to offer advice and support to women and children, with the intention of preventing sexual harassment and abuse. They concentrated particularly on the districts surrounding the railway stations, where procurers were said to be most active, and worked especially with Belgian refugees who arrived in large numbers in England in the early months of the war.[25]

Meanwhile another body of women, the Voluntary Women Patrols, had also been organized to act as unofficial policewomen, but from very different motives. Formed by the National Union of Women Workers, the aim of the patrols was to restrain the behaviour of women and girls who were said to be infected by 'khaki fever' and to be 'infesting' the neighbourhood of military camps. Nina Boyle was extremely alarmed at the use of women to restrict women's civil liberties, especially as the outbreak of war had led to calls for the revival of the infamous Contagious Diseases Acts. She was even more outraged when she discovered that some members of her own Women Police Volunteer Corps were being used for similar purposes. This led to a split within the Corps, with Damer Dawson and the majority of members voting for 'cooperation with the men'. Nina Boyle, Edith Watson, and Eva Christy reformed the Women Police Volunteers, announcing defiantly in *The Vote* that the WPV was now once again under the control of the Women's Freedom League, and that it would continue to work along the lines originally laid down, namely for 'the service of women'. They would absolutely refuse 'to assist the authorities in carrying out laws and regulations known to be unjust and improper'. Meanwhile Damer Dawson reformed the remaining forty or so women into the Women Police Service, thus founding what would eventually become an officially recognized force of policewomen.[26]

After the split the declared strategy of the WPV was to train women for duty in every Metropolitan Police and Assize Court, and there is evidence that they did at least start on this project. *The Vote* repeatedly criticized the work of Damer Dawson's women patrols, and the WPV under Nina Boyle made it absolutely clear that they saw their role as supporting women, and would under no circumstances collaborate in controlling women. Nevertheless the coopting of the women patrols isolated the WPV and it gradually faded away. Although there can be no doubt of Nina Boyle's and the WFL's implacable opposition to the policing of women by women in the service of patriarchal authority, they were perhaps naive in supposing that women police would be able to do otherwise. In their enthusiasm to establish a force of women who would serve the interests of women, they initially allied themselves with women from the 'social purity' movement, whose political motives were often ambivalent. The Criminal Law Amendment Committee, although it included a number of feminists and was committed to ending the sexual exploitation and abuse of women and girls, appeared unaware of the contradictions inherent in attempting to use patriarchal structures and institutions to promote greater freedom for women.[27]

The War, 'DORA' and '40D': The Contagious Diseases Acts Revisited

Unlike the WSPU, which abandoned its campaign for the vote shortly after the outbreak of World War I, the WFL, while suspending militant action, chose to continue the campaign for the vote and an equal moral standard. In 1915 the membership of the WFL's political and militant department was swelled by some former members of the WSPU, who disagreed with the direction the Pankhursts had taken. They also often worked with a group known as Suffragettes of the WSPU which split off from the 'official' WSPU. The war had brought the issue of the double standard of sexual morality even more to the fore, with, for example, the problem of 'war babies' (many of whom, feminists insisted, were the outcome of male sexual assault), the sexual harassment of women workers in munition factories, and the atrocities committed on women during wartime by soldiers. The mass rape and murder of women in Belgium and France by German soldiers provoked Nina Boyle to write an article on 'The Male Peril'. Feminists also had to be constantly on their guard against attempts to reintroduce the CD Acts by local Watch Committees, by the compulsory notification of VD, and by means of The Defence of the Realm Act (known as 'DORA'). This gave the military and police extraordinary powers and in areas near military camps they were using them to close public houses to women between 7 p.m. and 8 a.m. In some cases they were even imposing a total curfew on 'women of a certain class' during those hours.

In September 1916, Nina Boyle reminded readers of *The Vote* of the reasons why the WFL had severed its connection with the women police, and warned that the danger was drawing nearer that 'women might be used by men to do their dirty work'. Less than two months later a government-sponsored publicity campaign against VD was launched which called for the use of women police and women patrols to control prostitutes in order to 'protect' soldiers from infection. The WFL sent an immediate protest to the Home Secretary, deploring the government's intention to penalize prostitutes as a remedy against VD, while exonerating men. It called an emergency conference on compulsory notification, as a result of which a 'VD Manifesto of Women's Societies' was drawn up. The manifesto declared women's opposition to compulsory notification of VD, and compulsory detention and increased penalizing of prostitutes. It also listed the following demands: the provision of easily accessible treatment; stringent enforcement of the age of consent law; the raising of the age of consent to 18; soliciting to be an equal offence in men and women; an equal moral standard; the enfranchisement of women; and better military discipline in the camps. A deputation from the women's societies went to see Lord Rhondda, whose daughter Margaret (later Lady Rhondda) was a militant feminist. Her father claimed to be in sympathy and agreed that 'there was no real cure [for VD] other than chastity for men'. Within a month, however, a new twist was given to the affair by the publication by the government of the latest Criminal Law Amendment Bill. Feminists interpreted sections of this latest Bill as yet another attempt to revive the CD Acts, and there was a mass protest meeting at Central Hall, Westminster on 6 March, where it was reiterated that there should be no persecution of prostitutes and that 'our infallible preventative is chastity'. This resulted in a 'Drop the Bill' campaign and a demand to an end to all attempts to deal with prostitution by legislation until women were enfranchised.[28]

The 'Drop the Bill' campaign was briefly interrupted by news of the majority vote in Parliament for the partial enfranchisement of women. As far as the vote was concerned, the end now seemed to be in sight, and some feminists were optimistic that it would empower women to advance the cause of an equal moral standard. An article in *The Vote* expressed the hope that women's voting power would help to spread the idea that real sexual pleasure lay in forms of enjoyment that are not only harmless but beneficial. For the first time *The Vote* advertised a meeting about sex education, and printed an article promoting the idea of sex education as an alternative to legislation against sex slavery. Ethel Wedgwood argued that the notion of controlling instincts solely by prohibition and restraint was a legacy of outworn creeds. 'Physical love', she wrote, 'needs to be handled as part of physical science'. She believed that sex education needed to be based on 'knowledge of the laws of the human body, and on habits based on those laws', though she did not explain what the laws were. But she also insisted that sex education was best handled by mothers, and should definitely not be handed over to experts.[29]

The optimism regarding the vote seems to have inspired the WFL to intensify its campaigns against the double standard. At its eleventh annual conference in February 1918 the WFL passed a formal resolution:

> To insist on the recognition of an equal moral standard for men and women and to call upon the Government to establish such a standard in all its laws and enactments; to protest vigorously on all occasions against the victimization of women for certain offences while men go scot-free or have lighter punishment for similar offences; to press for a measure which will secure the publication of all names in every prosecution for immorality and indecency, and to insist that no man or woman shall be convicted upon police evidence only.

The 'Drop the Bill' campaign eventually succeeded in its aim. For some time, however, there had been rumours of a new regulation to be introduced under DORA, which would be even more punitive towards women: regulation '40D'. From this point until the war ended in November, when the order was re-voked, the slogan '40D Must Go' dominated the headlines in *The Vote*. There were numerous reports of protest meetings all over the country, and questions and debates on the subject in Parliament. All feminist organizations, and most other women's organizations, were unanimous in their opposition. *The Vote* urged its readers to use their recently acquired 'Woman Power' to defeat this latest assault on their civil liberties, just as they had in the case of the Criminal Law Amendment Bill. In order to underline the implications of '40D' for women *The Vote* devoted a whole issue to 'The Contagious Diseases Acts: Past and Present'. This outlined the history of feminist resistance to the state regulation of prostitution, from Josephine Butler to the present day, arguing that the effect of '40D' would be to revive the Acts, and reminding readers of the reasons why feminists had originally opposed them. Charlotte Despard pointed out that '40D' threw everything feminists had striven for into the melting pot, declaring: '40D spells slavery!' Margaret Wynne Nevinson reported cases under the regulation of women being coerced into internal medical examinations at the instigation of soldiers, who claimed to have been infected by them. 'What a gorgeous opportunity', she wrote, 'for the jealous lover, frenzied with thwarted passion, the rejected suitor, the scoundrel and the blackmailer!' The medical examinations were in theory voluntary, but in practice women were remanded again and again until their 'consent' was secured. Some women were reported as having committed suicide as a result of the compulsory internal medical examination, which the authorities in-sisted 'inflicted no hardship'.[30]

Alice Abadam, of Suffragettes of the WSPU, restated the feminist demand for an end to male soliciting and proposed that '40D' be replaced by a regulation making it illegal for any man to offer or give a woman money for the purposes of sexual intercourse. The government was deluged with over six hundred resolutions demanding the withdrawal not only of '40D' but of yet another Criminal Law Amendment Bill, and a new Sexual Offences Bill, both of which included clauses of a similar nature. '40D' rapidly developed into a national issue, with considerable support for feminists being expressed in the national press, including *The Star*, the *Yorkshire Observer*, the *Manchester Guardian*, the *New Statesman*, *The Herald*, and especially the *Daily News*. A resolution condemning it was also passed at the Labour Party Women's Conference. In November a mass protest meeting at Queen's Hall was organized by the WFL and the Association for Moral and Social Hygiene, with over fifty societies represented and Millicent Fawcett presiding. So great was the pressure that eventually the Government was forced to set up a cabinet committee to enquire whether any modification to '40D' was necessary.

A few days after the meeting at Queen's Hall, the war was at an end, and shortly afterwards '40D' was revoked. But that was very far from being the end of the matter. Almost at once new headlines appeared: 'Worse than 40D!' The WFL continued to campaign for an equal moral standard for some years after the war. This account, however, ends in 1918 because that year was a turning point in the history of the campaigns against the double standard. *The Vote*'s special feature on the CD Acts, past and present, was an indication that by 1918 the campaigns had come full circle. It seems deeply ironic that, just at the point of enfranchisement, feminists found themselves back where they started, in terms of the double standard. During the 1920s the campaign gradually withered away with the decline of feminist radicalism and the rise of reformism. This is another irony: that, just as feminists were in a position to wield their recently won political power, the radical impetus of the Women's Movement began to fade. The reasons for this, some of which will be discussed in later chapters, have yet to be fully explored.[31]

The sustained strength and determination of the feminist campaigns against the double standard, from Josephine Butler up to the end of World War I, is impressive. This is especially true of the militant feminists' campaigns, which must be viewed against the background of the broader struggle for the vote, the intense opposition which they encountered, and all that that meant, in terms of arrest, imprisonment, hunger-strikes, forced feeding, and persistent harassment under the Cat and Mouse Act. The fact that so many suffragettes were also able to pursue the struggle so relentlessly throughout the war, when there were so many other pressing demands on their time and energy, is also quite astonishing, and an important part of feminist history which deserves to be better known. This account of the whole struggle has shown that it was, in essence, a struggle to emancipate women from female sexual slavery, which militant feminists (and many non-militants as well) saw as central to male power. Despite the real problems caused by temporary alliances with the social purity movement, most feminists made it clear that their demand for an equal moral standard was a *political* demand. The slogan 'Votes for Women, Chastity for Men' was the culmination of over a century of feminist struggle to politicize sexuality, a struggle which was of great significance, in terms of promoting the concept of female sexual autonomy.

The challenge to the double standard was also a challenge to the core assumption of the patriarchal model of sexuality: the assumption that male sexual needs were 'natural' and beyond their control. By breaking the conspiracy of silence, and exposing what feminists saw as the *real* 'facts of life', male sexuality was revealed as a weapon of male power. This represented a radical redefinition of the natural as political, which had potentially revolutionary implications for the system of hetero-relations, as the following words of Emmeline Pankhurst suggest:

> If it is true – I do not believe it for one moment – that men have less power of self-control than women have, or might have if properly educated, if there is a terrible distinction between the physical and moral standards of both sexes, then I say as a woman, representing thousands of women all over the world, men must find some way of supplying the needs of their sex which does not include the degradation of ours.

The threat which this posed to male power was, in a sense, acknowledged by Frederick Pethick-Lawrence, a supporter of militant feminism and a member of the WSPU until it became women-only, who said that much of the male opposition to women's suffrage was based on the fear that women, if enfranchised, would impose upon men 'impossibly strict' standards of morality:

> In particular it was said . . . that on sex matters women were narrower and harder than men; and that if they were given power they would impose impossibly strict standards of morality, and endeavour to enforce them by penalties for non-observance.

The anti-feminist biologist, Walter Heape, whose anti-spinster views were noted in Chapter 1, was also well aware of the implications of the militant feminist challenge to male sexuality, and used his status as a scientist in an attempt to demolish their arguments and reassert the dominant definition of the natural:

> It is the fashion to talk glibly of the need for the suppression of brutal sexual instincts, of the control of sexual passion, and so forth. Such demands are made by women and addressed to man as a perverted creature, as an abnormal product of civilisation. The fact is that woman's sexuality is on quite a different plane to that of man; she is wholly ignorant as a rule of man's normal requirements, and

her virtuous demands, essentially designed for her own benefit as she conceives, are opposed to natural law.[32]

Although most feminists remained deeply committed to an equal moral standard, and some continued to campaign for it for many years after the war, we can begin to detect a change in strategy from 1918 onwards. We have seen that, for good reasons, many were becoming more and more wary about legislation as a means of empowering women in the sexual sphere. Even those who persisted with the legal struggle believed that, in the long run, changes in male sexual behaviour would only be brought about through education. Ethel Wedgwood's suggestion in *The Vote*, that feminists should in future look towards sex education as the means of overcoming the sexual exploitation and abuse of women and children, seems to have been generally regarded as a positive way forward. This of course raises crucial questions: what is meant by sex education, who controls it, what assumptions is it based on, what model of sexuality does it presuppose? Wedgwood's assertion that physical love should be handled as part of physical science, that it was subject to the 'ordinary laws of biology', implies that she believed that the science of sex, and sex education, were neutral or apolitical – though she did warn against what she called 'expertism'. But by 1918 scientific expertism in sexual matters had already begun to take over, and the publication in that year of Marie Stopes' *Married Love* heralded a flood of marriage manuals, teaching the 'facts of life'. The kind of 'facts' they purveyed, and their implications for feminism and hetero-relations, will be explored in later chapters.

A criticism which is sometimes made of the feminist campaigns against the double standard is that they were purely negative. Walkowitz, for instance, has argued that 'on the whole this attack on male dominance and male vice involved no positive assertion of female sexuality'.[33] What I have argued in this chapter is that the campaigns were not only an attack on male sexuality but a demand for female sexual autonomy, and were, in that sense positive. More importantly, they cannot be seen in isolation from the assertion of spinsterhood as a positive choice for women, a choice which, as I have already argued, has been mistakenly assumed to mean a denial of sexuality. There is also considerable evidence that many of the feminists involved in the campaigns against the double standard were also exploring the positive implications of female sexual autonomy, and attempting to construct a feminist model of sexuality. This evidence will be discussed in the following two chapters.

Notes

1   The principal secondary sources on the history of the militant struggle for the vote which include some reference, though mostly derogatory, to the campaign against the double standard, are Mitchell (1966; 1967; 1977) and Rosen (1974).

Feminist sources include Rover (1970) and Strachey (1978 [1928]). Sylvia Pankhurst's *The Suffragette Movement* devotes less than three pages to the subject, and she gives the clear impression that she wished to distance herself from it because it was not in accord with her socialist politics (Pankhurst, 1977 [1931], pp. 521–3).

2　When Emmeline and Frederick Pethick-Lawrence left the WSPU in 1912 as a result of political disagreements with the Pankhursts, it was agreed that they should continue to publish *Votes For Women* independently. The editorial line remained pro-militant. From October 1912 the new official organ of the WSPU was *The Suffragette*.

3　*The Vote*, 29 January 1910; 5 November 1910; 7 January 1911.

4　*The Vote*, 17 February 1912; 24 February 1912.

5　*The Vote*, 16 March 1912. For a detailed account of 'Black Friday' see Morrell (1981).

6　*Votes For Women*, 1 January 1915.

7　*The Vote*, 25 May 1910.

8　*The Vote*, 30 March 1912; *Votes For Women*, 17 November 1911, emphasis in original.

9　*Votes For Women*, 3 May 1912; 14 June 1912. One of the main sources of data was a recently published book by the American feminist Jane Addams, entitled *A New Conscience and an Ancient Evil* (1912). On the significance of W.T. Stead's death in reviving the campaigns, see Swanwick (1918).

10　*Votes For Women*, 26 July 1912; *The Vote*, 13 February 1914. For further details on the Criminal Law Amendment Committee on the subject of prostitution and male sexuality, see Chapter 4.

11　*Votes For Women*, 25 October 1912.

12　*The Suffragette*, 29 November 1912.

13　*The Vote*, 19 May 1913; Rosen (1974), p. 195.

14　*The Suffragette*, 11 April 1913; 18 April 1913. The article entitled 'The Government and White Slavery' was also reprinted as an appendix to *The Great Scourge*.

15　*The Vote*, 30 May 1913. For further discussion of this incident, see Mort (1987), pp. 153–63.

16　Martindale (1908), p. 8; pp. 70–1.

17　*The Suffragette*, 11 April 1913; *The Vote*, 19 May 1913.

18　There were several editions of this book, some entitled *The Great Scourge and How to End It*, some *Plain Facts about a Great Evil*, and some bearing both titles. Some had an appendix which included 'The Truth About the Piccadilly Flat' and 'The Government and White Slavery'. For a detailed analysis of *The Great Scourge* as theory see Elizabeth Sarah (1983).

19　Pankhurst (1913), p. 36; *The Great Scourge* was not an academic text, and there was no systematic list of sources on VD, but the main authorities cited included: Barrett, Ehrlich, Finot, Forel, Foster Scott, Fournier, Hallopeau, Marshall, Morrow, Mott, Noeggerath, and Tausig. Marshall and Morrow were cited the most frequently. Many critics, including some feminists, challenged these figures: see Billington-Greig (1913) and Pankhurst (1977 [1931]).

20　Pankhurst (1913), pp. 43–4.

21　Pankhurst (1913), p. 133; p. 33; p. 109; p. 154; p. 137. Many of the sources cited by Pankhurst agreed that prostitution was unnecessary, especially August Forel, who referred to it as 'the basest of all slaveries'.

22　*The Suffragette*, 18 July 1913; 25 July 1913; for further details on the Piccadilly Flat Case see Rover (1970).

23　Pamphlet in Fawcett Library; its authorship was not disclosed, but, judging by the style, it was probably Nina Boyle and/or Edith Watson or other members of the political and militant department.

24 Elizabeth Blackwell had in fact suggested in 1881 the introduction of 'a certain number of superior women into the police organization' to deal specifically with women offenders, especially prostitutes. However she insisted that the introduction of ordinary women 'corresponding to the common policeman', or 'in any way subordinate to lower officials', would be 'out of the question' (Blackwell, 1881, pp. 18–19). See Joan Lock (1979) for a fascinating history of the women police.

25 Lock (1979), p. 18. It is not certain who was the first woman to appear in public in uniform, but Lock believes it was probably Edith Watson, though it may have been Nina Boyle herself.

26 *The Vote*, 19 February 1915; the NUWW was shortly afterwards renamed the National Council of Women.

27 *The Vote*, 20 August 1915.

28 *The Vote*, 1 September 1916; 17 November 1916; 2 February 1917; 9 March 1917.

29 *The Vote*, 8 August 1917; 28 September 1917.

30 *The Vote*, 1 March 1918; 19 April 1918; 16 August 1918.

31 See, for example, Lewis (1975).

32 *The Suffragette*, 29 August 1913; Pethick-Lawrence (1943), p. 68; Heape (1913), p. 4.

33 Walkowitz cites only two exceptions to this generalization: Olive Schreiner, whose sexual ideology has already been discussed in Chapter 1; and Stella Browne, who will be discussed in Chapter 4.

Chapter 3

Towards a Feminist Model of Sexuality
Elizabeth Blackwell

the sexuality of women [is] the keynote to which all men's relations should be tuned, *Blackwell (1891) p. 5.*

The process of politicizing sexuality in which Victorian and Edwardian feminists were engaged necessarily entailed challenging both common-sense and scientific notions of what was or was not 'natural'. The power to define what is natural has always been absolutely crucial to the maintenance of any system of power relations. The allegedly 'natural' inferiority of black people, for instance, was a major justification for slavery, colonialism, and imperialism, and still operates today to legitimate more subtle forms of racism. In the nineteenth century the principal justification for denying women political, economic, educational, and legal equality with men was their 'natural' inferiority, physical and intellectual. The very existence of the Women's Movement, and the increasing achievements of women in various fields, such as education or medicine, posed a threat to patriarchal definitions of the 'natural' differences between the sexes; and the most common masculine response was to denounce women who refused to accept their place in the patriarchal order as 'unnatural'.

The charge of defying nature was directed with particular vehemence towards those women who resisted marriage, motherhood, or their confinement to the domestic sphere. Most feminists did not in fact demand the abolition of marriage; on the contrary they appear to have assumed that most women, given a free choice, would choose marriage and motherhood as their primary vocation. The very notion of free choice was nevertheless an implicit challenge to the belief that the desire to be wives and mothers was natural. Furthermore, by analyzing and exposing the ways in which women were coerced into marriage, feminism implicitly questioned the assumption that the institution was based on a *natural* impulse or desire, and hence was a *natural* relation. For if it really *were* natural, why would there be any need for coercion? As Harriet Taylor said: 'if women's preference be natural, there can be no necessity for enforcing it by law'.[1]

The campaigns against the double standard of sexual morality were, however, a far more direct challenge to patriarchal definitions of the natural. They represented a redefinition of male sexuality as *political* rather than natural. Although there was no attempt in the campaigns themselves to move beyond a critique of male sexuality, it is possible to see, emerging out of all these struggles, a radically new way of conceptualizing sexuality and hetero-sexual relations: an attempt to construct a feminist, as opposed to a patriar-chal, model of sexuality. The main purpose of this chapter and the following one is to sketch the main characteristics of this model by means of an exam-ination of the work of feminist sexual theorists: women whose political prac-tice included attempting to explore more theoretically the relationship between sexuality and male power, how it might be changed, and the possibility of constructing forms of sexual relationship and practice which presupposed female sexual autonomy. It is important to stress that these were no armchair theorists, and their work has never been dignified, even where it has been recognized at all, with labels such as 'science', 'psychology', 'sexology', or even theory, in the way that the work of some of their male contemporaries has. The ideas these feminists attempted to articulate in their writings devel-oped out of their active involvement in the Women's Movement, and many of them have already been discussed in that context. The aim here is to analyze them in greater depth, and to discuss to what extent feminists were involved, not only in redefining sexuality, but in a positive exploration of female sexuality.

One of the most neglected figures from this point of view is Elizabeth Blackwell. Although she is fairly well known for her pioneering work in opening up the medical profession to women, her work on sexuality has been almost entirely ignored. Where it has been mentioned it has been accorded only the most superficial consideration and she has usually been labelled as a sexual puritan.[2] Yet she was, as far as we know, the first woman in the nineteenth century to write specifically and explicitly about sexuality from both a feminist and a scientific perspective. For this reason alone her work merits serious attention, and it is hoped that the following analysis will con-tribute towards a reassessment of her significance in feminist histories of sexuality. I believe that she was the first to attempt to supersede the patriar-chal model of sexuality, and to begin to construct a feminist model of sexuality, predicated on the concept of female sexual autonomy. It was a model which was based on the assumption of human rationality articulated by Mary Wollstonecraft, and which stood the naturalistic assumption underpinning the double standard on its head. It was thus potentially revolutionary in its implications for hetero-relations.

Elizabeth Blackwell (1821–1910)

Elizabeth Blackwell was the first woman to qualify as a doctor. Born in Britain, she qualified in 1849 in the United States (sixteen years before

Elizabeth Garrett obtained her licence to practise in Britain) and was admitted to the British Medical Register in 1859.[3] She practised medicine in both countries and eventually settled in Britain from 1879 until her death in 1910. During the last forty years of her life she was actively involved in the feminist campaigns against the double standard of sexual morality, and was a founding member of the Moral Reform Union. She chose to remain a spinster and at the age of 35 adopted a 7-year-old orphan, Katherine Barry (known as Kitty), who remained her life-long companion. Her relationship to feminism was somewhat ambivalent: her decision to remain a spinster was at least partly a reflection of her antipathy to the institution of marriage and probably also to what it implied in terms of women's lack of sexual autonomy. She wrote in her memoirs that 'whenever I became sufficiently intimate with any individual to be able to realise what a life association might mean, I shrank from the prospect disappointed or repelled'. Indeed, there are strong indications from her memoirs and diaries that she thought initially of embarking on a medical career precisely in order to avoid marriage: 'I felt more determined than ever to become a physician, and thus place a strong barrier between me and all ordinary marriage'. She also had an intense hatred of domesticity, child care, being 'ladylike', and other 'feminine' accomplishments. Yet she was initially critical of the Women's Movement and tended to blame women themselves for their inferior position, and always considered marriage and motherhood to be woman's 'natural' and most important role. Nor was her decision to pursue a medical career made out of any desire to strike a blow for women's rights, though she did believe that women who suffered from specifically female complaints and disorders needed to be able to entrust their bodies to the care of other women.

As a young woman Blackwell distanced herself from feminism and dreamed of 'radical action' which would 'redeem the rising generation'. This radical action would be based on the power of women as mothers, using to the full their essential, innate maternal qualities, such as gentleness, sympathy, sensitivity, and, above all, altruism, to mould and influence the next generation. Even women who were not biological mothers reflected this power of maternity, since they carried their maternal instincts with them into medicine or whichever profession they entered. She always insisted to women medical students that far from trying to be like men they must strive *not* to be like men; their task was to humanize medicine by bringing to it feminine, maternal values. To a large extent she maintained this essentialist view of woman-as-mother throughout her life, even after she had become committed to an oppositional form of feminism, such as her work in the Moral Reform Union. Her commitment to motherhood was reflected in all her writings, but especially in the earlier works, in which she argued strongly that it was one of the fundamental 'laws of life' that the whole development of the female child should be towards one goal: motherhood. As Margaret Forster has pointed out, it was almost as though Blackwell, having herself deviated from the norm, felt compelled to reinforce it. It should be remembered however that it was Blackwell's medical training, with its heavy emphasis on the way the human body – and especially the female body – was governed by physiological laws, which to a large extent shaped her ideas and beliefs about women's maternal qualities and functions. This meant that she was deeply influenced by the patriarchal thinking which led to the construction of those laws. As I shall argue, the same influences can also be traced in her ideas about sex, and led to a number of contradictions in her model of sexuality, which, from a feminist point of view, to some extent limited its revolutionary potential.

Sexuality and the Relations of the Sexes: Standing the Patriarchal Model on its Head

Blackwell began writing about sexuality soon after returning to England in 1869, when she was introduced to the feminist campaigns against the Contagious Diseases Acts and the unequal standard of morality. She wrote later that it was at this time that her eyes 'suddenly opened to the purchase of women', and on her travels around Europe during the 1870s she became acutely aware of the dangers of ignorance and misinformation and the need for education in sexual matters. She soon became actively involved in the Moral Reform Union, and was also elected to the council of the National Vigilance Association, serving as a member of its Parliamentary sub-committee which was concerned with legislation. Her work in this field, together with her status among feminists as the first woman doctor and her long-standing friendships with some of the leading members of the Victorian Women's Movement, meant that she was very close to the core of feminist discussion and agitation around sexuality at this time, and thus in a position both to influence and be influenced by them.

Blackwell's motivation for writing about sexuality was both political and educational. She felt that the ignorance of parents, and especially mothers, in relation to 'essential physiological facts' was deplorable and the source of 'our gravest social evils'. She believed that women, because of their 'mighty potentiality of maternity', had a crucial role to play in educating the young, and a special responsibility in matters of moral welfare. She also believed that the most fundamental work which rested on the medical profession was 'the spread of physiological truth in its practical application to the education of both boys and girls'. As a woman physician and a 'Christian physiologist', who was deeply committed to justice and equality between the sexes, she felt under an obligation to counteract the 'false theories of human nature' which she believed most women had been taught and had uncritically accepted, especially those theories which legitimated the double standard of sexual morality. Referring to the Act of 1857 which had encoded into statute law the assumption that it was 'natural' for a husband to be unfaithful, she declared: 'In our own country the unjust condonation of adultery, by law, in 1857, against the strenuous opposition of far-seeing statesmen, has educated more than one generation in a false and degrading idea of physiology.' She believed that the medical profession could prove, 'through its knowledge of the physical and mental structure of the human race, that the great Christian doctrine of the equal standard of morality for our race is true doctrine based upon our human constitution'.[4]

In her first major essay, *Moral Education*, she attempted to combine her views on motherhood, her religious beliefs, her physiological knowledge, and her experience as a physician with her developing feminist consciousness, producing a characteristic blend of sexual theorizing and politics which she herself considered to be extremely radical, even daring.[5] Although not as daring as some of her later works it did contain some radical ideas which Blackwell was to develop into a coherent and challenging feminist critique of the patriarchal model of sexuality and heterosexual relations. Written when the campaign against the Contagious Diseases Acts had been in progress for about seven years, it was in essence an attack on the double standard of sexual morality which the Acts embodied, and which legitimated the sexual exploitation of women by men. She challenged the assumption underpinning both the double standard and the institution of prostitution – the assumption that the male sexual urge was natural and could not be controlled. This she did by setting out, carefully and logically, the 'laws of physiology' in the attempt to 'prove', not only that the sexual faculty *could* be controlled, but that *failure* to do so was *unnatural*. In other words she took the naturalistic argument which supported the double standard and stood it on its head. What was 'natural' according to the patriarchal view of sexuality, she alleged to be 'unnatural', and vice versa.

Blackwell accepted that the sexual instinct was the strongest force in human nature but argued that the essence of being human was the capacity to guide and control instinct by means of 'Reason, with the Will to execute its dictates'. Not only was the prevailing view of sex incorrect; so too was the prevailing view of the nature of 'man', and even the concept of 'nature' itself:

> Thought is often confused by a vague use of the term 'nature'. The educated man is more natural than the savage, because he approaches more nearly to the true type of man, and has acquired the power of transmitting increased capacities to his children. What is popularly called a state of nature, is really a state of rudimentary life, which does not display the real nature of man, but only its imperfect condition.

The great distinguishing marks of human beings, she continued, were their mental capacities and power of self-command. She argued that the fact that people were capable of exercising a high degree of control over the strongest of all cravings – hunger – showed the immense power of human intelligence and self-control. This faculty did not develop at the same rate as the sexual faculty, however; hence the necessity for parental, and especially maternal influence and guidance, which would eventually develop into self-control. This necessity existed 'as a law of human nature, unchangeable, rooted in the human constitution'. Failure to exercise the power of the Will and the control demanded by Reason would result in the 'blind instinctive elements' in human nature achieving 'complete mastery over the individual'. Such an individual was 'contrary to the true type of man', wrote Blackwell, and thus 'unnatural'.[6]

Blackwell was emphatic that physical passion was not in itself evil, but 'an essential part of our nature'; but because of its susceptibility to mental impressions it could become either an ennobling or a degrading force for both individual and society. The 'unnatural forcing' of sexual development during puberty and youth, and the 'immense provision . . . made for facilitating fornication' (not least by big business) constituted a grave danger to young men, who often became victims of physical sensation and suggestion. As well as being vulnerable to the common dangers of moral corruption they were often *advised* by those whom they respected to use prostitutes, a step which, once taken, was fatal. It led inevitably to the unnatural separation of physical sex from love and affection; and physical sex could be as addictive as alcohol, and lead ultimately to the destruction of the will:

> He has tasted the physical delights of sex, separated from its more exquisite spiritual joys. This unnatural divorce degrades whilst it intoxicates him. Having tasted these physical pleasures, he can no more do without them than the drunkard without his dram. He ignorantly tramples under foot his birthright of rich compound infinite human love, enthralled by the simple limited animal passion. His Will is no longer free. He has destroyed that grand endowment of Man – that freedom of the youthful Will, which is the priceless possession of innocence and of virtue, and has subjected himself to the slavery of lust. He is no longer his own master – he is the servant of his passions.

Blackwell especially deplored the actions of some parents whose incorrect views of sex and ignorance of physiological facts led them to provide mistresses for their sons, in order to keep them from resorting to prostitutes. She detailed the social and psychological effects on women of sexual exploitation, as well as the more general economic consequences of 'the degradation of female labour'. She believed that women, because of their maternal role, embodied to a greater extent than men the morality of a society, but criticized the hypocrisy of so-called Christian nations who upheld the double standard by claiming that the nature of men and women differed so radically that the same moral law was not applicable to the two sexes. 'Purity in woman cannot exist without purity in man', she declared.[7]

Moral Education represented, however, much more than a simple plea for purity and a single standard of sexual morality. It was an attempt to provide rational, scientific principles, derived from physiology, upon which the 'true relations of the sexes' should be based; it was offered as a 'Physiological Guide, showing the true laws of sex, in relation to human progress'. In Blackwell's view the laws of physiology pointed in one direction only: to marriage and the family, the only institutions which secured the observance of these laws. Thus her answer to the question with which she had begun – 'What is the true standard for the relations of men and women . . .?' – was: 'the early and faithful union of one man with one woman'. This she considered to be indisputably 'the true Ideal of Society', which secured 'the health and purity of the family relation' and was 'the foundation of social and national welfare'. This conviction was supported by another physiological law, the essential 'duality of sex' – the fact that the faculty of sex, unlike other human faculties, involved two people and resulted in parentage. 'No faculty', she wrote, 'can be regarded in the light of simple self-indulgence, which requires two for its proper exercise'; to disregard this fact was 'unscientific'.

The conservatism of Blackwell's conclusions to this essay, with the absolute insistence on the family and reproductive heterosexuality as the only foundation of human development and social progress, has led to her being dismissed by some historians and sexologists as a sexual puritan. Feminists, too, have tended to neglect her work on sexuality, and it is not difficult to see why: the combination of such moral absolutism and such a conservative view of woman's role in society is unlikely to endear her to those who are still struggling to change patriarchal values and power relations, particularly those which maintain and promote compulsory heterosexuality and the patriarchal family. At the same time it is important not to allow the conservative elements in the work to obscure its radical potential. To challenge the double standard by turning the naturalist argument on its head and critiquing the concept of human nature was extremely radical for its time and still has a radical ring today, when naturalism in sexual relations is in the process of being forcefully reasserted.

The Human Element in Sex

The radical ideas which Blackwell had introduced in *Moral Education* were developed more fully a few years later in what was to become her major work on sexuality. First published in 1880, *The Human Element in Sex*[8] contained all the principal elements of her thinking on sexuality, which were to remain essentially unchanged for the rest of her life. Her aim was to correct what she saw as a fundamental error in the prevailing view of human sexuality, namely the failure to recognize that 'in the human race the mind tends to rule the body, and that sex in the human being is even more a mental passion than a physical instinct'. She also argued that ignorance of the facts of sexual physiology was 'the greatest present obstacle to progress', and that a woman could neither educate her children nor play her proper part in society without this knowledge. Nevertheless the book was addressed not directly to mothers but to doctors, as an aid in the instruction of parents and guardians of the young. The medical audience was reflected in the general tone of the book, with its stress on scientific laws and evidence. The central theme remained the power of mind over body and the crucial importance of the distinction between the sexual organization of 'man' and that of the lower animals. Blackwell argued that while the sexual impulse in animals was 'a simple, imperative instinct', in humans it was a complex, 'compound faculty', involving thoughts and feelings, social ties, conscience and duty. Emphasizing that there was nothing inherently evil in physical sexual pleasure she insisted that it was these mental or moral aspects which characterized the sexual faculty in human beings, and which moulded and governed the human form of the sexual relations. Although she continued to define sexuality narrowly in reproductive terms she was not a biological determinist. On the contrary, her argument was that human sexual physiology had evolved in such a way as to reflect the demands made by the increasing complexity of the mental element in human sexuality.

According to Blackwell the essential features of human reproduction, namely ovulation and sperm formation, were governed by two laws, which she called 'the continuity of action' and 'the power of self-adjustment'. These were the distinctive marks of human sexual function, and both were necessitated by the growth of reason and its corollary, progressive civilization. The first, the law of continuity of action, signified that procreation in humans was not limited, as in lower animals, to any special season. This meant that men and women could be governed by *reason* as to the time and circumstances when they married and commenced the important work of founding a family. The sexual organs were thus the *servants* of the Will, not its masters: 'The physical organs are maintained in fit condition for reproduction by these functions of ovulation and spermation, as servants ready to obey at any time the superior intelligence of the master Will'. She added later that she looked forward to the time when woman would assume 'her due place as the regulator of sexual intercourse'. Throughout the animal world, she said, procreation was governed by the will of the female, and it was the task of physiology to show how this could be re-established amongst human beings. Amongst animals,

> Not violence, but gentleness is shown by the male to the female. Her refusal or desire guides sexual intercourse amongst the lower animals. To raise the human race to this higher animal level from which it has fallen is a special task of advanced physiology, which can show the physical method and reason of this redemption.

Like most feminists at that time she was opposed to artificial means of contraception, but considered that the periodic character of the female constitution enabled women themselves to regulate the probability of conception. She also maintained that in human marriage the satisfaction of physical desires formed a secondary, not a primary, part and that within the marriage relationship it must always be 'the woman's constitution which must determine the times of the special act of physical union'.[9]

The second law governing human reproduction was the law of self-adjustment. Blackwell argued that menstruation and nocturnal emissions were natural functions which endowed the individual with the power of self-adjustment and secured her or his independence by giving them control over their own nature. Every parent, she thought, would realize the beneficence of this law, since it pointed unequivocally to the dangerous and cruel error of condoning or advising the use of prostitutes and mistresses by young men, in order to maintain the 'health' of their sexual organs. She related how she had often been consulted by anxious mothers about their sons' 'unusual discharges', and how relieved they were when she told them they were natural and healthy. The mothers had accepted as a fact what they had been taught, namely that no young man who could not marry early could remain healthy without resorting to 'vice'. Blackwell countered:

> In the exercise of a faculty which requires the concurrence of two intelligent beings endowed with free will and reason, individual independence must be secured. It would strike at the root of human progress, and convert society into slavery, if the life and health of an adult could not be maintained by the self-guidance and independence of the individual.[10]

Female Sexuality

One of Blackwell's most radical contributions was her assertion that there was no essential difference between the sexes in terms of their capacity for physical passion. According to the dominant sexual ideology female sexuality was – in 'normal' women – either completely absent or very much weaker than in the male. William Acton's much-quoted pronouncement is probably the best known formulation of this view:

> I should say that the majority of women (happily for society) are not very much troubled with sexual feeling of any kind. . . . As a general rule, a modest women seldom desires any sexual gratification for herself. She submits to her husband's embraces, but principally to gratify him; and, were it not for the desire of maternity, would far rather be relieved of his attentions.[11]

Although Blackwell did not cite Acton or any other medical authority by name, there is no doubt that one of her main purposes in writing *The Human Element in Sex* was to mount a direct challenge to this claim:

Considering... the enormous practical edifice of law and custom, which has been built up on the very sandy foundation of the supposed stronger character of male sexual passion, it is necessary to examine closely the facts of human nature, and challenge many erroneous conclusions.

She emphasized the greater complexity and potential of both physical and mental aspects of female sexuality, exploding the 'common but mischievous fallacy' that the 'intense energy' needed on the part of the male in 'the special act of procreation' was an indication of 'the superior force of sexual attraction or passion in the male'. This ignored the fact, said Blackwell, that the chief sexual structures of the female were internal; furthermore, it also ignored the fact that 'sexual attraction is not limited by any isolated physical act'. She even went so far as to suggest that it was *female* sexuality which was stronger and less subject to control by the will. The female's more important share in the work of reproduction had resulted in the greater complexity and elaboration of her sexual structure and functions. The male's share involved 'only a passing act of stimulation'; this was significant, because it meant that female sexuality was *less* ruled by the will than male sexuality:

> The control possessed so largely by the male over the physical function of sperm-formation is not possessed by the female over the corresponding function of ovulation. In the female, nature apparently cannot venture to subordinate the simple physical functions of sex to the will, to as great an extent as in the male.

This was clearly intended as another nail in the coffin of the double standard, and she hammered it in by adding that it was an insult to men to suggest that they did not possess the power of self-control. Reassuring the reader that neither men nor women would ever become impotent 'through abeyance of function' – 'no such fear need ever disturb the mind' – she insisted that it was above all the laws of physiology which made such a suggestion untenable: 'The assertion that one human being is dependent on the degradation of another human being for the maintenance of personal health is contradicted by physiological facts, as well as social experience'.[12]

Blackwell also argued that those who denied sexual feeling in women confused passion with appetite. Appetite was a simple physical sexual instinct, as experienced by the lower animals, and was of little relevance when considering human sexual relations. The passion in human sexuality was not simply a physical faculty; it was a compound faculty, in which the mental, moral, or spiritual elements were just as important as the physical:

> The term passion, it should always be remembered, necessarily implies a mental element. For this reason it is employed exclusively in relation to the powers of the human being, not to those of the

brute. . . . In sexual passion this mental, moral or emotional principle is as emphatically sex as any physical instinct, and it grows with the proportional development of the nervous system.

According to Blackwell both physical and mental aspects of sex were at least as strong in woman as in man, and in some respects stronger. The fact that physical sensation took different forms in women and men had obscured the existence of sexual passion in women. Husbands often complained that their wives did not regard 'the distinctively sexual act' with the same intoxicating physical enjoyment that they themselves felt, and concluded, wrongly, that they lacked sexual passion. On the other hand, said Blackwell, clearly drawing on her experience as a women's physician, a wife often confided to her medical adviser that:

at the very time when marriage love seems to unite them most closely, when her husband's welcome kisses and caresses seem to bring them into profound union, comes an act which mentally separates them, and which may be either indifferent or repugnant to her.

Blackwell explained that terror or pain in either sex could temporarily destroy physical pleasure, and that a woman's apparent lack of sexual passion was often attributable to injuries suffered in childbirth, or to her husband's 'brutal or awkward conjugal approaches'. But in another radical departure from the patriarchal model she insisted that sexual pleasure was not reducible to (hetero)sexual intercourse. Although she believed that women who loved their husbands and were healthy and uninjured by childbirth might experience increasing physical satisfaction from 'the ultimate physical expression of love', she also believed that passion was distinguished by 'the profound attraction of one nature to the other', and 'delight in kiss and caress – the love-touch'. This, said Blackwell, was just as much physical sexual expression as 'the special act of the male' which was necessary for parentage.[13]

The fact that there was no fundamental difference between the sexes in terms of the nature and strength of sexual passion meant that there could be no possible justification for the physiological argument underpinning the double standard, viz., men's 'need' for regular (hetero)sexual release in order to maintain their health. Blackwell described fornication as 'the attempt to divorce the moral and physical aspects of human nature' and 'yielding to the domination of the simple physical impulse of sex', with no regard either for the mutual responsibility involved in sexual relationships or for their consequences. Although she sometimes tended to blame women almost as much as men for abusing their sexual powers, her support for the feminist agitation against the Contagious Diseases Acts was always unequivocal: 'Promiscuous intercourse can never be made "safe",' she declared. 'The resort of many men to one woman, with its results, is against nature'. As she became more deeply involved in the campaigns against the double standard, she developed a much stronger feminist analysis of men's responsibility for the sexual exploitation and abuse of women, insisting that it was men who must bear the direct responsibility for the conversion of women into merchandise.[14]

It is probably Blackwell's views on masturbation which more than anything else have led to her dismissal by modern sex researchers and historians as a sexual puritan. Blackwell regarded masturbation as potentially dangerous for two main reasons. First, it could lead to the development in the growing child of a 'precocious sexual consciousness' which, coming into play before the development of reason or a sense of responsibility, could result in the sexual instinct achieving an undue dominance over other human faculties. A precocious sexual instinct in the child might thus lead in the adult to fornication. Second, there was a risk that masturbation might become a real obsession, with the result that 'individual self-control, the highest distinctive mark of the human being, is abandoned'. Her views on masturbation were thus entirely consistent with her concept of human nature, her concept of sexuality as a compound faculty, her commitment to the abolition of the double standard, and her belief in the ability to control sexual behaviour through the power of reason and the exercise of the will. It should be pointed out, however, that although she believed that the habit of masturbation should be broken, she was emphatic that this should be achieved, not by punishment, force, or the inculcation of guilt, but by the tactful exercise of maternal influence and encouragement.[15]

The 'Debate' with Acton

Blackwell was clearly confident that she had been successful in demolishing the alleged physiological justification for the double standard: 'Physiology condemns fornication by showing the physical arrangements which support the moral law. . . . There is no justification in the physiological structure of humanity for the destructive practice of fornication'.[16] It seems that she had at least some support from within the medical profession for her views. There was an acknowledgement in *The Lancet* that the medical profession had too often been silent when they should have played a leading role in offering help and advice to young men 'in their conflict with temptation to sexual vice'.[17] This opinion was not shared by William Acton, the leading medical authority of the day on sexuality, who epitomized the patriarchal model of sexuality. Most of Blackwell's writings were in a sense a 'debate' with Acton, whose views on sexuality, and especially prostitution, were widely known though not universally accepted, even within the medical profession. Acton was considered by some male doctors, as well as by feminists, to be an apologist for the double standard, who implicitly sanctioned the use of prostitutes by men whose wives could not or would not gratify their husbands' sexual desires in the way Acton thought they should.

Acton's dogmatic pronouncement regarding woman's alleged lack of sexual passion has already been quoted. His concern with the nature of female sexuality did not stem, as has been suggested by some historians, from a desire to 'vindicate female nature from the vile aspersions cast on it by the abandoned conduct and ungoverned lusts of a few of its worst examples'. Rather he sought to reassure men that the sexual duties of marriage would not be too onerous for them. According to Acton, many men were reluctant to marry because they believed that marriage would make too many demands upon them sexually and they feared they would be unable to 'perform' as often as would be expected of them. As we have already seen in Chapter 1, there was during the nineteenth century increasing alarm at the low rate of marriage. Various reasons were put forward for this, one of which was the reluctance of some men to take on the responsibilities of marriage, including, if Acton is to be believed, the sexual responsibilities. He claimed that many young unmarried men formed their ideas of women's sensuous feeling from what they noticed among 'loose or, at least, low and immoral women', and that 'it is from these erroneous notions that so many unmarried men imagine that the marital duties they will have to undertake are beyond their exhausted strength, and from this reason dread and avoid marriage'. Evidently, then, the nineteenth-century belief in women's lack of sexual feeling was not universal. Acton's assertion that woman's periodic, if not total, lack of sexual desire constituted a natural protection against sexual 'excess' was intended to remove such objections to marriage:

> No nervous or feeble young man need, therefore, be deterred from marriage by any exaggerated notion of the arduous duties required from him. Let him be well assured, on my authority backed by the opinion of many, that the married woman has no wish to be placed on the footing of a mistress.[18]

At the same time Acton believed that one of the essential characteristics of the ideal English wife was a willingness to overcome her 'natural repugnance for cohabitation' and submit to her husband's embraces when he wished to exercise his conjugal rights. He severely castigated those women who failed or, more seriously, *refused* to gratify their husbands' sexual demands. He claimed repeatedly that married men often came to him with 'sad complaints' of the 'intense suffering' they had to undergo, and that during the last few years, 'since the rights of women have been so much insisted upon', numerous husbands had complained to him of the hardships they suffered by being married to women 'who regard themselves as martyrs when called upon to fulfil the duties of wives'. He cited one woman who maintained women's rights 'to such an extent that she denied the husband any voice in the matter, whether or not cohabitation should take place'. Apparently she maintained 'most strenuously' that since she had to bear the consequences, pains and risks of childbirth, a married woman had a perfect right to refuse to cohabit with her husband. Acton ventured to point out 'to this strong-minded female' that such conduct on her part might be, from a medical point of view, 'highly detrimental to the health of the husband, particularly if he happened to be strongly sexually disposed'. In other words it could lead to impotence: 'I regret to add that medical skill can be of little avail here. The more conscientious the husband and the stronger his sexual feelings, the more distressing are the sufferings he is doomed to undergo, ultimately too often ending in impotence'.[19]

In the case of unmarried men Acton believed that it was possible for them to control their sexual appetites by a combination of will-power, plenty of exercise, and medical supervision. However where married men were concerned he said he could offer little more than sympathy; a man of strong sexual disposition, 'debarred from the privileges of marriage', would inevitably be forced to endure almost unbearable sufferings, unless he happened to be endowed with a strong will, which was 'often found wanting in strongly-developed animal natures'. Was it surprising, then, asked Acton, 'that so many who, under more favourable auspices, would have continued to make the best of husbands, fall victim to a vicious mode of living, and seek in fornication some alleviation of their sexual sufferings?' He was careful to avoid actually recommending such a course of action; he relied instead on guilt-tripping and innuendo in the attempt to persuade women to become 'the soothers of man's woes' and to satisfy their 'imperious wants'. He suggested that there might be fewer divorces, and less need for wives to complain of marital infidelity, if they were more 'judicious' and 'waived their own inclinations'. He suggested too that in some women the knowledge that they would be deserted for courtesans if they did not gratify their husbands' passions might 'induce the indifferent, the passionless, to admit the embraces of their husbands'.[20]

It seems, then, that for Acton, women's alleged lack of sexual feeling was a good thing in so far as it relieved husbands of responsibilities which would otherwise be too onerous and exhausting.[21] Moreover he shared Blackwell's view that 'man' was distinguished from the lower animals by 'his' intellectual and moral capacities; he believed that man was formed for higher purposes and that 'to devote the whole energy of his nature to sensual indulgence was to degrade himself to the level of a brute'. But the failure or refusal of the wife to minister to the husband's 'imperious wants' was dangerous and inexcusable, and the numerous husbands who so frequently complained to him about 'this spirit of insubordination' alleged that it had become more intolerable since it had been backed by the opinions of John Stuart Mill. As we have seen in Chapter 1, Mill had complained that the wife did not even have the privilege of the female slave, who at least in theory if not in practice had the right to refuse her master 'the last familiarity'. According to Acton, Mill had committed the cardinal sin of 'inducing the sex to believe that they are "but personal body-servants of a despot" '.

It is clear, then, that the differences between Blackwell and Acton were quite fundamental. Acton made no distinction between sexual appetite and sexual passion; for him sexuality was essentially a male characteristic and little more than an animal instinct, subject only to limited control. He compared it sometimes to a match, waiting to be struck, and sometimes to gunpowder, which 'remains harmless till the spark falls upon it'. Despite his acknowledgment of the distinction between humans and the lower animals, he played down the significance of distinctively human characteristics such as will-power, self-control, and the capacity for rational action, implying that a man with a strong sexual disposition was almost by definition lacking in a strong will. The concepts of reason and responsibility had no place in this patriarchal model of sexuality. Although Acton disapproved of sexual 'excess', this was because of its supposed exhausting and draining effects on men, rather than its harmful effects on women. He saw prostitutes as a 'social pest', and men as their victims, rather than as persons responsible for their own actions. He objected strongly to the attempts by some women to exercise a degree of control over sexual activity within marriage, and insisted that since they had been created as 'helpmeets' to their husbands they should submit to their husbands' control. The ostensible reason for this was the harm that would be done to the husband's health by abstinence; but one does not need to scratch far below the surface to see that what he was really saying was that any change in the sexual power relationship within marriage would result in male *impotence*. Impotence means not merely inability to perform coitus, but loss or lack of power, an ambiguity which in sexual-political terms is not without significance!

Blackwell's Model of Sexuality

The complexity and sophistication of Blackwell as a sexual theorist, in comparison with Acton, is striking. Despite the fact that hers was essentially a reproductive model, in which sexuality was defined as an imperative procreative instinct, subject to the 'laws' of physiology, it was not biologically determinist in any simplistic sense. Because the capacity to reason, to exercise the will, and thus to change were built in to her concept of human nature, the possibility of rational control of sexual behaviour was integral to her model of sexuality. The power of mind over body, of reason over appetite, and the mental element in sex – all were key components in her model and applied equally to women and men. Thus she was able to argue logically and persuasively that there was no rational or physiological justification for the sexual double standard, and to debunk the notion that sexual intercourse was necessary to health and abstinence harmful. 'Chastity' and 'continence' for her did not mean the imposition of a repressive code of sexual morality but 'the government of the sexual instinct by the higher reason or wisdom'. Chastity was itself a 'development or differentiation of the primitive sexual instinct', a positive quality of human civilization, ultimately rooted in the power of habit over nature which human beings had acquired in the course of evolution.[22]

Blackwell shared with the rest of the medical profession, with contemporary scientists, and with all those who wished to give scientific legitimation to their views, a fondness for making frequent reference to the 'laws of nature'. This was a common feature of both conservative and radical sexual ideologies throughout the nineteenth century. But Blackwell's concept of human nature was far from static or absolute; nature could be *changed* by the combined forces of habit and heredity:

> Habit can so change the nature as to make what was difficult easy; it can so strengthen the tendencies in directly opposite directions as to both govern, and to a great extent change the action of the physical organization itself; and the fact of heredity will transmit these changed tendencies to succeeding generations.

Habit exercised its power over human nature by modifying the physiological character of the nervous system to create a 'second nature':

> It is in this way, through a change in the nervous system itself, that habit becomes literally a second nature; and in this way habits most opposite to the natural or rudimentary state are introduced into our human organization, and 'nature is dominated by or absorbed in habit'.[23]

Chastity was thus, for Blackwell, not an arbitrary, externally imposed moral doctrine, but an idea and a practice which had 'grown up from a physiological basis' and was 'inseparably interwoven with the essential structure of our physical organisation'. She believed that 'the law of chastity must gradually extend its sway over the human race' by means of the forces of habit and heredity, but that 'the choice between inevitable degeneracy and sure improvement [was] left to our relatively free will'. At the same time, however, she believed that the consequences of that choice could not be avoided, because 'the violation of nature's laws leads inexorably to gradual but inevitable degeneration of the race'.

By far the most radical characteristic of Blackwell's model of sexuality was her inversion of the naturalistic assumption underpinning the double standard of sexual morality. Her central thesis was that adult human beings of both sexes were naturally endowed with the capacity to guide and control the sexual instinct, provided that the capacity to reason and exercise the will had been allowed to develop normally. This formed the foundation of a new way of conceptualizing sexuality and heterosexual relations which, from the point of view of feminist sexual politics, was potentially revolutionary in its implications. All the main themes of her writing flowed from this central thesis: the mental element in sex, the equivalent strength of female and male sexuality, the distinction between sexual appetite and passion, the danger of separating sex from affection, the inability of continence to cause impotence, the notion that sex was not reducible to coition, and the insistence that procreation should be governed by the will of the female. Taken as a whole what these elements pointed to was a feminist model of sexuality, which was predicated on the concept of female sexual autonomy. For the best part of a century feminists had protested against a system and an ideology which forced them to be the slaves of men's imperious sexual nature, and which defined sexuality essentially in male terms; what this new model of sexuality implied was that 'the sexual nature of woman [was] the keynote to which all men's relations should be tuned'.[24]

While Blackwell herself remained firmly committed to the ideal of marriage, and never questioned the assumption that heterosexual relations were ultimately natural, her model of sexuality implied such a major shift in the balance of power between the sexes that it could be said to constitute a potential threat, not merely to marriage, but also to what feminists today would call the institution of heterosexuality. It is not difficult to imagine the insubordinate wife, of whom Dr Acton so bitterly complained, consulting Dr Blackwell instead and returning home so empowered that her marriage became impossible to sustain! It is also doubtful whether she would be able to find a 'new man' who would be willing to work out a truly equal relationship with a sexually independent woman – a woman who believed that sex was not reducible to coition, that continence was perfectly healthy, and that it was the woman who should ultimately regulate heterosexual activity! It is ironic that Blackwell, though a spinster by choice, placed such great value on marriage and motherhood; and doubly ironic that her model of sexuality pointed in a direction which would surely have earned her the approval of the most ardent champion of spinsterhood! Cicely Hamilton, for instance, must surely have found in Blackwell, if she had read her work, some confirmation of her view that 'sexual intercourse was not for every woman an absolute necessity'.[25]

There are, however, several tensions and contradictions within Blackwell's model which in political terms limited its revolutionary potential. Given that the concept of female sexual autonomy was integral to the model, one would expect at least some consideration of lesbianism, if not of homosexuality in general. Yet on both these subjects Blackwell was absolutely silent. One reason for her silence might simply have been homophobia: she may have had such a fear or hatred of homosexuality that she could not even bring herself to mention it; or perhaps she feared that discussing it would harm the feminist cause even more than discussing subjects such as birth control or free love – subjects which, like most feminists at the time, she also avoided. It is undeniable that the political climate was hardly conducive to the discussion of either lesbianism or male homosexuality: the vilification of the spinster, the notorious case of Oscar Wilde, and the Labouchere Amendment to the Criminal Law Amendment Act of 1885, which outlawed male homosexuality, all combined to make the subject of lesbianism a very dangerous one indeed for a feminist spinster to approach.

At a more theoretical level Blackwell's silence points to a contradiction within the model of sexuality she constructed: that although the concept of female sexual autonomy points logically towards the possibility of lesbianism, there could be no place for it in a model which was essentially reproductive and therefore heterosexist, except as a deviation or perversion. If she had categorized lesbianism as a perversion it would have contradicted the principle of female sexual autonomy; but if she had considered it as a positive possibility it would have been in contradiction to her reproductive model of sexuality, as well as her strong Christian beliefs. Whether Blackwell was aware of this contradiction is a matter of pure speculation. We shall probably never know why she chose, if choose she did, to avoid the subject. It is possible that since the definition of homosexuality as a violation of nature's laws is implicit in the model, she simply thought it unnecessary to define it explicitly in those terms.

This contradiction may also reflect to some extent the tension in Blackwell's writings, and perhaps also in her personality, between the feminist and the physician. Blackwell the feminist was concerned to emphasize the mental element in sex, and the unity of the physical, emotional, and spiritual aspects which underpinned her definition of sex as a compound faculty. On the other hand, she was very conscious of her position in the medical profession, especially as she was the first woman to qualify as a doctor, and to Blackwell the physician the laws of physiology were paramount. She clearly felt that to base her opposition to the double standard on political or moral arguments alone, or on evidence derived from her own experience and knowledge as a feminist and a woman, would not carry sufficient weight. As a physician she felt compelled to 'prove' scientifically that men's uncontrollable sexual urges were a myth, and to demonstrate that there was no physiological justification for the double standard.

The strategy of standing the naturalistic fallacy on its head was indeed radical, but in substituting her own laws for those she overturned, Blackwell limited the political effectiveness of her redefinition of the natural. One problem inherent in appealing to the 'laws of nature' to justify political claims is that laws by definition set limits to human possibilities, and new laws may give rise to new tyrannies. Another problem is that whether or not a particular proposition becomes generally accepted as a law is a matter, not merely of 'proof', as Blackwell understood it, but of politics. Blackwell's implicit belief in the value-free nature of science appears to have made it impossible for her to comprehend that her medical credentials and scientific evidence were not enough to endow her 'laws' with credibility or legitimacy in the patriarchal scientific community. Otherwise it might have been she, rather than Havelock Ellis, who was accorded the status of founding mother of sexology. As it was, her position as a woman and a feminist ensured only that her contribution to the theorization of sexuality became distorted and all but erased from history.

Notes

1 See Spender (1982), p. 142.
2 See, for example, Brecher (1970); McLaren (1978); Mort (1987).
3 The main sources of the biographical details which follow are: Nancy Sahli's unpublished PhD dissertation, *Elizabeth Blackwell: A Biography* (Univ. of Pennsylvania, 1974); Blackwell's own account of her work in opening up the medical profession to women (Blackwell, 1895); Alice S. Rossi's discussion of the Blackwell 'clan' in Rossi (1974), pp. 323–45; and Margaret Forster's biographical essay (1986). On Blackwell's work in the Moral Reform Union see Chapter 1, pp. 28–9.
4 Blackwell (1902), p. 58; p. 69; p. 72.
5 The full title of the essay was *The Moral Education of the Young, Considered under Medical and Social Aspects* (1876); a revised edition was published in 1879, entitled *Counsel to Parents on the Moral Education of the Young in Relation to Sex*, from which the quotations used in this chapter have been taken.
6 Blackwell (1879), p. 5; most nineteenth-century feminists do not appear to have objected to the use of the generic 'man' and 'he' in the way that modern feminists do, and the usage has been retained here in order to convey the style and 'flavour' of Blackwell's writing.
7 Blackwell (1879), pp. 38–9.
8 *The Human Element in Sex* went through several new editions with very minor revisions between 1890 and 1894, eventually being reprinted in 1902 as part of a two-volume collection of Blackwell's writings entitled *Essays in Medical Sociology*; the following quotations are from the 1894 edition.
9 Blackwell (1894), p. 22; p. 78. In common with the medical opinion of the day she thought – erroneously – that conception was most likely to take place around the time of menstruation. For a discussion of her views on birth control, see McLaren (1978).
10 Blackwell (1894), p. 23.
11 Acton (1875), p. 210. Some medical authorities considered on the contrary that women were 'tyrannically governed by sex', a view which Blackwell repudiated because it was based on a concept of sex which was exclusively physical.
12 Blackwell (1894), p. 46; p. 29.
13 *Ibid.*, pp. 49–50.
14 *Ibid.*, p. 43.
15 *Ibid.*, p. 40.
16 She also added that in this respect modern physiology merely endorsed 'the profound insight of the fathers of Christianity'. There was nothing unusual, in the late nineteenth century, in the integration of evolutionary science with religious and moral concerns. As Frank Mort has pointed out, Darwinism had initially shaken religious beliefs, but by this time most clerics believed there was nothing incompatible between evolutionary science and religion. Darwin's *Descent of Man* (1871) showed how the growth of moral faculties like self-control, love, and altruism were key elements in progressing towards higher moral culture (Mort, 1987, p. 110).
17 The extract from *The Lancet* was a statement of the following 'physiological facts': (1) that occasional involuntary emissions of semen during sleep were natural and

healthy; (2) that sexual continence did not cause impotence, and that the main cause of impotence was 'prolonged sexual excess'; it was a fallacy that lack of use of a physical organ necessarily led to atrophy (and to underline the point the writer drew an analogy with the breast, which did not atrophy if it was not used for feeding infants); (3) that no function of the body was so influenced and controlled by the higher nerve-centres as the sexual; it followed that immorality could not be banished by any rules of diet or exercise, for 'vice is voluntary, and it is only by the exercise of a resolute self-will that virtue is maintained'.

18 Acton (1875), pp. 209–10. For discussions of women and 'passionlessness' in the nineteenth century, see Cott (1978/9) and Degler (1974).

19 Acton (1875), p. 212.

20 *Ibid.*, pp. 213–14.

21 Acton did concede that some women became, after each period, *capable* of experiencing sexual excitement, but only to a limited degree. He still believed that women could only be aroused as a result of a positive effort on the part of the husband, and even when aroused (which was often impossible) female sexual excitement was still very moderate compared with the male.

22 Blackwell (1902), p. 63.

23 *Ibid.*, pp. 59–61. This argument was based on Lamarck's theory that attributes gained during an individual's lifetime could be passed on to the next generation. The unattributed quotation may possibly be from Lamarck.

24 Blackwell (1891), p. 5.

25 See Chapter 1, p. 20.

Chapter 4

'Sex Freedom' or Female Sexual Autonomy?
Tensions and Divisions within Feminism in the Late Nineteenth and Early Twentieth Centuries

There are striking similarities between Elizabeth Blackwell's model of sexuality and the ideas of a number of feminists who were analyzing sexuality around the turn of the century and who questioned the coital imperative underpinning the patriarchal model of sexuality. Given Blackwell's status as the first woman to qualify as a doctor, her active involvement in the Women's Movement, and the fact that she was the first feminist to write about sexuality from a scientific perspective, one would expect her ideas to have been quite widely read and discussed within feminist circles. It is, however, difficult to assess the extent of her influence with any precision. It is known that Ellice J. Hopkins, a feminist active in the social purity movement, admired her essay on *Moral Education*, and helped her to find a publisher. Millicent Fawcett thought *Purchase of Women* so important that she had it reprinted during the agitation surrounding the 'White Slavery' Bill of 1912. Blackwell herself discussed her ideas at the Men and Women's Club, a mixed 'progressive' discussion group which included in its membership Olive Schreiner and other feminists. She must also have discussed her ideas in the Moral Reform Union and other women's and feminist groups, especially those with a particular interest in sexuality, and, as we have seen, the views expressed in the militant feminist newspapers were obviously consistent with hers. There is, however, no direct evidence from feminists' writing, in the form of quotations or references, of how they used or considered her ideas. The conventions of the time regarding the citing of sources were extremely loose, and it was not at all unusual for writers, feminist or otherwise, to refer to or borrow from other writers, including well-known medical, scientific, or political authorities, without actually naming them.

Continence, Psychic Love, and the Coital Imperative

Towards the end of the nineteenth century some feminists began to develop what Sheila Jeffreys has described as a 'complex philosophy of sex', central to which were the concepts of 'continence' and 'psychic love'. Prominent amongst them were Elizabeth Wolstenholme Elmy and Frances Swiney, both of whom were active in the suffrage movement and supporters of militant feminism. The central and unifying theme of their writings was the right of women to control their own bodies; to live, in the words of Wolstenholme Elmy, 'free from all uninvited touch of man'. Like Blackwell, these were no armchair theorists but feminist activists with long experience of campaigning against the double standard. Both were married, and it seems reasonable to assume that they did not view their struggles for sexual self-determination as separate from their personal sexual relatonships.[1]

Wolstenholme Elmy, who sometimes wrote under pseudonyms such as Ellis Ethelmer and 'Ignota', produced two sex education books, in which she used analogies with plants and animals in order to convey the basic facts of human reproduction to children. In the book for older children she clearly stated her belief in the right of the married woman to decide, not only whether or not to have children, but whether or not to have sexual intercourse:

> the conviction is every day growing that under no plea or promise can it be permissible to submit the individuality, either mental or physical, of the wife, to the will and coercion of the husband; the functions of wifehood and motherhood must remain solely and entirely within the wife's own option. Coercion, like excess, is in itself a contravention and annihilation of the psychic nature of the sexual relation.[2]

What she meant by 'the psychic nature of the sexual relation' was virtually identical to Blackwell's concept of 'the mental element in sex'. Like Blackwell, she wanted to shift the emphasis away from the male definition of sex as a purely physical function, synonymous with sensual appetite, towards the more spiritual aspects of human passion. In a book called *Phases of Love* she traced the historical evolution of human love, documenting the 'bodily servitude' and 'carnal oppression' of woman by the 'blind and selfish sensuality' of man, and arguing optimistically that man was now learning to know and to prize the psychic rather than the physical in his relationship with woman. She felt that it was now possible to detect 'a swiftly advancing and ever loftier concept of the newer and higher faculty – the psychic emotion and impulse between two human beings of different sex, to which the name of "love" is specially and worthily applied'. She considered that this advance had been brought about mainly by 'the growing emancipation and autonomy of woman', and affirmed that justice and equality were the necessary preconditions for such love to exist.[3]

Wolstenholme Elmy and Blackwell shared fundamentally the same model of sexuality, in which 'the sexual act' was displaced in favour of female sexual autonomy. Wolstenholme Elmy looked forward to an ideal form of heterosexual relationship which centred not on sexual intercourse but on psychic love, and which recognized 'the wife's continuing right of physical inviolability'. 'True love', she wrote, 'admits of no physical expression but as sanctioned by the equal will and psychic purpose of both parties'. Like Blackwell, she also believed that the primary purpose of sexual intercourse was reproduction, though she did acknowledge that some couples might wish to engage in it occasionally for pleasure, and recommended the 'safe period' in order to avoid conception.[4] In general, though, her concept of psychic love assumed the capacity, on the part of both sexes, for rational action, and the ability, not to suppress, but to control their physical passions. One problem with the concept of 'psychic love' is that it might suggest, to the modern reader, the complete avoidance of all forms of physical sexual expression. Wolstenholme Elmy's poetic and rather flowery descriptions were very vague and inexplicit, making it difficult to interpret with any precision what she actually meant by psychic love in practice. There can be little doubt that it did include physical expressions of love and affection, similar to what Blackwell described as 'delight in kiss and caress' and 'the love-touch'. It also seems to have included sexual intercourse, as long as it was 'sanctioned by the equal will and psychic purpose of both parties' and practised with 'prudence' and 'temperance'. But it was clearly not Wolstenholme Elmy's intention to be prescriptive about the sexual behaviour of married couples, merely to establish the right of the married woman to control her own fertility and sexuality. She sought to do no more than set out what she believed were the fundamental parameters within which women and men, who were committed to 'true psychic love' and 'equal psychic fellowship', could explore for themselves what they wanted from their relationships, and how they wished to express their sexual feelings.

The same basic principles were evident in the writings of Frances Swiney. Swiney was much admired by Wolstenholme Elmy, and her works were advertised in *The Suffragette*, the journal of the Women's Social and Political Union. Her essay, *The Bar of Isis*, went through four editions between 1907 and 1919. Little is known of Swiney's background, but the copious references to scientific and medical literature in her work suggest either that she had received some kind of medical or scientific education, or that she had embarked upon independent research in these fields. It is highly likely, therefore, that she would have been familiar with the work of Elizabeth Blackwell, and it is surprising that, although Swiney was unusually careful about citing her sources, there were no specific references to Blackwell in her writing. There was a strong scientific slant to Swiney's analysis, which, like Blackwell's, relied heavily on physiological evidence and laws. She was also a theosophist who believed in the evolution of humans from physical to spiritual beings, and the complementarity of science and religion. The League of Isis, a theosophical society which she founded, had as its emblem the Bar of Isis, an ancient fertility symbol, representing the gravid and inviolate womb and designating what Swiney called the Law of the Mother: the right of women to control their own fertility by controlling men's sexual access to their bodies. This theme was central to all her writings and was developed in tandem with a critique of the notion of men's imperious sexual 'needs', which she referred to as 'man's necessity', or his 'incontinent' and 'perverted' sexuality.

Swiney believed that 'woman's redemption from sexual slavery could only be achieved through man's redemption from sex-obsession'. She argued that there was 'no living organism so completely under the tyranny of sex as the human male', and that the majority of men were 'utterly incapable of freeing themselves from the limitations of masculinity'. She dismissed as 'sex-sophistry' the double standard of morality, and sought to expose it as 'the illogical device by which man has cloaked masculine licentiousness under the specious plea of sexual necessity'. Men had made their laws fit in and give license to their 'stimulated predilections'. Like Blackwell, she stood the naturalistic argument on its head, drawing on evidence from biology, physiology, and anthropology in order to show that male sexual 'incontinence', far from being natural, was a *violation* of natural law and a 'perversion of physiological truth'. She pointed out that the sexual exploitation and abuse of females by males simply did not occur, either in sub-human species, or in simple societies which retained vestiges of the earlier matriarchate. But in men, repeated artificial stimulation of sexual desire had resulted, through heredity, in changes in the structures of their brains, 'until an abnormal tendency to indulgence in sex-relations has been engendered quite contrary to and subversive of natural law'.[5]

Swiney's articles and papers were published around the turn of the century, when there was much official alarm being expressed about the problems of the low birth rate and 'race degeneracy', for both of which women had been made the scapegoats. Women were blamed, either for refusing to breed in sufficient numbers, or for being bad mothers. Swiney countered by producing quantities of medical and scientific evidence, culled from authoritative sources, in the attempt to 'prove' that the real cause of these problems was men's failure to observe the 'natural law of continence'. Like Wolstenholme Elmy, she argued that it was the 'abnormal and fostered sensuality of the human male' which was responsible, not merely for venereal disease, but for all of the diseases of women's reproductive system, including cancer. She considered human sperm, in excess, to be poisonous: 'if limited its power is for good: in excess it is a virulent poison'.[6]

Swiney explicitly challenged the coital imperative which is intrinsic to the patriarchal model of sexuality. She argued that it was *natural* for the female to regulate sexual activity and *natural* for the male to experience long periods of continence or 'latent sexuality' when he was able to live a life free of sexual obligations. The physiological law which made this possible she called the 'law of adjustment', a concept which, as we have seen, was a key element in Blackwell's model of sexuality. Swiney viewed the act of coition purely as an act of fertilization which had only one purpose, 'that of aid to the reproduction of kind by the procreatrix, the mother'. 'Fertilisation', she wrote, 'is for the male an episode, not a habit'; and 'what is more', she added, 'Nature destined man for a higher purpose than that of a mere fertiliser'. As a theosophist Swiney believed that the body was a kind of chemico-physical laboratory, capable of changing one form of energy into another. This process, which was known as 'transmutation', also applied to sexual energy, and was the source in humans of great mental and spiritual achievements. There was thus no biological reason why the male should find it difficult to follow the law of adjustment, even when this involved an absolute prohibition on sexual activity, as she argued it naturally would during pregnancy and lactation. She considered that those men who insisted on resuming sexual intercourse with their wives within a fortnight of confinement were 'below the brutes', adding: 'to term them *human* is a misapplication of a definition'.[7]

Swiney launched a scathing attack on the self-appointed experts who dared to 'anathematize' the mother for her rebellion against motherhood. She declared that it was unnatural for most women to have more than four children, and suggested that the 'experts' would do better to turn their attention to a more profound study of nature's laws and teach their own sex the 'science of life'. The science of these honourable gentlemen, she wrote sarcastically, was as false as their morality, and their abysmal ignorance of physiology was only equalled by their utter disregard of elementary ethics. Her castigation of the medical profession was particularly severe. When, she demanded to know, had the majority of medical practitioners prescribed to the husband moderation, self-control, and 'the natural instinctive chivalry of the brute'? Why did they not go into hysterics over the husband who had rendered the wife a life-long invalid, 'a worn-out machine, broken down under the strain and stress, mental and physical, of repeated sexual exactions'? The average practitioner, male or female, was so fearful of encroaching upon the 'rights of the husband' that they preferred to condone male sexual indulgence. The day was dawning, however, when no reputable doctor would countenance any infringement of nature's law:

> For woman, herself, is happily learning the natural law of reproduction with the natural restrictions placed on sexual relations, and she is gradually teaching man self-respect, self-reverence, self-control, and the exercise of a love that worketh no evil.[8]

For Wolstenholme Elmy and Swiney, the concepts of continence and psychic love represented the unequivocal rejection of a male-defined, phallocentric model of sexuality, geared to the husband's physical rights and allegedly natural needs, with the consequent 'bodily slavery' and exploitation of the wife. At the same time, by insisting on female sexual autonomy, the right of the wife to define her own needs and desires, and questioning the centrality of penile penetration in heterosexual intercourse, these feminists were clearly making positive attempts to explore ways of relating sexually to men which would empower women within heterosexual relationships. The concepts of continence and psychic love represented an attempt, not to deny or repress sexuality, but to supersede the patriarchal model, with its separation of the physical and psychic elements of sexuality, and its reduction of sex to a purely physical function – a coital imperative. The emphasis on the psychic or spiritual aspects of sex constituted a rejection not of physical expressions of sexuality but of physiological reductionism. It was an insistence that sexuality be recognized as, in Blackwell's terms, a 'compound faculty' a highly complex unity of physical and emotional needs and desires which were not reducible to a single physical goal.

Not all those who were critical of male sexual violence and exploitation or used the terms continence and psychic love necessarily shared the same model of sexuality. Olive Schreiner, for instance, wrote in *Woman and Labour* that 'the New Woman's conception of love between the sexes is one more largely psychic and intellectual than crudely and purely physical, and wholly of an affection between companions'. Yet she viewed sex as essentially an animal instinct, which she often described as 'primordial', and compared to hunger and thirst. Although she believed that it was as strong in women as it was in man, her notion of female sexual autonomy was rather confused. She believed that sexual relationships should not necessarily be tied to reproduction and that any woman over 30 should be allowed to have a child without disgrace, even if she was not married, but she had no critique of heterosexual intercourse. On the contrary, she described it as 'the great sacrament of life'. Schreiner's model of sexuality had its roots, not so much in the Women's Movement, as in the Men and Women's Club, and the men's Darwinian insistence on the 'master dominance' of the (hetero)sexual instinct. Karl Pearson, the founder and dominant member of the Club, to whom Schreiner was strongly attracted, sexually and intellectually, believed that evolution had implanted in women a desire for children and in man a desire for women. As Judith Walkowitz has pointed out, his model of sexuality was essentially male: aggressive, compulsive, and compulsory, 'a spermatic economy harnessed to a Darwinian racial imperative'. It epitomized the patriarchal model of sexuality, with its assumption of uncontrollable male sexual 'needs', underpinned by the coital imperative. Walkowitz's research, and a study by Lucy Bland, have shown that the women in the Club attempted to develop a critique of male sexuality, and to explore a more woman-centred model of sexuality, but that the power struggles with the men made this process very difficult.[9]

The Men and Women's Club consisted of about twenty members, with equal numbers of men and women, most of the latter being spinsters. It held regular meetings between 1885 and 1889, and those invited to speak on sexual matters included Elizabeth Blackwell and Annie Besant. Although there was a wide range of opinion amongst the women, and they were sometimes sharply divided, they repeatedly challenged the men for treating male sexuality as given and only female sexuality as problematic. Letitia Sharpe, for instance, considered that the worst disability that women suffered was that they were still 'judged and valued by their bodies rather than their minds', and most of the women members agreed with Blackwell that 'if men controlled themselves women would at last be able to express themselves'. Several women attacked male sexual coercion within marriage, and criticized sexual intercourse. Henrietta Müller maintained that 'to many women intercourse is an unpleasant and fatiguing obligation'; another woman characterized 'coition on the part of the man' as 'a violent action, bordering on convulsions and causing great exhaustion' (Walkowitz, 1986, p. 49). Maria Sharpe objected to Pearson's treatment of sexual intercourse as 'on a footing with other pleasures' such as mountain climbing, and thought that expressions such as 'harmless physical pleasure', a 'mere transient pleasure', or 'purely physical pleasure', which Pearson used to describe sexual intercourse, were misleading because they ignored the grave personal consequences which sexual intercourse implied for women.[10]

Henrietta Müller attacked Pearson's model of sexuality in a paper of her own, in which she argued that male sexual licence had been transmitted over generations and had made men morally inferior to women. She argued that self-control was the moral basis of life, and it was the absence of sexual passion, gained over centuries of self-restraint on the part of women and transmitted to subsequent female generations, that made women free. Women did not need men. As long as society had depended on physical strength, men had wielded power. But now that moral strength was the new criterion of social power, the dominion of man would be replaced by that of woman. Müller resigned when a male member of the club defended prostitution on the grounds that it served male needs. In a letter to Pearson she complained that it was the same old story – the men were dogmatic and dominated the discussion, 'the women resenting in silence, and submitting in silence'. Whenever women differed from men, their voice of protest was immediately stifled, and the presence of 'the enemy' made genuine discussion impossible: 'Even when one who is bold opens her lips, they feebly admire her courage but do not venture to follow her example because the enemy is present' (Bland, 1986, p. 132). Müller declared her intention of forming a women-only club, and shortly afterwards joined the women-only Moral Reform Union, where she worked with Elizabeth Blackwell in the campaigns against the double standard.[11]

It was not only the domination of the men, but the rule of science which made it difficult for the women of the Men and Women's Club to explore their own ideas about sexuality. As Walkowitz has pointed out, they were 'expected to work within a scientific ideology that denied the validity of female subjective experience, and over which the largely "untrained" female members had only an uncertain command'. In other words, in order to participate they were forced to renounce their feminist politics and deny the reality of male sexual exploitation of women. They were also forced to learn a new language, the language of patriarchal science, a language which they found inadequate to the exploration of complex thought and feeling. The evidence presented by Walkowitz and Bland suggests that the language of patriarchal science, which prohibited the expression of emotion and subjectivity, often silenced them, constrained their thinking, and undermined their attempts to explore the implications of female sexual autonomy.[12]

Jeffreys (1985) has identified several more feminists, such as Margaret Sibthorp, Lucy Re-Bartlett, and Effie Johnson, who expressed ideas similar to the concept of psychic love, which was almost invariably linked to the concept of voluntary motherhood. Some were also advocates of 'free love', but took care to point out that theirs was a feminist rather than a libertarian version of this ideology. As we have seen in Chapter 1, the feminist version of 'free love' was based on opposition to the concept of 'conjugal rights' with its implicit sexual ownership of the wife by the husband, and meant the assertion of a woman's absolute right to control sexual access to her own body. During the 1870s and 1880s Annie Besant was committed to the libertarian version of 'free love', along with the advocacy of artificial methods of birth control. But by the 1890s Besant had completely rejected her beliefs about free love and birth control and turned to theosophy and celibacy. She now believed that men's excessive sexual instinct, which had reached its present abnormal development as a result of self-indulgence in the past, was 'one of the most fruitful sources of human misery'. Her answer to the problem of birth control was no longer contraception but self-restraint:

> To hold this instinct in complete control ... is the task to which humanity should set itself.... It follows that Theosophists should sound the note of self-restraint within marriage, and the restriction of the marital relation to the perpetuation of the race.

In making such a statement Besant was coming into line with mainstream feminist opinion, which until the 1920s would remain implacably opposed to artificial means of birth control – a topic considered by many to be too controversial to be mentioned in public.[13]

The reasons for this have been explored by a number of historians, who have pointed out that the prevention of conception by artificial means was in contradiction with the feminist demands for female sexual autonomy, voluntary motherhood, and male continence. The feminist argument was basically that while contraception might provide some protection against unwanted pregnancy, it undermined their insistence that men could and should learn to control their sexual appetites. Artificial contraception made it much more difficult for women to resist men's excessive demands for sexual intercourse, and made them into what Henrietta Müller called 'an instrument for the use of the man'. It therefore undermined feminist attempts to redefine sexuality by shifting the emphasis away from the physical towards the psychic or emotional aspects. Artificial contraception reinforced the coital imperative and the patriarchal model of sexuality. A correspondent who wrote to the feminist journal *Shafts* protested that it was 'truly a *man's* remedy to look towards "scientific checks" rather than the elimination of male lust to eliminate "enforced maternity" '.[14] In short, feminist opposition to the promotion of artificial methods of contraception was based on the fear that its effect would be to strengthen male power within heterosexual relations and to undermine female sexual autonomy.

Militant Feminists, 'New Moralists', and the Sexuality Debates

The critique of male sexuality was taken up by militant feminists as part of their campaign against the double standard of sexual morality. Although all feminists, militant and non-militant, were opposed to the double standard, some disagreed with the tactics used by the militants, and felt that in demanding a single moral standard they were merely intent on imposing on men the same repressive code of sexual morality which men had imposed upon 'respectable' women. What many of these critics of militancy wanted instead was a 'new morality' in which women and men would be free to enjoy the sexual relationships they desired, without regulation or restriction by Church or State. These feminists found a vehicle for their ideas in a new journal, *The Freewoman*, which began publishing in 1911, and soon became a battleground for competing sexual ideologies, particularly in the correspondence columns. *The Freewoman* was founded by Dora Marsden, a former suffragette who left first the Women's Social and Political Union and then the Women's Freedom League because she felt their leaders were too autocratic. It was published as a 'weekly feminist review' between November 1911 and May 1912, when it changed its subtitle to a 'weekly humanist review'. In the following October it collapsed, owing to lack of finance, but resurfaced briefly in 1913 as *The New Freewoman: An Individualist Review*. After another collapse it finally reappeared in January 1914 as *The Egoist*.[15]

These changes in title and subtitle are a good indication of the direction which editorial policy took during a period of less than two years. From the beginning it was extremely hostile, not merely to militancy, but to the importance placed by militants and non-militants alike on securing votes for women. Dora Marsden, who controlled the editorial policy, believed strongly in the ideal of individual, spiritual freedom, and made it clear in the very first issue that this was far more important to her than 'externals' such as politics and economics. The first leading article distinguished between 'Freewomen' and 'Bondwomen', defining the former as individuals in their own right, and the latter as merely complementary to men. The journal's initial feminist stance became progressively displaced by an increasing emphasis on freedom of speech, freedom of thought, and the freedom of the individual in general.

Within less than a year it was announced that, as a humanist paper, its purpose was 'to show that the two causes, man's and woman's are one', and by June 1913 it had declared: 'Women's Movement forsooth, . . . why does not some-one start a straight nose movement . . . or any other movement based upon some accidental physical contournation?' The journal was also strongly influenced by anarchism, syndicalism, and libertarian socialism, and many of its contributors were men, including H.G. Wells, Edward Carpenter, and Guy Aldred. Prominent female contributors included Stella Browne, Rebecca West, Teresa Billington-Greig, Ada Nield Chew, and Rose Witcop.[16]

The debates around feminism and sexuality in *The Freewoman* are extremely interesting because they bring together most of the strands of feminist sexual theorizing which had emerged up to that point in history. They also highlight some of the political differences and tensions within feminism which could only be expressed to a limited extent in the militant feminist press. Although *The Freewoman* had, in its early stages, a clear editorial line which might be characterized as 'libertarian-feminist', and from which the debates were initiated, contributions expressing conflicting viewpoints were included, mainly in the form of correspondence. The oppositional and often acrimonious nature of the debates suggests that the political differences and tensions had their source in something far more fundamental than mere differences of political opinion or emphasis. What it suggests is that the various protagonists in the debates were engaged in a struggle between conflicting sexual ideologies, each underpinned by incompatible models of sexuality.

The journal opened in November 1911 with a two-pronged attack on militant feminism and the politics of spinsterhood. Within the first few months the debate broadened out to include the issues of celibacy and continence, the double standard and sexual freedom, and it soon became clear that what was being debated was not simply the politics of spinsterhood but the nature of sexuality itself. The debate was fuelled by the struggle around the Criminal Law Amendment Bill of 1912, which had begun as a feminist-inspired attempt to curb the trafficking in women and girls, but in the process of becoming law was virtually sabotaged and resulted only in increased harassment of working-class prostitutes by the police. The controversy surrounding the bill exacerbated differences and tensions between feminists who were already divided over issues such as the role of legislation in controlling sexual behaviour, and the 'new morality' which was to replace the double standard.[17]

Since the spinster was a symbol, both of the feminist revolt against patriarchal marriage and of female sexual autonomy, it was appropriate that the debate should begin with her. The leading article (unsigned) which sparked it off was entitled 'The Spinster – By One'. Essentially it was a plea for an end to the restrictions which condemned unmarried women to celibacy, and an attack on the alleged dangers of chastity, which was defined in terms of denying the sex instinct. It was heavily ironic in tone and obviously intended to be provocative, since it presented an extremely negative and misogynistic caricature of the spinster:

> I write of the High Priestess of Society. Not of the mother of sons, but of her barren sister, the withered tree, the acidulous vessel under whose pale shadow we chill and whiten, of the Spinster I write. Because of her power and dominion. She, unobtrusive, meek, soft-footed, silent, shamefaced, bloodless and boneless, thinned to spirit, enters the secret recesses of the mind, sits at the secret springs of action, and moulds and fashions our emasculate society. She is our social Nemesis.[18]

According to the writer all spinsters were middle-class, and spent their time 'haunting' libraries and theatres. She also accused spinster schoolteachers of making children breathe in every day 'the atmosphere of her violated spirit'. This must have been very shocking and offensive to all those feminist spinsters who had worked so hard to challenge the patriarchal stereotype of the spinster as bitter and twisted and a danger to society because of her thwarted sexual instincts. They must have felt that this was a deliberate attempt to undermine the positive image of the spinster which they had struggled for the best part of a century to construct. That a journal calling itself feminist should publish something so vicious and antagonistic to basic feminist principles must have felt like a double betrayal. At least one suffragette cancelled her subscription immediately, saying she was 'amazed at any modern woman countenancing the contents'. She considered that the article on the spinster was 'ludicrous' and 'morally objectionable', and suggested that 'Bondwoman' would be a more appropriate name for the paper than 'Freewoman'.[19]

The article on the spinster was quickly followed by several others on the 'new morality' and related topics such as divorce, marriage reform, illegitimacy, birth control, and 'sex freedom'. The correspondence columns revealed a range of responses, from praise for their courage and frankness, to flat reassertions of the 'old morality' and the desirability of self-control. Many tried to avoid polarization by expressing their misgivings or criticisms in a thoughtful and reasoned way. E.M. Watson, for instance, who was probably Edith Watson of the Women's Freedom League and a prominent campaigner against the double standard, found some of the articles 'excellent' and wished the journal prosperity. At the same time she criticized the elitism of the leading articles and 'the tendency in your paper towards a glorification of freedom in all that concerns sex impulses'. While she supported wholeheartedly any changes which would give women greater equality within marriage, and enable it to be a real choice based only on love, she thought it a mistake to encourage men and women to believe 'that any satisfactory society can be built up on the basis of complete freedom in sex matters'. Like many other correspondents, she feared that what the new sex freedom heralded was a morality based on existing male values and practices, especially the separation of the physical aspects of sex from the emotional and spiritual aspects. Watson pointed out the anti-social implications of such a separation:

One might as well try to build an edifice on an active volcano, for nothing in nature is more unstable, unreasonable, and capricious than the sex-instinct when separated from any idea of duty, honour, or spiritual-mindedness.

Another (anonymous) correspondent attributed the promotion of the new morality precisely to the fact that men were afraid that when women were enfranchised, their sexual freedom under the double standard would come to an end:

> It is noteworthy how anxious men are to safeguard their incontinence in the coming age of the Freewoman. They are expecting trouble, as your columns show, and by paying heed to them, Freewoman will be leaving the frying-pan for the fire.[20]

The topic which provoked the most heated exchanges during the first few months of publication was abstinence, and the question of whether it was harmful to the health of either sex, and especially, in the light of the article on the spinster, to the health of women. Margaret Hill, for example, insisted that 'woman is physically complete. Though she is a necessity to man, he is not necessary to her'. Edith Watson demanded to know what evidence there was to support the theory that abstinence was, in the words of one (male) writer, 'painful and physiologically injurious'. She maintained 'that this conception has done more harm to women in marriage and more to foster the horrors of prostitution than any other of the theories of sex'. She also wanted to know 'what proof is there that the enforced abstinence of many single women has been injurious to them?' Replying to her own question, she wrote: 'I affirm, on the contrary, that there is a greater percentage of nervous and physical wrecks among married than among single women'. Kathlyn Oliver, drawing on her own experience, expressed her support of Watson:

> I am an unmarried woman, nearly thirty years of age, and have always practised abstinence, and although not a powerful person, I enjoy the best of health, and have never troubled a doctor since I was six years old. My married women friends, on the contrary, have always some complaint or something wrong.
> Who has not seen the girl married at twenty almost immediately degenerate into a nervous wreck? I deny absolutely that abstinence has any bad effect on my health.

Oliver, who was a working-class spinster and former secretary of the Domestic Workers Union of Great Britain, insisted that she was 'neither a prude nor a Puritan', but 'an apostle of the practice of self-restraint in sex matters'. 'How can we possibly be Freewomen', she asked, 'if, like the majority of men, we become the slaves of our lower appetites?'[21]

A 'New Subscriber' entered into a personal and highly antagonistic debate with Oliver, accusing her and Watson and other women like them of being 'sexually anaesthetic', and insisting that for those women who *were* 'capable of intense sexual emotion', abstinence from 'normal sexual relations' was unnatural and had ruined their lives. She agreed that many women had been made 'ill and wretched by the unrestrained indulgence of married life with ignorant or brutal husbands', but argued that 'the abuse of a natural pleasure does not make it entirely injurious and to be deprecated'. 'There is surely a middle path', she wrote, 'between total abstinence and excess'. Her letter made several references to the scientific study of sex and specifically cited Havelock Ellis and August Forel as authoritative sources. She referred to the 'far greater range of variation sexually among women than among men' and claimed to have known 'specimens of all varieties intimately'. She also suggested that those single women who claimed that sexual abstinence was not harmful probably resorted to various forms of 'auto-erotism' or 'onanism', implying that they were hypocritical because they were not abstaining totally from 'sexual indulgence', merely substituting masturbation for 'normal sexual relations'.[22]

Oliver retaliated by accusing 'New Subscriber' of being of the 'male persuasion', adding that she had anticipated that she would be accused of 'not being normal'. She asserted that she had experienced sexual desire when she first 'fell in love' and, though unable to marry, she had on occasions continued to experience 'the sex feeling' ever since. She acknowledged that the fact that she was unable to give expression to her feelings sometimes affected her spirits, making her sad and depressed, but denied that it had an adverse effect on her health. She made a clear distinction between *experiencing* sexual desire and being *governed* by it: for her the capacity to exercise rational restraint over one's instincts and desires was a mark of being human:

> [the sex feeling] never did, and it never will, govern me as it governs and enslaves the majority of men. My intellect and reason rules my lower instincts and desires, and it is this fact which raises me above the lower animals (including man).

'New Subscriber''s response was to reiterate her distinction between women like Oliver, who were 'of cold temperament' and 'undersexed', and those, like herself, who were of 'ardent temperament'. She emphasized that the latter did not imply 'indulgence in indiscriminate promiscuity', but deplored the influence of women like Oliver on the Women's Movement:

> It will be an unspeakable catastrophe if our richly complex Feminist movement with its possibilities of power and joy, falls under the domination of sexually deficient and disappointed women, impervious to facts and deeply ignorant about life.

This clearly upset Oliver, who wondered what she had done to deserve such contempt, and protested that she did not want to prevent others from enjoying all the laxity in sex matters that they desired, provided that they did not interfere with her and did not injure anyone but themselves. 'New Subscriber''s reply was extremely patronizing, merely underlining what she considered to be Oliver's ignorance of life, and it was clear that by now the level of mutual antagonism and personal animosity was so high that there was no possibility of constructive debate between these particular parties. 'New Subscriber' eventually decided to identity herself as Stella Browne on 11 July 1912, but though they both continued to write to the journal, they no longer responded to each other's letters.[23]

There were many other contributions to the debate, including numerous articles and letters from men protesting that abstinence was unnatural. Most of the female correspondents raised broader questions about the nature of female sexuality, male sexuality, and heterosexual relations. Edith Watson argued that many great geniuses were ascetics and poured scorn on the notion that men were constitutionally unable to endure abstinence. She believed that the main reason men were now preaching 'sterilization' (i.e. contraception) was because they saw this as a way of meeting feminist demands without having to practise self-restraint:

> Considering the vast amount of suffering that their sex imposes first and last on women, whether married or celibate, we may be forgiven for holding very cheap the 'suffering' that abstinence imposes on men. To liken it to hunger or thirst is an absurdity, for men cannot live a week without food or drink, but are known to be capable of remaining celibate for a lifetime. Yet it is on this theory of male 'suffering' that the present marital relation is based, and women sacrifice themselves to it daily. The movement for freedom among women bade fair to do it some injury, but men have met the difficulty by preaching and teaching sterilization – anything rather than practise self-restraint.

She thought that the sexual impulse in women was probably greater than in men, and that they were just as tempted to 'indulgence', but restrained by considerations of fear or prudence. She could not believe that the 'Freewoman''s ideal of freedom would take the form of a 'loose licence', and saw no advancement for women 'along the lines of a laxity in sex matters equal to that which characterizes men'. She believed that the highest forms of development were the outcome of habitual self-control, and that the 'Freewoman' would seek to teach men 'the restraint that Nature has taught her to impose on herself', by seeking 'to raise marriage to the standard of a spiritual and intellectual as well as a physical union – a union, indeed, in which physical intercourse *cannot* exist without a spiritual affinity'.[24]

The question of the allegedly irresistible impulses of sexual passion, and the relationship between mind and body, was taken up by Mary Bull, who asked:

> Are our dual natures, then, nine-tenths body and one-tenth mind? so would the specious argument of 'man's necessity' imply. Are we to sink below the level of the brute creation? for even the creature has periodical times of mating, particularly shown in bird and insect life.

She claimed that it was a well-known fact that the mind governed the body, citing many instances, such as physical healing by means of mental sugges-tion, and argued that if the powers of the mind were enlisted to conquer the impulses of the body, venereal diseases could be eliminated. Man's 'neces-sity' was nothing more than a convenient invention:

> If, then, the effect of mind on matter is a physical law, and the power of the mental over the physical proved beyond doubt by prophets, thinkers and teachers, why should sexual impulse be a thing apart from the law? Because man, for his convenience, has made it so![25]

One leading article took the form of a review of a recently published novel about the trafficking in women. The article was untypical in that it included a strong critique of male sexuality, arguing that men had been encouraged to let their impulses run riot: 'passion has remained with the majority of them mainly an impulsive physical affair, capable of being aroused by next to nothing, and of being satisfied with about as much'. The writer suggested that women would have to provide men with incentives and social rewards for 'monogyny', for instance by demanding a certificate of health from any man they chose as long-term partners, and by demanding the same fidelity from men that husbands demanded from wives. On the other hand, C. Gasquoigne-Hartley, in another book review, took the opportunity to criticize feminists for attempting to impose upon men 'the same false code of repression which has in the past held back the growth and development of women'. She asserted that chastity for women was a 'false god' and wrote: 'There seems to be a very widespread opinion that to use the divine gift of sex for pleasure is wrong'.[26]

Several women attempted to explore the nature of female sexuality by going beyond Stella Browne's rather simplistic categorization of women as either 'cold' or 'ardent'. One suffragette, who used the *nom de plume* Cailin Dhu, agreed with Edith Watson that a woman's desire was 'in general, no mean second to a man's', but did not think that 'to make our morality on a plane with a man's would improve our position'. She said she did not believe that it was necessary to 'play every note in the sexual scale' in order to be complete. She thought that women should 'stop beating around the bush', because they were now far enough advanced to decide what they wanted. At the same time, she appeared to believe that women and men had been 'created' monogamous and polygamous respectively, and it was not clear how this was to be overcome by her recommendation of 'medical regulation of marriage', or indeed what the latter might entail. Another correspondent, who signed herself 'A Grateful Reader', made the point that 'the absolute indifference or dislike of the sexual act in many women' did not necessarily mean either that they lacked 'sex attraction' or that they disliked 'love-making'. She suggested that it might be due, either to ignorance, or to girls' life-long training in personal modesty, or to the fact that men knew 'exactly what they want' while women did not. 'It is quite impossible', she wrote, 'to "explain" to people what they can know nothing about, till they experience it'. She also thought that Weininger's theory – that many women despised themselves because they felt instinctively that men despised them and held them in contempt – might have considerable truth in it, and hoped that more women would write in about their experience.[27]

Some women felt that most of the correspondents viewed the sexual aspect of womanhood rather morbidly. 'Hibernian' wrote: 'They make of woman a woman first and a human being afterwards; that is to say, they will not allow that she can be a complete normal human being unless her sexual side has had full scope'. She believed that there were 'many doors into the palace of full, vivid, ecstatic life'. This opinion was heartily endorsed by a woman who signed herself, tongue in cheek, 'A Deficient and Disappointed Woman', and refused to see sexuality as a political issue at all. She said she did not mind being categorized as 'impervious to facts and logic, and deeply ignorant of life' – such abuse could not possibly eradicate her sense of humour! She urged readers to stop 'this worship of sex' (as 'the one ultimate world-power'), and to 'come out to play in the fresh air', suggesting that perhaps 'we who are "undersexed" are the balance on the wheel of life'.[28]

The agitation surrounding the Criminal Law Amendment Bill of 1912 (the 'White Slavery' Bill) added further fuel to the debate about 'man's necessity' and the resulting 'sex slavery'. There was a crop of articles and letters by men protesting at what they saw as the repressive nature of the proposed legislation, which had originally included a feminist-inspired clause making soliciting of women by men an offence. The male correspondents insisted, either that the cause of prostitution was economic, or that men's need for prostitutes was natural and inevitable. Katharine Vulliamy responded that as long as there were large profits to be made out of the demand for women, it was impossible to know to what extent the demand was natural. 'The least observant person', she wrote, 'can see how the public can be made to feel all sorts of artificial needs when it is "good for trade" '. She added that bringing up boys to think that women exist for the convenience and comfort of men, and teaching girls to be parasites, docile and obedient, was one of the principal contributory causes of prostitution, and still an ideal which the educational system officially promoted. Vulliamy, who was a member of the Criminal Law Amendment Committee which had been formed in order to apply pressure on MPs to pass the Bill, also responded to the accusation that feminists were again trying to make people moral by Act of Parliament and encouraging the punishment and persecution of prostitutes. Her reply highlights very clearly the distinction between the feminist approach to this issue and the 'social purity' approach, and explains why many feminists considered such legislation to be necessary:

> The problem for legislation is not so much the 'making people moral by Act of Parliament' as the protection of members of the community from being preyed on for commercial profit. The white slave traffic is essentially like any other form of slavery, and it is not at all necessary that a Bill aimed at it should consider the causes of prostitution, which are as irrelevant to the criminal Law Amendment Act as the wholesome effects of work on cotton plantations, so freely dragged into the controversy, were to negro slavery.
>
> I should not be on the 'Pass the Bill' Committee if its objects were to punish prostitutes without inquiring into the causes of prostitution; its object is merely to obtain Government facilities for the C.L. Amendment Act. The Act itself is directed solely at procurers, landlords of disorderly houses, or persons who exploit or control prostitutes for their own profit. It will not touch the question of prostitution, except inasmuch by eliminating some of its exploitation for commercial purposes it may simplify the problem.

Vulliamy conceded that one objection to the Bill was that it gave power to arrest on suspicion for procuring, and that arrest on suspicion had its dangers. But she argued that people could be arrested on suspicion of theft and that girls should be given at least as much protection as property. It was a question of balancing one right against another: 'If helpless girls are not to be protected against procurers', she asked, 'why should protection against "persecuting faddists" be claimed for procurers?' She acknowledged that the Bill did not go very far, but pointed out that a Bill which did go far had no chance of passing. She thought that if an effective law could not be passed all at once, it was a 'practical expedient to divide it up, and pass it one thing at a time'. The most that they could expect, she added, was that it would make the administration of the existing law more effective, and that 'the agitation connected with it will have carried public opinion a few steps forward'.[29]

Another male contributor who proposed the introduction of Japanese-style palaces of prostitution received a sharp response from Edith Watson:

> Oh, how sick we are of man's 'necessity' and all his disloyal excuses for the exploiting of womanhood! For Heaven's sake let us know something of that necessity. Let sincere men speak honestly, and tell us the truth about their necessity. Have we been lied to from the first? Is purity really impossible to man? Have there never been any genuine ascetics, any pure priests? Do Arctic explorers take their

wives with them? And to those to whom sex is an obsession, is there no possibility of their indulging it alone, without obtruding their 'necessities' upon women?.

This provoked the accusation from the author of the article that Watson was openly recommending 'self-abuse'. She countered that he was glorifying and idealizing prostitution, and said that while she did not 'recommend' self-abuse, she was 'certainly strongly of the opinion that where an abuse is inevitable it is infinitely better to abuse ourselves than other people, and to bear alone any consequences of our abuses'. In support of her argument she cited the sexologist Forel, whom she had heard lecture, and who considered masturbation to be harmless and infinitely preferable to prostitution. '*My* case for self-abuse', she continued, 'would be that it strikes even men as degrading, and reveals the sexual "necessity" in all its ugly nudity'. 'Let men be reduced to self-abuse for all their sexual "necessities" outside of passionate love', she continued, 'and perhaps their "necessity" will become less evident to them. I certainly think it better than any form of prostitution or sexual coercion in marriage'.[30]

Kathlyn Oliver took up the cudgels again, this time in response to an article on marriage reform, in which the (male) author appeared to advocate child marriage. Although the author strenuously denied this, Oliver pointed out that it was implicit in his argument that self-restraint in sex matters was incompatible with human nature; he could not both forbid boys to marry as soon as they experienced sexual desire, and also deny that they possessed the capacity for self-restraint. Essentially, the debate was not so much about child marriage as about 'human nature' – more precisely, *men's* human nature:

> His absurd and utterly false reasoning that a plea for self-restraint in men is, in other words, a desire to change human nature makes him an impossible person to debate with. I deny that self-control in sex matters is incompatible with human nature; the man or woman who is incapable of sexual self-control should be walking about on four legs, and not on two, because lack of self-control is incompatible with human nature.

Oliver, too, cited Forel as her authoritative source: 'To quote Dr Forel, "Only that man is truly free" (and I would add truly human) "who has become the master of his lower instincts" '. She also pointed out that the reason so many women were averse to marriage was the loss of sexual autonomy which this entailed:

> Mr Woods evidently declines to believe that any wife ever desires to be free from the embraces of her husband, that she ever desires to be alone, or perhaps he doesn't think about it at all, but holds that

access to a wife's body at any and all times in a man's indisputable (or divine) right.[31]

By September 1912 Dora Marsden had decided to curb the articles on sexuality because she was worried by W.H. Smith's ban on the sale of *The Freewoman*. Meanwhile the militant feminist campaign against the double standard of sexual morality was escalating, fuelled by the subversion of the feminist intent behind the Criminal Law Amendment Bill of 1912. In the spring of 1913 Christabel Pankhurst's series of articles, subsequently reprinted as *The Great Scourge and How to End It*, began to appear in *The Suffragette*. This shared many features of the emerging feminist model of sexuality articulated by Blackwell, Wolstenholme Elmy, Swiney, and many of the contributors to the debates in *The Freewoman*. Central to the work was a critique of the concept of 'human nature' and the notion that men's sexual needs were natural. If venereal disease was to be prevented, argued Pankhurst, then prostitution must go. At this, she wrote, there will be 'shrieks of protest' and 'we shall hear the usual balderdash about "human nature" and "injury to man's health"'. But why, she demanded, was 'human nature' to have full scope only in the one direction of sexual vice? It was part of 'human nature' to rob and kill; even cannibalism was in the 'nature' of some human beings. Yet these activities were not generally tolerated or regarded as socially acceptable. And why was the 'human nature' of men so different from the 'human nature' of women? According to man-made morality, a woman who was immoral was a 'fallen' woman and unfit for respectable society, while an immoral man was simply obeying the dictates of his 'human nature'. Similarly, according to man-made law, a wife who was unfaithful to her husband only once could raise no plea of 'human nature' in her defence; whereas a man who consorted with prostitutes throughout the whole of his married life was apparently acting only in accordance with 'human nature'. One was forced to the conclusion, said Pankhurst sarcastically, that women's nature must be very much cleaner, stronger and higher than men's. 'But Suffragists, at any rate, hope that this is not really true. They have more faith in men than men have in themselves, and they believe that a man can live as pure and moral a life as a woman can'.[32]

Pankhurst poured scorn on the theory that prostitution was necessary and inevitable, and on the notion that an equal moral standard was an impossible dream. She underlined the point with a reference to an eminent medical authority (male) who stated there were 'no organs in a man's body that can be better controlled than the sexual organs'. In a passage which closely echoed the words of Blackwell and Swiney, Pankhurst hit back at those who insisted that men who used prostitutes were simply 'exercising their natural functions'. Such statements, she wrote, no longer had the power to deceive women, now that they were arming themselves with the necessary medical knowledge. It was not suffragettes, but incontinent men who were defying Nature:

Women know that, as one doctor has expressed it, man's physical nature is accurately adapted to the needs of his moral being, and that . . . prostitution and immorality are not in accordance with Nature, but are a violation of Nature's laws. Chastity and continence for men are natural and healthful; it is unchastity and incontinence which destroy men morally and physically.

Now that women were aware of these facts, she said, they would 'treat with contempt the gross cant about men's sexual needs'. The need for prostitutes only arose 'because of that exaggerated development of the sex instinct which is supposed to be natural where men are concerned'. Prostitution not only exploited some women but degraded all women by poisoning men's idea of the (hetero)sexual relationship. It separated the physical aspect of sex from the spiritual and emotional aspects, reinforcing the pernicious doctrine that 'woman is sex and beyond that nothing . . . that women are created primarily for the sex gratification of men'.[33]

Pankhurst had no doubt that the majority of men were naturally just as capable as women of exercising rational control over their sexual desires. What was needed was a massive programme of re-education in sexual matters, to sweep away ignorance and superstition, and to teach men, from youth upwards, 'the rightness and possibility of an equal moral standard for men and women', as well as the responsibilities of husbandhood and fatherhood. At present their sexual appetites were artificially stimulated and inflamed by a variety of physical and mental causes, including the fallacious theories about their own sexual nature. Pankhurst looked to the medical profession to 'come to the rescue of men whose willpower fails them', arguing that it was the doctors' primary duty to instruct men in sex hygiene: 'It would indeed be an extraordinary thing if the medical profession, which has discovered means of regulating every other bodily function, should be unable to tell men how to regulate the sex function'. Athough she was aware that most of the medical profession had up to now viewed sexual issues from a masculine perspective, she believed that the power of the vote would widen women's sphere of influence, including within the medical profession. When doctors were in a position to view sexual matters much more from women's perspective, they would be able to help men, 'if need be by medicinal means, to live as befits a highly-evolved and self-respecting human being'. This allusion to 'medicinal means' indicates a tension in Pankhurst's model of sexuality between the natural and the social or political. While she clearly believed that men's excessive sexual 'needs' were socially constructed rather than natural, and that men were just as capable as women of controlling their sexual desires, she seems to have thought that there might be a small number of extreme cases where natural self-control might be lacking. She made one other passing reference to this when she wrote: 'Prison doctors administer medicine which keeps under control the "human nature" of men prisoners who have no natural self-control'. Apart form these two instances the whole emphasis was on the importance of the re-education of men, a matter which she seems to have viewed with some optimism. To those men who continued to insist that prostitution was necessary and inevitable she retorted: 'We think better of men than this'.[34]

There is no actual evidence that Pankhurst read *The Freewoman* or was aware of the debates on sexuality which took place within its pages. But it is highly probable that she *was* aware of them, since the journal acquired a certain notoriety in suffrage circles. Millicent Fawcett, for example, thought it 'objectionable and mischievous', and Maude Royden (also of the NUWSS) called it 'nauseous', though there were some suffragists who approved of it. Edith Watson of the Women's Freedom League was critical not only of its tendency to glorify sexual freedom but also of its elitism, and deplored the personal attacks on the leaders of the Women's Social and Political Union. Nina Boyle, her close friend and political ally, wrote to the paper in a tone of sarcastic hilarity, poking fun at its 'portentous intellectuality' and 'lofty disregard for the ordinary facts of life'.[35] Olive Schreiner was appalled by it; she complained that nearly all the articles were written by men, and thought it should be called 'The Licentious Male'. There was certainly a strong similarity between the ideas expressed by Pankhurst in *The Great Scourge* and those of correspondents to *The Freewoman*, such as Watson and Oliver, who opposed its editorial position. The fact that Pankhurst also chose to address the questions of sex freedom and spinsterhood in her series of articles on VD suggests that she may have seen this as an opportunity to make her own contribution to these debates. She observed that certain men, alarmed by the dangers of prostitution (not to mention the expense), were now trying to persuade women to adopt a looser code of morals than hitherto:

'You are asking for political freedom,' women are told. 'More important to you is sex freedom. Votes for women should be accompanied, if not preceded, by wild oats for women. The thing to be done is not to raise the moral standard of men, but to lower the moral standard of women.' To this proposal the women reply by a firm and unqualified negative. Votes they certainly intend to have, and that quickly, but they know too well what is the harvest of wild oats, and having that knowledge, they refuse to sow any.

When women have the vote, they will be more and not less opposed than now to making a plaything of sex and of entering casually into the sex relationship.

As we have already seen in Chapter 1, Pankhurst also laid great stress on the dangers of marriage to women's health, and declared that spinsterhood was a rational, political response to female sexual slavery and male sexual behaviour. She also refuted the claim that single women suffered from being 'unmated', and that the 'unsatisfied desires' of women were in any way a problem. Nowadays, she affirmed, the life of the single woman was full of joy and interest and in every way complete. Only if she found a man worthy of her, a man fit physically and morally to be her husband, would she contemplate marriage.[36]

'Sex Freedom' or Female Sexual Autonomy?

The conflict between the views of the militant feminist campaigners against the double standard and those of the self-styled 'Freewomen' or 'new moralists' suggests that feminists were deeply divided over the issue of sexuality. It would be simplistic and misleading, however, to characterize the division as one between 'progressives' or 'radicals', represented by members of *The Freewoman* circle, and 'conservatives' or 'purists', represented by those, such as Watson and Oliver, who opposed them. In the first place, there were certain elements of feminist sexual radicalism which were common to both: in particular the opposition to the double standard, and the critique of marriage as an institution. They also shared a belief in the right of women to 'refuse maternity', though for the 'new moralists' this meant the right to use artificial means of contraception, which most other feminists, militant and non-militant, felt would only reinforce female sexual slavery. At a fundamental level, both groups also appeared to share a common commitment to female sexual autonomy. Stella Browne, despite her hostility to Kathlyn Oliver and her supporters, expressed this in a most uncompromising manner, asserting that 'our wills are ours, our persons are ours', and that the sexual experience is the right of every human being not hopelessly afflicted in mind or body and should be entirely a matter of free choice and personal preference, untainted by bargain or compulsion'.[37]

But a closer examination of their views suggests that female sexual autonomy had a very different meaning for the different groups. For the 'new moralists' it seems to have been very close to the libertarian notion of 'free love', with its connotations of freedom from restriction by Church or State, and sometimes from social constraints and responsibilities of any kind. The 'new moralists' tended to avoid using the term 'free love', probably because of the negative implications of sexual licence or 'excess' with which it was inevitably associated. Nevertheless, as several critics pointed out, it was difficult to see the distinction between 'free love' and the 'new morality'. Dora Marsden, for instance, attacked monogamy as 'a grossly unfair monopoly' which she believed to be 'based on the intellectual apathy and insensitiveness of married women'; and some other 'new moralists', though not all, did go so far as to advocate transient sexual encounters. Isabel Leatham summed up the 'Freewoman''s concept of 'sex freedom' and the 'new morality' as follows: 'the Freewoman will not enter upon the sex relationship for any such conscious purpose as that of reproduction, but rather . . . will find passionate love between Men and Women, even if that be transient, the only sanction for sex intimacy'.[38]

Radical though this position appears, it failed to take sufficient account of the power imbalance between women and men in a patriarchal society, and how this might be reflected in, or constituted by, heterosexual relationships based on particular sexual practices. Further, it failed to question the masculine, phallocentric definition of sex as a natural, physical instinct, which 'needed' to be satisfied by means of heterosexual intercourse. On the contrary, it seems that some sought to define female sexuality in the same terms. This was especially evident in the denigration of the spinster, the strictures on the alleged dangers of celibacy or abstinence from heterosexual intercourse, and the labelling of women who denied that the latter was harmful as 'undersexed', 'cold', or 'sexually anaesthetic'. It was also evident in the following anonymous contribution: 'all natural functions require exercise, even when not employed on purely utilitarian purposes'. A 'vicar's wife' also suggested that there were some women to whom sex was as much a necessity as it was to men, and who were equally capable of separating the physical and spiritual aspects of sex: 'there are women who disassociate the spiritual from the bodily appetite, and satisfy the latter without the former, just as a man can. There are some in fact, to whom it is a necessity of health to do so'.[39]

In these respects there was a crucial difference between the concept of sexual freedom which the 'new moralists' propounded, and the concept of female sexual autonomy as expressed in the writings of the feminist sexual theorists discussed earlier. Blackwell, Wolstenholme Elmy, and Swiney started from a radical critique of male sexual practices and the ideology which legitimated them as 'natural'. Although they did not use the terminology we use today, they clearly recognized that male sexuality was socially constructed, and how it functioned in the social control of women. For them the attainment of female sexual autonomy entailed both a radical redistribution of power within heterosexual relationships *and* a radical redefinition of the nature of sexuality. It included the right of women to refuse, not merely maternity, but heterosexual intercourse itself, a right which they believed the use of artificial methods of contraception would undermine. By emphasizing the unity of the physical and psychic aspects of sexuality, and affirming the natural ability of human beings to exercise rational control over their physical instincts, they were attempting to move towards a form of sexual expression which would enable women to retain their autonomy within heterosexual relationships. Although they appear to have assumed that heterosexuality and the desire for motherhood were natural, there was nothing in their model of sexuality which undermined the validity of spinsterhood. On the contrary, their insistence on the right of women to refuse heterosexual intercourse, as well as on the naturalness of continence and celibacy, lent implicit support to those feminist spinsters who were struggling to validate spinsterhood as positive and fulfilling.

It was this model of sexuality which underpinned the arguments of those feminists such as Watson, Oliver, and Pankhurst, who opposed the 'new moralists' concept of sexual freedom. It was a model of sexuality which was firmly rooted in more than a century of feminist struggles to emancipate women from female sexual slavery, and to displace the patriarchal model of sexuality which legitimated it. It was a feminist model of sexuality in the sense that it represented, not only a radical inversion of what men had defined as 'natural', but a positive attempt to redefine sexuality in a way which would reflect women's experience and women's interests as autonomous human beings. The sexual ideology of the 'new moralists', on the other hand, had its source in a quite different tradition, namely that of sexual libertarianism or male sexual radicalism. In this sense, Oliver's description of Browne as being 'of the male persuasion' was not inappropriate. The weakness of this position has always been that it ignores or underplays power differences between participants in sexual relationships and is based on an uncritical acceptance of the patriarchal model of sexuality. The divisions between feminists which have been described here were essentially about how the female sexual autonomy which all feminists desired was to be achieved. Some thought it could be achieved by extending the sexual freedom which men already enjoyed to women; others though it necessary to bring about a fundamental change, not only in heterosexual relations and practices, but in the way sexuality itself was conceptualized.

Despite the significant progress which feminists had made towards the development of a feminist model of sexuality the patriarchal model remained remarkably resilient. We have already noted a tendency for protagonists on all sides of the debates to legitimate their arguments and assertions by reference to the 'laws of nature'. Feminists as well as anti-feminists appear to have found it increasingly necessary to rely, not on argument alone, but on medical and scientific 'proof'. This has been noted especially in the writing of Elizabeth Blackwell, Frances Swiney, Christabel Pankhurst, and some of the contributors to *The Freewoman*. Several of the latter cited specifically the work of sexologists in support of their political positions. Stella Browne was a great admirer of the work of Havelock Ellis, though she also mentioned August Forel, who seems to have been particularly favoured by militant feminists, probably because he was extremely forthright in his condemnation of prostitution and the double standard. In the following chapter I shall argue that it was the development of sexology, and in particular the work of Havelock Ellis, which was largely responsible for sustaining and increasing the resilience of the patriarchal model of sexuality, in the face of such a persistent and determined feminist challenge. It represented, in effect, the appropriation of the sexual by male scientific 'experts', overturning more than a century of feminist struggle to politicize sexuality, to take it out of the sphere of the 'natural'. What feminists had defined as political, the experts redefined as 'natural'. By endowing the patriarchal model with scientific legitimacy, the feminist challenge was undermined, and further development of the feminist model of sexuality was effectively blocked.

Notes

1 Jeffreys (1985), especially ch. 2. Elizabeth Wolstenholme's 'free union' with Ben Elmy was strongly disapproved of by leading suffragists and when she became pregnant she came under great pressure to marry him. When she eventually did so they both took the name Wolstenhome Elmy as a gesture against the patriarchal nature of marriage.

2 Wolstenholme Elmy [Ethelmer] (1892), p. 43.

3 Wolstenholme Elmy (1897), p. 5.

4 We now know that the period recommended, though in accordance with contemporary medical opinion, was in fact unsafe.

5 Swiney (n.d.) 'Man's Necessity'.

6 Swiney (1912), p. 39. Feminists such as Swiney were already suggesting a possible link between heterosexual intercourse and cervical cancer, a suggestion which is now supported by medical evidence. On the problem of the birth rate in relation to imperialism and motherhood, see Davin (1978).

7 Swiney (1912), p. 8.

8 *Ibid.*, p. 45.

9 Schreiner (1978 [1911]); Walkowitz (1986); Bland (1986); for further details on Schreiner's model of sexuality see also Chapter 1.

10 Bland (1986), pp. 128–31; Walkowitz (1986), p. 49.

11 Bland (1986), p. 132.

12 Walkowitz (1986), p. 144; my interpretation of this evidence differs in some respects from those of Walkowitz and Bland. Walkowitz in particular considers that despite these difficulties the women gained confidence in their ability to take command of the tools of Darwinian, evolutionary social science.

13 Besant (1901), p. 6. See also Jeffreys (1985), ch. 2. Margaret Sibthorp edited a feminist journal, *Shafts*, which was strongly opposed to artificial methods of birth control.

14 Dyhouse (1989), p. 170; for detailed discussions of feminism and birth control see Gordon (1977) and McLaren (1978).

15 Information on the life of Dora Marsden may be found in the biography of her life-long friend, Harriet Shaw Weaver, by Lidderdale and Nicholson (1970).

16 *The Freewoman*, May 1912; July 1913.

17 See Chapter 2, pp. 37–44.

18 *The Freewoman*, 23 November 1911.

19 *The Freewoman*, 21 December 1911.

20 *Ibid.; The Freewoman*, 15 February 1912.

21 *The Freewoman*, 30 November 1911; 8 February 1912; 15 February 1912.

22 *The Freewoman*, 22 February 1912.

23 *The Freewoman*, 29 February 1912; 7 March 1912. For information on Stella Browne see Rowbotham (1977); for a more critical view see Jeffreys (1985), especially ch. 6. It is mainly because of her belief in the separation of sexual pleasure from reproduction by means of access to contraception and abortion that Browne has been seen by Sheila Rowbotham and others as radical. I discuss the contradictions implicit in this view in Chapter 6.

24 *The Freewoman*, 8 February 1912, emphasis in original.

25 *The Freewoman*, 7 March 1912.

26 *The Freewoman*, 15 February 1912; 7 March 1912. Mrs Gasquoigne-Hartley was also known as Mrs Walter Gallichan (see Chapter 1). She was vice-chairman of the *Freewoman* Discussion Circle, and addressed one of their meetings on 'The Problems of Celibacy'.

27 *The Freewoman*, 21 December 1911; 9 May 1912. For a discussion of the ideas of the anti-feminist Otto Weininger, see Klein (1946).

28 *The Freewoman*, 7 March 1912; 9 May 1912.

29 *The Freewoman*, 13 June 1912; 20 June 1912.

30 *Ibid.; The Freewoman*, 4 July 1912.

31 *The Freewoman*, 1 August 1912.

32 Pankhurst (1913), pp. 5–8; see also Chapter 1, pp. 20–1 and Chapter 2, pp. 46–9.

33 Pankhurst (1913), p. 62; pp. 122–3; p. 137; pp. 19–25.

34 Pankhurst (1913), p. 12; p. 22; p. 11; p. 33.

35 '*Please* go on!', implored Boyle. 'You cannot have any idea how funny you all are. I haven't laughed so much since I was young' (*The Freewoman*, 21 December, 1911, emphasis in original). The editors replied that her hilarity was infectious, but seemed at a loss to understand its cause.

36 Pankhurst (1913), pp. 130–2.

37 *The Freewoman*, 1 August 1912; 21 March 1912. On the 'progressives' versus 'purists' dichotomy see especially Gordon and Dubois (1984) and other articles in the collection of papers given at the conference held at Barnard College, New York in 1982, edited by Carol Vance (1984). Walkowitz (1982) also inclines to this view, as do Weeks (1982), Coward (1984) and Mort (1987). See also the collection edited by Snitow, Stansell, and Thompson (1984). For a critique, though still within the same dichotomy, see Jeffreys (1985), especially ch. 10.

38 *The Freewoman*, 4 January 1912; 11 January 1912.

39 *The Freewoman*, 1 February 1912; 21 March 1912.

Chapter 5

Eroticizing Women's Oppression
Havelock Ellis and the Construction of the 'Natural'

The life and work of Havelock Ellis have been extensively researched and documented, and there is a high degree of consensus concerning his place in the history of sexuality. He is regarded not merely as one of the great torchbearers of sexual 'enlightenment', who helped to blaze the trail of the sexual revolution, but as one of the most influential sexual thinkers of this century, who stands in the same relation to modern sexual theory as Albert Einstein to modern physics. As the founding father of sexology Ellis is credited with having placed the study of sexuality on a scientific footing and, together with Freud, Kinsey, and Masters and Johnson, with providing the basic framework within which sexuality in modern times is conceptualized. His reputation is essentially that of a naturalist, who observed rather than judged, and whose commitment to sex reform did not impair his objectivity as a scientist. In the opinion of his most recent biographer he was 'a revolutionary, one of the seminal figures responsible for the creation of a modern sensibility'.[1]

The particular features of Ellis' work which have contributed most to his popularity, especially with sexual 'radicals', are: first, his recognition of the existence of female sexuality and the importance of female sexual pleasure; and second, his contribution towards greater tolerance of sexual deviance, particularly homosexuality. Sheila Rowbotham, for example, has argued that Stella Browne's sexual 'radicalism' owed much to Ellis, and relates that people sat round reading Ellis in Communist Party branches in the 1930s, and that this was seen as very progressive. Jeffrey Weeks has examined Ellis' contribution to the liberalizing of attitudes towards homosexuality, as well as to the more general formulation of liberal sexual ideology. His assessment of him is as 'ultimately, a cautious sex reformer rather than a sexual radical', though he sees this as heightening rather than diminishing his importance. Weeks has, however, acknowledged Ellis' failure to challenge stereotypes of masculinity and femininity, in relation to both sexuality and the respective social roles of men and women, and has noted serious weaknesses in his discussion of lesbianism. He has also drawn attention to the apparent para-dox that Ellis, on the one hand, recognized the necessity of women controlling their own sexuality, while arguing, on the other, that nature defined woman's true sphere as motherhood. He points out, for instance, that while Ellis ad-vocated contraception and abortion, he was strongly opposed both to women's employment outside the home, and to the idea of nursery provision. He also insisted that every healthy woman ought to exercise her reproductive func-tion at least once in her lifetime, and asserted that women's brains were 'in a certain sense . . . in their wombs'. Furthermore, as we shall see later, although Ellis claimed to be pro-feminist, he was extremely hostile to militant feminism, and in particular to the Women's Social and Political Union.[2]

Weeks has suggested that Ellis' reactionary views on woman's role stemmed partly from a failure to appreciate a socialist analysis of the rela-tionship between capitalism and the position of women, and partly from the fact that he was trapped within stereotyped images that he had inherited. It seems to me, however, that Weeks has failed to take sufficient account of the sexual-political context in which sexology in general, and the work of Havelock Ellis in particular, emerged. As we have seen, the last two decades of the nineteenth century and the first two decades of the twentieth were a period of considerable upheaval in the relations between the sexes, and feminists were making significant progress in politicizing sexuality and heterosexual relations. This was precisely the period when Ellis was researching and writing about sexuality, and it would be very odd indeed if his ideas were not pro-foundly affected by these struggles and changes. Weeks' uncritical accept-ance of Ellis' reputation as a champion of woman's right to sexual pleasure, and the notion of sexual 'liberation', has also prevented him from appreciat-ing the *anti*-feminist implications of much of Ellis' work. During the 1970s and 1980s the Women's Liberation Movement has produced a considerable body of analysis and research which shows that the relationship between sexual liberation and women's liberation is much more problematic than implied by Weeks. As part of this process feminists have begun to subject sexology to much more critical scrutiny, pointing out the contradictions and sometimes straightforwardly anti-feminist implications inherent in much of the sexological literature.[3]

A major impetus to the development of a feminist critique of sexology stemmed from the rediscovery of female friendships and support networks before the twentieth century. Carroll Smith-Rosenberg documented the in-tensely emotional and often sensual bonds between middle-class women in nineteenth-century America, and began to explore why it was that such re-lationships were openly expressed and tolerated at that time, but later became invisible. She suggested that in the twentieth century cultural taboos evolved, 'to cut short the homosocial ties of girlhood and to impel the emerging women of thirteen or fourteen toward heterosexual relationships'. Nancy Sahli argued that these networks of female friendship came under increasing stress towards the end of the nineteenth century, when a new definition of what constituted 'normal' female relationships developed in both America and Europe. Love between women, irrespective of whether it actually involved physical or genital contact, became defined as abnormal, as a perversion – as lesbian. Sahli suggested that Ellis was strongly implicated in this process. He explicitly linked the alleged increase in lesbianism in the late nineteenth century to the influence of the Women's Movement, arguing that it developed 'the germs' of lesbianism by means of 'hereditary neurosis'; and also that it promoted a 'spurious imitation' of lesbianism, a form of 'pseudo-homosexuality'. This morbidification of love between women has been fully explored by Lillian Faderman, who argues that the sexologists provided a weapon against love between women at a time when women's increasing independence threatened the patriarchal social structure and especially the institution of marriage. 'If [women] gained all the freedom that feminists agitated for', she asks, 'what would attract them to marriage?' Sahli has also pointed out that the label 'lesbian' became synonymous with female autonomy and commitment between women, because feminism and women's independence constituted a threat to the established (patriarchal) order:

> and one way to control these sexless termites, hermaphroditic spin-
> sters, or whatever one might call them, was to condemn their love
> relationships – the one aspect of their behaviour, which, regardless of
> their other social, political, or economic activities, posed a basic threat
> to a system where the fundamental expression of power was that of
> one sex over another.[4]

The evidence already presented in this book supports the hypothesis that feminism and women's increasing independence constituted a threat to the institutions of marriage and hetero-relations, and therefore to the patriarchal social structure. This analysis of Ellis' model of sexuality attempts to show that, although the morbidification of lesbianism was undoubtedly a key factor in undermining feminism, this was only one side of the coin. The other was the eroticization of women's oppression by means of the 'art of love'. The sexological model of sexuality which Ellis constructed was in essence no more than the re-packaging, in scientific form, of the patriarchal model of sexuality which feminists were struggling to deconstruct. What feminists had argued was political, Ellis redefined as 'natural' and therefore unable to be changed.

Studies in the Psychology of Sex

Ellis' sexological writings spanned the last decade of the nineteenth century and the first four decades of the twentieth. The *Studies in the Psychology of Sex*, which constitute the core of his scientific enterprise, were first published during the period 1897–1910. Their importance for feminism lies in the fact that they represent, as Andrea Dworkin has pointed out, the first codification – though I would qualify this with the words 'explicit' and 'scientific' – of male sexual values. There is ample evidence that Ellis was aware, both through his contacts with sexual radicals, such as Edward Carpenter, and through his relationships with feminists, especially Olive Schreiner, of the impact of the nineteenth-century Women's Movement on the relations between the sexes. He certainly knew about the feminist campaigns against the double standard, and must also have been aware of the debates within feminism about sexuality. Indeed, given the evidence assembled in the last seven chapters, no-one researching and writing about sexuality in the late nineteenth and early twentieth centuries, particularly someone as thorough as Ellis is said to have been, could have been unaware of the feminist challenge to the patriarchal model of sexuality.[5]

This analysis of the *Studies* highlights the key themes and concepts of Ellis' model of sexuality, interpreting them in the light of the feminist challenge to the patriarchal model. The two most important themes which are interwoven throughout the work may be summarized as follows:

1   the notion that normal heterosexual sex is based on a power relation which is biologically determined; male domination and female submission are therefore not only inevitable but essential to sexual pleasure;

2   the notion that all forms of abnormal sex are merely extensions of the normal; even the most violent and dangerous forms of sexual perversion are ultimately rooted in 'innocent and instinctive impulses', and thus, it is implied, harmless and acceptable.

These themes emerge from the very first essay in Volume I, in which Ellis discussed the evolution of modesty, which he defined as an instinctive fear, originating in a primitive animal gesture of sexual refusal on the part of the unreceptive female, i.e. the female who is not physiologically ready for mating. Feminine modesty was necessary, according to Ellis, to arouse masculine passion and was an essential element in courtship, the key concept and linchpin of the whole work. What Ellis meant by courtship was the pursuit and conquest of the female by the male, which he claimed was re-enacted in every heterosexual act. The fact that courtship could be observed in animals and 'savages', as well as in 'civilized' men and women, proved, according to Ellis, that pursuit and conquest of the female by the male was natural, a biological inevitability. Modesty was also the clue to understanding the nature of female sexuality. It represented inhibition, which courtship was designed to overcome. The sexual impulse in woman was, according to Ellis, 'fettered by an inhibition which has to be conquered . . . her wooer in every act of courtship has the enjoyment of conquering afresh an oft-won woman'. He argued that because women, unlike other mammals, do not come into oestrus, there can be no way of being certain whether they want sex or not, implying that although women sometimes give the *impression* that they are not interested in heterosexual sex, this is not necessarily the case. This begins to bear an uncanny resemblance to the familiar patriarchal justification of rape. Modesty, according to Ellis, was essentially there to be overcome. It was an 'inevitable by-product of the *naturally* aggressive attitude of the male in sexual relationships, and the *naturally* defensive attitude of the female'. The biological evidence for this lay in the existence of the hymen, which he claimed to be the physical representation of modesty. Here we have the first suggestion that the process of courtship may well involve pain for the female, which heralds the emergence of the second theme: the normalization of sexual perversions based on male sexual violence. 'The masculine attitude', wrote Ellis, 'in the face of feminine coyness may easily pass into a kind of sadism, but is nevertheless in its origin an innocent and instinctive impulse'. It was an important aspect of male sexual desire, claimed Ellis, that the woman's 'favours' should be gained by surprise, and not by mutual agreement; the more 'modest' the woman – in other words, the more frightened she was – the more sexually exciting she was to the man. The exhibitionist, for example, almost invariably exposed himself to 'innocent, respectable girls', and the urolagnist was chiefly excited by catching the young woman unawares in the act. As if to forestall possible objections that such behaviour constituted assault, Ellis argued that since feminine modesty was itself an expression of the female sexual impulse, the more modest and timid the girl, the more ardent her desire. He did in fact argue later, in Volume III, that even if heterosexual intercourse did take place against a woman's will, it was usually with the 'consent' of her unconscious instinct, which sided with her attacker against her own conscious resistance.[6]

Ellis was one of the first men to examine the idea that female sexual desire fluctuates according to the menstrual cycle. He also applied the notion of periodicity, which had in fact been proposed by Olive Schreiner, to the sexuality of men.[7] He was forced to admit that the evidence regarding a monthly cycle in men was inconclusive, but he claimed that there was evidence to suggest an annual sexual rhythm in men. Records of the behaviour of inmates of prisons and lunatic asylums apparently showed that there was a disturbance of the metabolism at certain times of the year, which was reflected in the sexual impulse of men and probably some women. Ellis linked this with the universal phenomenon of spring and autumn festivals, which he believed to be a reflection of periods of sexual excitement, and which often included orgies. The fact that Ellis was prepared to make such dubious inferences on the basis of so little, and such unconvincing data, is somewhat puzzling. It suggests that the notion that sexual desire in men is periodic was very important to him. The explanation for this probably lies in the sexual-political context: specifically, the feminist campaigns against the double standard, and the demand that men could and should exercise sexual self-control. The implications of Ellis' argument seem to be that not only is it in men's nature to be aggressive, but that sometimes their sexual urges *really are* beyond their control. Furthermore, the cyclical nature of female sexual desire implies that women also have uncontrollable urges. Whatever may have been Ellis' real motives here, his emphasis on the periodicity of sexual desire in both sexes certainly provided biological ammunition to counter the key element in the feminist challenge to the double standard of sexual morality, namely the insistence that men were capable of exercising rational control over their sexual instincts.

In this introductory volume, then, Ellis laid the foundation of the analysis of the sexual instinct, which would eventually culminate, at the end of Volume VI, in a section entitled 'The Art of Love'. The *male* sexual urge was defined as essentially *a desire to conquer the female*. Female resistance, far from being real, was the manifestation of *female* sexual desire – *the desire to be conquered*. Conquest and resistance, dominance and submission, were defined as *natural*. In both sexes sexual desire manifested itself periodically and spontaneously; it was thus inappropriate to blame or criticize men for the sexual exploitation of women, or for sexual 'excess'. If the female experienced pain, this, too, was defined as *natural*; it was rooted in impulses which were essentially 'innocent', and thus not inherently harmful or problematic. This model of normal heterosexual sex was to become the springboard for promoting both a woman's right to sexual pleasure, and the acceptability of sado-masochism and all forms of sexual activity based on pain and humiliation.

Sex and Power: The Legitimation of Male Sexual Violence

The relationship between pain and sexual pleasure was fully explored in Volume III, the kernel of the *Studies*, where Ellis examined in detail the processes of sexual arousal and orgasm. These he termed tumescence and detumescence, comparing them to the loading and discharge of a gun. The problem which concerned him was that tumescence was not necessarily automatic, but often had to be brought about by the most prolonged and elaborate means, which he documented in detail, with extensive use of anthropological data. Ellis did not explain why it was that the male sexual urge was spontaneous, while tumescence was not; nor did he seem aware of the contradiction between the 'uncontrollable' nature of the male sexual urge and the inability to achieve spontaneous tumescence. If tumescence is not necessarily spontaneous, this raises the question of what it is that men are experiencing when they have sexual 'urges': what is it they feel an urge to do? The assumption inherent in the patriarchal model of sexuality is that it is a biological urge to have heterosexual coitus. But if this were so, tumescence would surely be spontaneous.

According to Ellis' model of sexuality, the process by which tumescence was normally achieved was courtship: the *conquest* of the female by the male. This suggests that, for men, sexual urges are not merely about sex but also about *power*, which would tend to confirm the feminist view of male sexuality as a social construct: as political rather than natural. Ellis, however, chose not to pursue this line of reasoning. He turned instead to evolutionary theory in the dogged pursuit of his argument that sexual urges were biological. He maintained that force was a necessary part of courtship, and that this was the origin of the close connection between love and pain. Courtship was, in fact, from an evolutionary perspective, a form of combat, and was consistent with the law of natural selection, since it ensured that only the best and most vigorous males succeeded in passing on their genes. The very existence of the hymen suggested that nature wished 'to reinforce by a natural obstacle the moral restraint of modesty so that only the most vigorous male would insure his reproduction'. Male aggression and the use of force were therefore not merely natural, but positively valued by women:

> Force is the foundation of virility and its psychic manifestation is courage. In the struggles for life violence is the first virtue. The modesty of women – in its primordial form consisting in physical resistance, active or passive, to the assaults of the male – aided selection by putting to the test man's most important quality, force. Thus it is that when choosing among rivals for her favours a woman attributes value to violence.

To give added scientific authority to this view he quoted at length from Lloyd Morgan, endorsing the latter's conclusion that '"Courtship is thus the strong and steady bending of the bow that the arrow may find its mark in a biological end of the highest importance in the survival of a healthy and vigorous race"'.[8]

For Ellis, then, there was indeed an association between sex, power, and violence, but the zoological history of the human race 'proved' scientifically that it was 'natural', rather than political; and what is 'natural' is, by implication, inevitable. There were five main constituents to this argument, which may be summarized as follows:

1 the female's primary role in courtship is the playful but serious one of the hunted animal who lures her pursuer, not with the aim of escaping, but in order to be finally caught;
2 the male's primary role is, by display of energy and skill, to capture the female, or *'arouse in her an emotional condition which leads her to surrender'*; this in turn arouses even greater excitement in the male;[9]
3 these two roles bring about the tumescence necessary for ultimate detumescence and discharge, leading to propagation;
4 because both sexes are ultimately seeking the same end, i.e. sexual union, there can be no *real* conflict, only the appearance of conflict and cruelty;
5 when there is rivalry between males for possession of one female an

element of real violence and cruelty may be introduced – inflicted by the male on his rival, and viewed by the female with delight.

These fundamental elements of the sexual impulse still persisted in the present day, according to Ellis, in the masculine tendency to delight in domination, and the feminine tendency to delight in submission.

Ellis' comments on the close connection between male sexuality, power, and violence are extremely revealing. At certain points the distinction between the sexual impulse and the impulse to exert force almost disappears:

> The infliction of pain must inevitably be a frequent indirect result of the exertion of power [in courtship]. It is even more than this; the infliction of pain by the male on the female may itself be a gratification of the impulse to exert force.[10]

He noted that in normal men, sexual excitement might be induced by reading exciting accounts of battle and war, and that this could give rise to unconscious longings for satisfaction in warlike games, such as football and wrestling. He agreed with Freud that there was a sexual element in the playful combat of boys, and argued that the tendency to criminal violence during youth was a by-product of the sexual impulse, and might even be regarded as a tertiary sexual character. He claimed that the instinct of cruelty was awakened in boys by the first sexual relationship and often led to acts such as the torturing of animals or younger boys. Whether or not such observations are correct is not at issue here; the point is that Ellis was apparently determined to prove that the connection between male sexual desire and the impulse to exert power was biologically determined and therefore inevitable.

Equally significant was his insistence that women found sexual pleasure in both the idea and the reality of violence and pain, whether inflicted by them or upon them. Furthermore, the fact that women deliberately aroused the greatest desires in men at the same time as withholding their favours, was in itself, he explained, a form of cruelty and power. He listed quantities of highly dubious 'evidence' from countries all over the world which purported to show how women enjoyed being beaten, raped, and sexually brutalized, and had no respect for weak men. Thousands of women, he claimed, wrote love letters, including proposals of marriage, to convicted rapists and sadistic murderers. He cited numerous examples from anthropology of ritual marriage by capture, in which it was the bride's role to 'pretend' extreme reluctance. What this allegedly showed was that she really *enjoyed* being taken by force, because if she *really* wanted to get away she could! The fact that Ellis went to such extraordinary lengths to 'prove' that women need pain in order to experience sexual pleasure, even if they claim they do not, suggests that he was engaged, not in the disinterested pursuit of truth, but in an attempt to destroy an opposing argument. He asserted that pain and pleasure were indistinguishable in women: 'the normal manifestations of a woman's sexual pleasure are exceedingly like pain'. He also claimed that women's genitals were less sensitive than men's, citing medical texts, which reported cases such as a 'nymphomaniac' who allegedly had an orgasm when subjected to clitoridectomy, as did a 'prostitute' when growths were removed from her vulva. The inference the reader was clearly intended to draw was that pain was not only a 'normal' constituent of sexual intercourse, but for most women as well as men, essential to sexual pleasure. In men, it was a normal manifestation of power, which, in Ellis' model, was itself normal and natural: 'to exert power, as psychologists well recognise, is one of our most primary impulses, and it always tends to be manifested in the attitude of a man towards the woman he loves'. He hastened to add that the normal, well-balanced man only inflicted physical pain on the woman he loved 'if he felt it was part of his love', and 'if she liked it'. Given that Ellis had so cleverly blurred the distinction between power, pain, and sexual pleasure, how the 'normal man' was supposed to tell the difference is something of a mystery.[11]

That Ellis was well aware of the political implications of his arguments, especially in the light of feminist campaigns against the double standard, is revealed by the following quotation:

> I am well aware that in thus asserting a certain tendency in women to delight in suffering pain – however careful and qualified the position I have taken – many estimable people will cry out that I am degrading a whole sex and generally supporting the 'subjection of women'. But the day for academic discussion concerning the subjection of women' has gone by. The tendency I have sought to make clear is too well-established by the experience of normal and typical women – however numerous the exceptions may be – to be called into question. I would point out to those who would deprecate the influence of such facts in relation to social progress that nothing is gained by regarding women as simply men of smaller growth. They are not so: they have the laws of their own nature; their development must be along their own lines, and not along masculine lines. It is as true now as in Bacon's day that we only learn to command nature by obeying her. . . . We can neither attain a sane view of life nor a sane social legislation of life unless we possess a just and accurate knowledge of the fundamental instincts upon which life is built.[12]

The message to feminists was clear: one of man's fundamental 'instincts' is to exert power over woman; one of the 'laws' of woman's 'nature' is not merely to submit, but to enjoy it, to experience the resulting pain as pleasure!

The Normalization of the Sexual Perversions

Having established the inevitable, biological association between sexuality, power, and pain, it was but a short step to the normalization of those sexual perversions which ritualize and celebrate that association – sadism and maso-chism. It was Ellis' stated intention in Volume III to establish 'the normal basis on which rest the extreme aberrations of love', and to show that

> indeed, in their elementary forms [they] may themselves be regarded as normal. In some degree they are present, in every case, at some point of sexual development; their threads are subtly woven in and out of the whole psychological process of sex.[13]

The difference between sado-masochism (and most other sexual perversions) and the 'normal' association of love and pain was thus merely one of degree. Even such an apparently innocent activity as the 'love-bite' could be seen as bordering on the abnormal, argued Ellis. In essence it was no different from the most extreme forms of sadism and masochism. Ellis supported his thesis with numerous examples drawn from case histories and letters from anony-mous people described vaguely as 'friends' or 'correspondents'. Space prevents a detailed analysis of them here. Most of them concerned men, and Ellis admitted that there were very few female sadists, and far more male than female masochists. Yet he quoted extensively from women's letters, many of which expressed, not sexual excitement at experiencing or inflicting pain, but frustration with their lovers' selfishness, anger at men's domination and con-trol of heterosexual activity, and the determination of the women to define their own sexual needs and desires. He did include a letter from a woman who distinguished carefully between sexual excitement at the *idea* of pain, and the reality of it. She agreed that the desire to inflict pain seemed almost universal among men, but maintained that 'no woman has ever told me that she would like to have pain inflicted on her'. She continued:

> Perhaps a woman's readiness to submit to pain to please a man may sometimes be taken for pleasure in it. Even when women like the idea of pain, I fancy it is only because it implies subjection to the man, from association with the fact that physical pleasure must nec-essarily be preceded by submission to his will.[14]

Ellis chose not to comment on or explore the complexities in this contribution, such as the implications of the word 'necessarily', which he appeared to equate with 'naturally'.

Another strategy he repeatedly used to 'prove' women's love of sadism was inference from the behaviour of other animals, which he claimed to be almost invariably characterized by cruelty on the part of the female towards the male. He argued that, if in 'man' it was the other way round, this was a 'very slight counterpoise' to the female cruelty which has always existed in nature. As Andrea Dworkin (1981) has pointed out, in order to give yet more legitimation to male violence against women, he appeared to contradict his main thesis – that woman wants to be conquered by force – by positing a more fundamental female sadism. But there can be little doubt that it was the legitimation of male sexual violence which was his main purpose. As I pointed out at the beginning of this analysis, his definition of courtship bore an uncanny resemblance to the usual patriarchal justification of rape. In Volume III the implications of women's 'eagerness to submit' and 'delight in physical pain' were made explicit. Ellis claimed that offences such as rape, sexual assault, and the sexual abuse of children were extremely rare, citing research which allegedly showed that reported cases were often based on lies and false accusations. He also asserted that women probably 'raped' men just as often as the reverse, and that women often 'cried rape' to cover up voluntary sexual exploits.[15]

Ellis subsequently devoted two whole volumes to the analysis of various forms of sexual perversion, which he preferred to call 'erotic symbolism'. His fascination for this topic was probably connected with the fact that his particular sexual preference was urolagnia, a perversion, he claimed, 'which has been noted in men of high intellectual distinction', and was usually, as in his own case, linked to difficulties in achieving tumescence. Irrespective of the specific sexual practice under consideration, the basic argument remained the same: that the difference between normal and abnormal was merely one of degree. As I have argued elsewhere, this has remained one of the basic tenets of sexology right up to the the present day. It rests ultimately on the belief, legitimated by scientific argument and evidence, that masculine dominance and female submission in sexual activity have biological origins and are thus inherent in all forms of sexuality and sexual pleasure.[16]

Female Sexuality, 'Frigidity', and the 'Art of Love'

The fundamental elements of female sexuality that emerge from the above analysis may be summarized as follows:

- female sexual desire is as spontaneous as that of the male;
- it manifests itself in the desire to be conquered;
- there may be a pretence of resistance;
- there is in most women a tendency to delight in suffering pain.

According to Ellis' model, pleasure in submission to male domination is inherent in female sexuality. How was it, then, that on Ellis' own admission, most women had an aversion to sexual intercourse? The prevailing Victorian medical view, as expressed by William Acton, was that women were congenitally sexually anaesthetic, except, that is, for 'fallen' women. Ellis countered this by arguing that women did have strong sexual impulses, but that they were repressed, partly because of the failure of their husbands to arouse them, and partly because the element of pain, which was normal in establishing coitus, failed to become merged with sensations of pleasure. Furthermore, women were slow to become aroused; men, on the other hand, were often clumsy and brutal, because they failed to understand the complexity of the process of arousing their wives, and attempted coitus before they were 'ready'. Ellis compared the penis and the vagina to a lock and key: 'a lock not only requires a key to fit it, but should be entered only at the right moment, and, under the best conditions, may only be adjusted to the key by considerable use'.[17]

Ellis considered it of paramount importance that 'sexual anaesthesia' or 'frigidity' be cured in order to maintain the institution of marriage. Expressing concern at the rising divorce rate, he declared that, while he agreed that divorce should be easier to obtain when absolutely necessary, it was important to counterbalance this by increasing the stability of marriage. He strongly advocated training for marriage, not merely to combat ignorance and prevent sexual aversion, but in order to teach men the skills necessary to give their wives sexual pleasure. As we shall see below, his concern to cure 'frigidity' was closely bound up with a much broader concern about the feminist threat to the institution of marriage, and about the politics of spinsterhood. One of his correspondents, 'a lady who has written largely on the woman question', argued that sexual coldness was not necessarily to be regretted, in either sex, but Ellis insisted that it was unnatural:

> a state of sexual anaesthesia, relative or absolute, cannot be considered as anything but abnormal ... the satisfaction of the reproduction function ought to be at least as gratifying as the evacuation of the bowels or bladder ... an act which is at once the supreme fact and symbol of love and the supreme creative act cannot under normal conditions be other than the most pleasurable of all acts, or it would stand in violent opposition to all that we find in nature.

According to Ellis, part of the problem was the apparent passivity of female sexuality; but he reiterated that the female's 'reluctance' during courtship was designed by nature to increase sexual desire, which meant that she was not *really* passive. Ellis compared female sexual passivity to a magnet: it appeared to 'do' nothing, but really exerted tremendous power. This apparent passivity obscured the fact that women suffered from prolonged sexual abstinence just as much as men. It is one of Ellis' major claims to fame that he helped to break the Victorian taboo on 'self-abuse'. In Volume I of the *Studies* he devoted a whole essay to the subject, showing that it was universal, natural, relatively harmless, and could even be beneficial. His attitude towards masturbation was, however, ambivalent. He also believed it could be damaging if carried to excess, particularly in women, because it trained the sexual orgasm 'to respond to an appeal which has nothing whatever to do with the fascination normally exerted by the opposite sex'. Later, in Volume

III, he explicitly warned that masturbation by women could lead to an aversion to coitus.[18]

How then, was 'frigidity' (defined as aversion to coitus) to be cured? One possibility was hypnosis, already being practised by at least one doctor to Ellis' knowledge, with considerable success. The hypnotist would suggest to the woman that

> all her womanly natural feelings would be quickly and satisfactorily developed during coitus; she would experience no feeling of disgust or nausea, would have no fear of the orgasm not developing; *that there would be no involuntary resistance on her part.*[19]

Ellis did not disapprove of such a method, but proposed his own, more subtle, means of overcoming the woman's resistance: the 'art of love'. This he considered to be the 'primal foundation' of marriage, and the only possible way of ensuring its stability. It was not enough that wives should endure coitus out of duty to their husbands; they must learn to actively participate and enjoy it. Their teachers were to be their husbands. This might appear at first surprising, especially since Ellis castigated husbands severely for their clumsiness and brutality, conceding that defloration on the wedding night frequently amounted to rape, sometimes even causing serious injury. He borrowed a musical image from Balzac, who had compared the average husband to an orang-utan trying to play the violin. Ellis aimed to transform him into a producer of sweet music and harmonious melodies; the instrument being his wife: 'she is, on the physical side, inevitably the instrument in love; it must be his hand and his bow which evoke the music'. It was thus quite consistent with Ellis' model of sexuality that the orchestration of female sexual pleasure should be under male control. As we have seen, the male's role in courtship was, by display of energy and skill, to capture the female; to 'arouse in her an emotional condition which leads her to surrender'. Just as, biologically speaking, it was the task of the male to overcome the resistance of the female, so it was the task of the man 'to gain real possession of a woman's soul and body', a task, he considered, 'that requires the whole of a man's best skill and insight'. The capture of the female usually entailed the use of force. Ellis argued that this created difficulties for men because, although women admired men's strength, and indeed *wanted* to be forced to the things they desired, they revolted from any exertion of force outside certain narrow boundaries. It was thus very hard for men to know when to stop, especially at the moment when their emotions were least under control. In the last analysis, however, force was not really a problem; for, as Ellis pointed out, the fact that human coitus took place face to face symbolized that humans had outgrown the animal sexual attitude of the hunter seizing his prey in flight, from behind. 'The human male may be said to retain the same attitude', he wrote, 'but the female has turned round; she has faced her partner and approached him, and so symbolises her deliberate consent to the act of union'.[20]

It is difficult to understand how anyone could interpret this model of sexuality as 'progressive', in the sense of promoting women's right to define and control their own sexuality. The 'art of love' might be more accurately termed the art of conquest and control. Yet it was the logical conclusion of the model of sexuality that Ellis constructed, in which power, pain, and pleasure were inseparable. He may have helped to liberalize attitudes towards masturbation, male homosexuality, and sexual perversions. But his definition of dominance and submission, power and pain, as normal, natural, and essential to heterosexual pleasure, provided scientific legitimation of male sexual violence, undermining the feminist critique of male sexuality and the campaigns against the double standard. Feminists had emphasized the unity of the psychic and physical, and the ability of humans to exercise rational control over their instincts. Despite the title of Ellis' work – *Studies in the* Psychology *of Sex* – he defined sex as essentially a physical, animal instinct, a coital imperative, largely beyond the control of human will. This depoliticized male sexual violence and paved the way for the pathologizing of rape and the sexual abuse of children, as medical conditions requiring treatment, rather than as manifestations of male power.[21]

In essence, what feminists had argued was political, Ellis defined as natural, and the fact that this was presented as science, and by implication objective, neutral, and value-free, made it much more difficult to challenge. The sexological model was little more than the patriarchal model of sexuality, re-packaged in scientific form. Although it seemed to hold out the promise to women of sexual liberation, it promoted as 'natural' a form of heterosexuality and sexual pleasure which eroticized male dominance and female submission. The 'art of love' was a strategy for teaching women to accept male violence as inevitable, male sexual demands as normal, to experience submission as pleasure, to 'consent' to conquest – in other words, to 'enjoy' precisely that form of male sexuality and heterosexual sex which feminists had struggled long and hard to challenge. It reinforced the coital imperative, blocking their search for alternative forms of heterosexual intercourse which were safe and pleasurable and carried no risk of pregnancy. It led instead to the promotion of artificial, unsafe, and ultimately dangerous forms of contraception, which further undermined women's right to refuse coitus. Fundamentally, the 'art of love' represented the eroticization of women's oppression, and, together with the morbidification of love between women, the denial of female sexual autonomy. It thus had profoundly anti-feminist implications. Whatever the actual motives of the individual man who constructed this model of sexuality, it could hardly have been better suited to subverting the emerging feminist model, and restoring the balance of power within heterosexual relationships and between the sexes. While it appeared to offer sexual liberation to women, in effect it offered to men a means of reconstituting male power and the structure of hetero-relations.

The Sexological Model and Feminism: Divide and Rule

Ellis was not single-handedly responsible for the construction of the sexological model, though there is no doubt that the publication of the *Studies* established him as the leading sexologist of his day. The other two 'founding fathers' of sexology were the German Iwan Bloch and the Swiss August Forel, whose ideas were very similar and who repeatedly acknowledged their debt to Ellis. Forel and Ellis were, with Magnus Hirschfeld, joint presidents of the World League for Sex Reform, of which Bloch was also a member. Bloch, Forel, and Ellis all shared essentially the same patriarchal model of sexuality, expressed in terms of 'scientific facts' and 'natural laws'. Forel, for instance, defined sex as a 'purely animal instinct' and described heterosexual desire in masculine terms as 'penetrating' the whole nervous system. He saw it as a desire so powerful that it laid hold of the male's whole organism, urging it to penetrate the female, making it feel 'as if it had for a moment become a germinal cell'. Everywhere in nature the male pursued the female with implacable tenacity, at the risk of his own life, employing sometimes cunning, sometimes dexterity, and sometimes force to attain his object. 'The ardour of the female is not much less', he wrote, 'but she uses coquetry, pretending to resist, and simulates repulsion. The more eager the male, the more coquettish the female'. His description of male sexuality is remarkably similar to that of modern sociobiologists, who see men as biologically driven to pass on their genes:

> If there were no other difficulties or consequences, man would without the least doubt be instinctively inclined to copulate with as many women as he could, and procreate as many children as possible. The more he is capable of satisfying his procreative instinct, the more he becomes self-exalted, as he thus sees himself multiplied and feels his power extended by the possession of a great number of wives and children.

Women, according to Forel, were even more the slaves of their instincts than men, and the instinct to procreate was inextricably bound up with the instinct to surrender to the male:

> The instinct of procreation is much stronger in woman than in man, and is combined with the desire to give herself passively, to play the part of one who devotes herself, who is conquered, mastered and subjugated. These negative aspirations form part of the normal sexual appetite of woman.

Because this instinct was thwarted in 'old maids', they had much greater need than bachelors of compensation for sexual love, otherwise they became 'dried-up beings or useless egoists'. With chilling simplicity Forel asserted: 'Without [heterosexual] love woman abjures her nature and ceases to be normal'. Bloch's view of female sexuality was even more aggressive. 'The author of "Splitter"', he wrote,

> has very well characterized this fact when he says:
> 'Women are in fact pure sex from knees to neck. We men have concentrated our apparatus in a single place, we have extracted it, separated it from the rest of the body, because *prêt à partir*. They (women) *are* a great sexual *surface* or target; we *have* only a sexual *arrow*.'[22]

The anti-feminist implications of the sexological model of sexuality become even more apparent when viewed in relation to the attitudes of the 'founding fathers' towards feminism and women's role in society. Ellis, Bloch, and Forel all expressed their theoretical support for the emancipation of women but were in fact highly selective about the forms of feminism they would support, and often attacked the Women's Movement for turning women away from what they considered to be the 'laws of their nature', which were heterosexuality, marriage, and motherhood. In Ellis' first major book, *Man and Woman*, which was intended to clear the ground and act as an introduction to the *Studies*, he set out to prove that there was a biological basis to the separate spheres that feminists were struggling to break down. 'Woman's special sphere', he asserted, 'is the bearing and the rearing of children, with the care of human life in the home. Man's sphere remains the exploration of life outside the home, in industry and inventions and the cultivation of the arts'. For Bloch, the ultimate rationale for sexual differences lay in the sperm and the ovaries: 'The sperm cell represents the *active*, the germ cell the *passive*, principle in sexuality. Already in this *most important* act in the process of procreation the natural relations between man and woman are very clearly manifested'. He also argued that the sexual double standard was rooted in the natural differences between the sexes, and that the one and only way to end prostitution and its attendant social evils was by free love. He did distinguish, however, between 'wild love', by which he meant sexual promiscuity, and 'free love', by which he meant monogamous free unions, as advocated by the Swedish feminist, Ellen Key.[23]

Ellen Key's form of feminism was in fact the *only* kind of feminism which the sexologists were prepared to endorse wholeheartedly, for reasons which are not difficult to fathom. It was a form of feminism which was based on the belief that femininity and masculinity were biologically determined, on the celebration of heterosexual love, and on the glorification of motherhood. It was particularly influential in Scandinavia, Holland, Italy, Austria, and Germany, where the *Bund für Mutterschutz* originated, of which Bloch was a committee member. Ellen Key was also admired by some British feminists, especially those who were in favour of free love. Although most feminists broadly agreed that it was important to raise the status of motherhood and to recognize the social value of women's work in rearing the new generation, they also insisted on a woman's right to refuse marriage and motherhood, and sought to raise the status of the spinster. It was this aspect of feminism above all which Ellis, Bloch, and Forel were quite unable to accept. Ellis in particular, though he tended to shun direct political involvement, clearly felt so strongly on this point that he had to intervene, metaphorically cheering on from the sidelines those feminists whose ideas he approved, and providing them with scientific ammunition to promote their ideals. In the *Studies* he applauded Ellen Key's suggestion of a year's compulsory service to train girls in housekeeping and infant care. He believed not only that every healthy woman ought to exercise her reproductive function at least once in her lifetime but that motherhood was 'woman's supreme function'. He attacked the Women's Movement for tempting women away from following one of the most fundamental laws of their nature, declaring emphatically: 'The task of creating a man needs the whole of woman's best energies'.[24]

At the same time Ellis strove to undermine those who threatened his definition of woman's role, by declaring their ideas unscientific. As time went on he enthused more and more about the new 'teutonic' movement, because it was based on what 'marks the woman as unlike the man', and was in tune with his own aims, set out in *The Task of Social Hygiene*, which were 'to breed a firmly-fibred, clean-minded, and self-reliant race of manly men and womanly women'. Among animals which lived in herds under the guidance of a leader, he argued, this leader was nearly always male, and so it should be with humans. He repeatedly criticized the Women's Movement in Britain for confining itself to 'imitating' men, to obtaining the same work and the same rights as men, and for aiming to 'secure women's claims *as a human being rather than as a woman*'. He described the idea that women should have the same education as men, and the same occupations as men, as 'the source of all that was unbalanced, sometimes both a little pathetic and a little absurd, in the old women's movement'. The banner of equality under which they had fought, he insisted, had no biological foundation. Bloch was equally emphatic that all attempts to 'obliterate' the differences between the sexes should be seen as *'futile, and as antagonistic to human development'*. He regarded the formation of a so-called 'third sex', in which these differences were obscured, as a markedly retrogressive step and described women who competed with men in the world of work as 'barren and stunted'. 'Such types', he insisted, who could be distinguished by 'aberrations' such as smoking and wearing masculine clothes, were 'certainly not the final goal of the woman's movement'. They were caricatures, 'products of a false and extreme conception of woman's development'. Like Ellis, Bloch blamed the Women's Movement for the spread of 'pseudo-homosexuality', declaring that heterosexuality was 'the only condition in harmony with the progressive tendency towards perfection'.[25]

The sexologists approved and encouraged the 'new feminism', with its emphasis on woman's role as wife and mother, and Ellis argued strongly for the endowment of motherhood, on the grounds that if women were economically independent they would be better able to fulfil their role as 'mothers of the race'. Although the 'new feminism' did not become established until the 1920s, the ideas on which it was based were beginning to circulate before the war when divisions between feminists were becoming more apparent. As the above quotations suggest, sexologists exacerbated these divisions, by fuelling the anti-spinster backlash, and by putting the weight of their scientific authority behind those feminists who opposed militant feminism, the campaigns against the double standard, and political spinsterhood. The sexological model also sharpened the division between the wife-mother and the spinster, whom the sexologists 'smeared' insidiously with the 'taint' of lesbianism. Ellis' distinction between the 'true invert' and the 'pseudo-lesbian', which was universally accepted by sexologists, was very useful in this respect. Those spinsters who renounced the 'old feminism', with its 'absurd' notion of equality with men, and supported the 'new feminism', could be tolerated, even though their 'sexually incomplete' state rendered them objects of contempt, and essentially unnatural. Even if they happened also to be lesbians, they could still be tolerated as a small minority of congenital 'freaks' who posed no serious threat to the social order. But those spinsters who persisted in challenging male power were isolated and marginalized by the implication that they were carriers of a contagious disease – pseudo-homosexuality – whether or not they actually had sexual relationships with women. Thus 'real' lesbianism was depoliticized, while 'political' lesbianism was pathologized.

The 'new feminism', which sexologists helped to promote, represented in effect the redefinition of feminism as 'freedom to follow woman's nature', a 'nature' which was largely male-defined and represented no threat to male power. In essence, it was the 'nature' from which most Victorian and Edwardian feminists had been struggling to emancipate themselves. It is perhaps a measure of the success of feminism that, as Cicely Hamilton shrewdly pointed out, once women were no longer forced into marriage and motherhood by economic necessity or fear of 'old maidism', a 'new inducement' would have to be found in order to persuade them to become wives and mothers. Sexology provided this inducement by holding out the promise, not of 'equal rights', but of 'erotic rights'; in other words, sexual pleasure, in a form defined by men and controlled by men, and a form which eroticized male dominance and female submission.[26]

The increasing divisions between feminists which have been discussed in previous chapters now become somewhat easier to understand. These divisions emerged sharply in the early twentieth century, in the context of the campaigns against the double standard and the debates about sexuality and spinsterhood. The divisive influence of sexology was especially apparent among the supporters of *The Freewoman*, and an illustration of this is provided by one of the members of its circle, Mrs Gasquoigne-Hartley. She was married to Walter Gallichan, a prominent sex reformer and popularizer of sexology, whose vicious attack on 'man-hating' spinsters has already been quoted. Mrs Gasquoigne-Hartley appears originally to have been an 'old feminist' who, at around the time of her marriage to Gallichan, renounced what she called her 'masculine' ideals of equality with men and became a 'new feminist'. She developed a marked hostility to spinsterhood and came to understand that 'no freedom can be of service to women unless it is a freedom to follow her own nature', which was to be wife and mother. She became fiercely opposed to militant feminism and insisted that the feminist motto should be 'Free *with* Man'. She explicitly acknowledged her debt to Ellis, as well as to Ellen Key, both of whom apparently enlightened her about 'all those facts of woman's organic constitution which make her unlike man'. She also confessed that she had been 'compelled' to give up her view that it was 'men and their un-controllable passions' which were chiefly responsible for the sexual exploita-tion of women and girls. She was aware that hers was very much a minority view amongst feminists at that time, but insisted 'against all the Feminists' that 'the real need of the normal woman is the full and free satisfaction of the race-instinct'.[27]

Another feminist who was heavily influenced by sexology, especially by Ellis, was Stella Browne, whose notion of 'sex freedom' and anti-spinster views were discussed in Chapter 4. Browne was a socialist and an active campaigner for birth control and abortion, and became directly involved with sexology and sex reform through her membership of the British Society for the Study of Sex Psychology, which was founded in 1914 to campaign for better public education on the scientific facts of sex. Ellis was also a member of the BSSSP, and Browne's indebtedness to him was evident, and often explicitly acknowledged, in all her writings. In a paper which she presented to the society in 1915, she developed the point she had made in *The Freewoman*: that militant feminist campaigns against the double standard were led by women who were 'sexually deficient' or 'anaesthetic' and 'deeply ignorant about life'. She argued that it was women's sexual variability which was the cause of so much cant and bitterness between them. What particu-larly concerned her was the 'considerable and pretty steady percentage of cold natures, who may yet be very efficient and able and very attractive to men'. In a clear allusion to the militant feminist challenge to male sexuality, she asserted:

These cold women generally have a perfect mania for *prohibition* as a solution for all ills. But surely, we do not want the new world to be built up only by women who have long ago forgotten what sex means, or who have never experienced strong sexual emotions, and regard them as a sign of grossness or decadence.

I think no one who knows the 'personnel' of many social reform movements, can doubt that this is a very real danger.

The danger to women of (hetero)sexual abstinence was another theme which she had introduced in her letters to *The Freewoman*, and which she now expanded:

> I would even say that after twenty-five, the woman who has neither husband nor lover and is not under-vitalised and sexually deficient, is suffering mentally and bodily – often without knowing why she suffers; nervous, irritated, anaemic, always tired, or ruthlessly fussing over trifles; or else she has other consolations, which make her so-called 'chastity' a pernicious sham.

She was later to make her own major contribution to the promotion of the joys of heterosexual intercourse for women, by translating into English Van de Velde's *Ideal Marriage*, which was to become 'the Bible' of marriage manuals.[28]

Meanwhile Browne warned of another danger of (hetero)sexual abstinence, the spread of 'pseudo-homosexuality' amongst women:

> Careful observation and many confidences from members of my own sex, have convinced me that our maintenance of outworn traditions is manufacturing habitual auto-erotists and perverts, out of women who would instinctively prefer the love of a man, who would bring them sympathy and comprehension as well as desire. I repudiate all wish to depreciate or slight the love-life of the real homosexual; but it cannot be advisable to force the growth of that habit in heterosexual people.

She also maintained that 'artificial or substitute homosexuality – as distinct from true inversion – is very widely diffused among women, as a result of the repression of normal gratification and the segregation of the sexes, which still largely obtains'. In 1923 she presented another paper to the BSSSP in which she described five case studies of 'feminine inversion', analyzed in terms very similar to Ellis' own case studies of lesbians. Here she made explicit the previously implied link between militant feminist hostility to men, sexual anaesthesia, and 'repressed inversion': 'I am sure that much of the towering spiritual arrogance which is found, e.g. in many high places in the suffrage movement . . . is really unconscious inversion'. She believed that the true 'inverted impulse' should be recognized 'as frankly as we recognize and reverence the love between men and women'. But she deplored the 'repression and degradation of the normal erotic impulse' which forced women of 'strong passions and fine brains' into relationships with women. These pseudo-homosexual relationships were, she insisted, 'makeshifts and essentially substitutes, which cannot replace the vital contact, mental and bodily, with congenial men'.[29]

It is interesting that militant feminists such as Christabel Pankhurst and

Edith Watson occasionally cited Bloch and Forel with approval, whereas the only feminists who cited Ellis with approval were those who, like Browne and Gasquoigne-Hartley, opposed the militants on the question of the double standard. This was probably because Bloch and Forel were extremely forthright in their condemnation of state regulation of prostitution, and because their writings contained snippets which the militants could use to support their arguments and campaigns. One example is Forel's view, quoted by Pankhurst in *The Great Scourge*, that the buying and selling of sex led to the perversion of the sexual instinct and the degradation of women 'in the basest of all slaveries'. Forel regarded prostitutes as hardly more than 'automata trained for the use of male sensuality', and wrote that when men looked among prostitutes for the sexual psychology of woman 'they only found their own mirror'. The fact that even militant feminists were prepared to use sexological evidence, albeit very selectively, in support of their arguments, is an indication of the increasing influence of the scientific approach to questions of sexuality during the Edwardian period. Although they were extremely critical of male bias in science and medicine, and very wary of the dangers of 'expertism', some feminists appear to have felt that the use of scientific evidence would lend greater legitimacy to their arguments. Some may even have felt that, apart from specific and relatively superficial instances of male bias, science was essentially objective and neutral, and could therefore be used as a weapon in the struggle for female sexual autonomy. Alison Neilans, for instance, former suffragette and later secretary of the Association for Moral and Social Hygiene, referred to Ellis in 1914 as the leading scientific authority on sex. Somewhat naively, she hoped to enlist science in the attack on the double standard, especially on the artificial, commercial stimulation of men's sexual instinct, and looked to sexologists for help in defining what was 'normal', or 'what normal sexual instinct really requires'.[30]

Feminists such as Browne and Gasquoigne-Hartley were clearly convinced that sexology was based on pure 'fact'. But the status of science was such that there seems to have been a general failure on the part of feminists to appreciate the ideological and political nature of science in general and the sexological model of sexuality in particular. It was not until the 'second wave' of feminism in the 1960s that a feminist critique of science began to develop, and feminists began to recognize that the structures of science and scientific knowledge were not only controlled by men but saturated with fundamental patriarchal values and assumptions.[31] In the absence of such a critique, which was made possible, partly by developments in the philosophy of science and the sociology of knowledge, as well as by the increasing participation of feminists in scientific work, it was not surprising that many feminists embraced the sexological model uncritically. There may well have been some who recognized at some level its anti-feminist implications, but felt that they lacked the tools with which to oppose it, or even to articulate their objections. They were simply not in a position to compete with the power of patriarchal science to define what was 'natural' or 'normal'.

During the 1920s and 1930s there was a concerted effort to popularize the new science of sex, and to teach the 'facts of life' to 'ordinary' people. This was achieved mainly by means of 'marriage manuals', which will be analyzed in the following two chapters. Some of the writers and translators of marriage manuals were women, a few of whom were feminists. I shall argue that the adoption by some feminists of the sexological model gave rise to serious contradictions in their understanding of sexuality and its relationship to women's liberation, and undermined their feminism. Nowhere are these contradictions more evident than in the work of Marie Stopes, who is the subject of the next chapter.

Notes

1 The most recent and important biography of Ellis is generally agreed to be Grosskurth (1980). On his role in the history of (patriarchal) sexual thought, see Robinson (1976); on his role in the history of modern (patriarchal) sexology, see Brecher (1970). Earlier and shorter versions of my analysis of Ellis' model of sexuality were published in Jackson (1981; 1983).

2 Ellis (1913a), vol. III, p. 253. Rowbotham and Weeks have both produced much more critical assessments of his role as a sex reformer than other historians. See Rowbotham and Weeks (1977); and Weeks (1977; 1981; 1985), which discuss his relationship to the sexual 'radicalism' of the late nineteenth century, especially Edward Carpenter and the Fellowship of the New Life (see also Grosskurth, 1980).

3 There have been numerous feminist critiques of the concept of sexual liberation and its relationship to women's liberation, and many disputes about the subject within feminism. For sharply contrasting views compare Campbell (1980); Coote and Campbell (1982); and Coward (1978); with Egerton (1985); Coveney *et al.* (1984) and Jackson (1985). See also Jackson (1981; 1983; 1984); and Jeffreys (1981; 1983; 1985).

4 Smith-Rosenberg (1975), p. 27; Faderman (1981), p. 237; Sahli (1979), p. 27.

5 Ellis was born in 1859 and died in 1939, a few months before Freud. Volumes I–VI of *Studies in The Psychology of Sex* were first published between 1897 and 1910, and revised and reprinted between 1913 and 1915. Volume VII was added in 1928, and new editions were published in 1936–7. On Ellis' relationship with Olive Schreiner, see First and Scott (1980); and Grosskurth (1980, ch. 5), who also discusses his relationships with other feminists, especially Margaret Sanger and Edith Lees, who became his wife.

6 Ellis (1913a) vol. III, p. 3; p. 40 (my emphasis); p. 42. To illustrate his concept of modesty he compared woman to a bitch; when in heat she would throw modesty to the winds, but when not she would refuse the dog's attentions and squat firmly on the floor, concealing her sexual parts. At the same time, he argued, this was also an invitation to the dog, and, in the human male, mixed up with his ideas of what was sexually desirable in the female. Even in heat the bitch, having first chased the dog, might turn to flee, thus appearing to refuse him, and perhaps submitting to his embrace only after much persuasion. With reference to the point about urolagnia it should be noted that Ellis' own sexual preference was in fact urolagnia (see Grosskurth, 1980).

7 See Grosskurth (1980), ch. 5.

8 Ellis (1913a), vol. III, pp. 32–4. The notion that male sexual aggression is an

inevitable consequence of his being biologically driven to pass on his genes, and that the more aggressive males are in evolutionary terms the more successful, is still a widely held scientific view. It is not only a core assumption of sociobiology and related disciplines but is repeatedly asserted as 'fact' in popular television programmes about the natural world. For an excellent feminist critique of sociobiology see Bland (1981).

9 Ellis (1913a), vol. III, p. 69, my emphasis.
10 *Ibid.*, p. 67.
11 *Ibid.*, pp. 82–4.
12 *Ibid.*, p. 103.
13 *Ibid.*, p. vii.
14 *Ibid.*, p. 90.
15 See, for example, Ellis (1913a), vol. III, p. 226.
16 See Jackson (1984; 1987).
17 Ellis (1913a), vol. III, p. 235. On the sexual ideology of William Acton see Chapter 3.
18 Ellis (1913a), vol. III, p. 219; vol. I, p. 261.
19 Ellis (1913a), vol. III, p. 240, my emphasis.
20 Ellis (1913a), vol. VI, p. 539; p. 531; p. 554.
21 Most sexologists were, like Ellis, members of the medical profession. For further discussion of this point, see Chapter 7.
22 Forel (1908), pp. 73–4; p. 117; p. 94; p. 129. Forel did acknowledge that for women, heterosexual desire was not always to be equated with the desire for coitus, which he believed was often absent in young girls and only developed some time after they actually experienced coitus. But even the emotional desire was, he asserted, essentially a desire to be dominated, a desire to surrender: the sentimentalism of the young girl produced in her 'a state of exultation which often borders on ecstasy and then overcomes all the resistance of will and reason' (*ibid.*, p. 130). Bloch (1909), p. 84, emphasis in original.
23 Ellis (1934 [1894]), p. iii; Bloch (1909), p. 9, emphasis in original.
24 Ellis (1913a), vol. VI, p. 7. The *Bund für Mutterschütz* began in Germany in 1905 as a society for the protection of mothers, especially unmarried mothers, led by Helene Stöcker of Berlin. It had links with the international movement for sex reform and in the 1920s and 1930s developed a strong bias towards eugenics, as a result of which it gained support from the growing fascist movement.
25 Ellis (1913b), p. 46; p. 63, my emphasis; Ellis (1946), p. 247; Bloch (1909), pp. 12–13, emphasis in original.
26 See the discussions of Cicely Hamilton in Chapter 1. On the 'new feminism' see Lewis (1975; 1984), and, for a different view, Jeffreys (1985), chs. 7, 8, and 9.
27 Gasquoigne-Hartley (1913); see especially p. 364 and p. 263. See also earlier references to her views in Chapter 1 and Chapter 4.
28 Rowbotham (1977), p. 87; p. 101. The initiative behind the BSSSP and much of its membership derived from a secret male homosexual reform organization called the Order of Chaeronea. The Chairman was Edward Carpenter. Browne also translated several other works by sex reformers, such as Max Hodann's *History of Modern Morals* (1937).
29 See Rowbotham (1977), pp. 102–3; Browne (1923), pp. 57–8, Sheila Jeffreys has suggested that Browne's confusion about lesbianism might be due to anxiety about the nature of her own relationships with women (Jeffreys, 1985, ch. 6).
30 Marie Stopes made use of this quotation from Forel in her marriage manual *Married Love* (see Chapter 6). On Alison Neilans see *The Shield*, vol. XIV, no. 4, June 1914.
31 See especially Bleier (1984) and Wallsgrove (1980).

Chapter 6

The Unhappy Marriage of
Feminism and Sexology
Marie Stopes and the 'Laws of Love'

'The Art of Love', the title of a chapter of Volume VI of Ellis' *Studies*, has been termed the prototype of the countless how-to-do-it sex manuals of the twentieth century. In this and the following chapter I explore the popularization of the sexological model of sexuality by means of the marriage manuals published during the inter-war period. Aimed at the general reader, marriage manuals offered advice to 'ordinary people' on sexual technique and problems such as sexual 'maladjustment' and frigidity. During this period it was extremely difficult for a member of the general public to gain direct access to the works of the sexologists, since both libraries and booksellers restricted their availability to doctors, lawyers, scientific researchers, and scholars. In most cases, therefore, those who knew anything at all about sexology and the 'facts of life' would have acquired their knowledge from marriage manuals.

The first and probably most important of these, in terms of its popular impact, was Marie Stopes' *Married Love*. First published in 1918, it was listed in 1935 as sixteenth out of the twenty-five most influential books of the previous fifty years. Over 2,000 copies were sold in the first fortnight, and over 400,000 by the end of 1923. By 1955 it had gone through numerous reprints and twenty-eight editions, amounting to 1,032,250 copies, and had also been translated into fourteen languages.[1] Its companion volume on birth control, *Wise Parenthood*, published eight months later, had sold over 300,000 copies by 1924 and was translated into twelve languages. These two books, together with the publicity associated with Stopes' campaign for birth control, resulted in a deluge of letters from all sections of society asking for advice, not merely on birth control, but on a wide range of sexual problems. In 1928 the sequel to *Married Love*, entitled *Enduring Passion*, was published. This was not such a best-seller as the earlier texts, but by the outbreak of World War II it had gone through eleven reprints and six editions. It was translated into nine languages, and the eighth and final edition was published in 1956. Although Stopes' impact was at its strongest during the period 1918 to 1928, the popularity of these texts certainly continued well into the post-war period.[2]

Married Love and *Enduring Passion* were partly inspired by the sexual difficulties Stopes experienced in her two marriages. Stopes herself wrote in the preface to *Married Love* that she had paid such a terrible price for sexual ignorance that she felt that knowledge gained at such a cost should be placed at the service of humanity. It seems appropriate, therefore, to preface the following analysis of her model of sexuality with a few biographical details. Born in 1880, Marie was the daughter of a feminist, Charlotte Carmichael Stopes, who supported the militant wing of the women's suffrage movement. Marie initially considered the suffragettes immodest and unladylike but admitted later that she had some sympathy with the militants, but feared to get involved lest it damage her career as a scientist. In 1912 she did in fact join the Women's Social and Political Union and is on record as hotly defending militancy, though there is no evidence that she actually took part. She was educated at the North London Collegiate school where she obtained a scholarship in science, and at University College, London, where she achieved a BSc with honours in both botany and geology. She was the only student to pass with honours in geology, thus surpassing all the other – male – students. Marie did her postgraduate research in Munich and became fluent in German, as well as being the first woman in Germany to gain a doctorate in botany. She was also the first woman to be appointed to the science faculty of Manchester University, and in 1905 she became the youngest Doctor of Science in Britain. By the age of 30 she was established as one of the leading palaeobotanists of her day.[3]

Her first major heterosexual relationship lasted about five years, but her hopes of marriage failed to materialize. Her first marriage, to Reginald Ruggles Gates, took place in 1911 at the age of 30. Five years later she succeeded in having the marriage annulled on the grounds of non-consummation. Her husband's impotence appears only to have become an issue when Marie, unable any longer to put up with his unreasonable and abusive behaviour, tried to find grounds for divorce. She had never received any kind of sex education and had never experienced sexual intercourse, so had no reason to believe that sexually her marriage was in any way unusual. Her friend and first biographer, Aylmer Maude, appears to have enlightened her on this point, though not until after she had already decided to seek a divorce. She consulted doctors and solicitors and, finding them unhelpful, decided to take up her own case as a piece of scientific research. In Maude's words she 'went to the British Museum and read pretty nearly every book on sex in English, French or German'.[4] The authors specifically mentioned in Ruth Hall's biography include Ellis, Forel, Carpenter, Alice B. Stockham on 'Karezza', Marshall on the physiology of reproduction, and Starling on hormones, but many others would of course have been available, including works by feminists such as Blackwell, Swiney, and Wolstenholme Elmy. She was apparently much impressed by Carpenter's 'nature-sex mysticism' and his theory that both male and female benefited physiologically through the mutual absorption of secretions during coitus. Hall considers, however, that the most formative influence on Stopes at this time was probably Ellis. She seems to have been particularly impressed by his emphasis on the dangers of sexual abstinence and 'frigidity', as well as his material on the sexual perversions, which she read with extreme distaste. Her scientific education had ensured that she was already steeped in Darwin, and she was also strongly influenced, as were most scientists, sexologists, and sex reformers at that time, by eugenics.

Stopes began her scientific research into sex in 1913 and by 1915 she already had a second draft of *Married Love*, then entitled *They Twain*. In the same year she first met Margaret Sanger, who had recently arrived in Britain from America to avoid prosecution under the Comstock Law for offering information on contraception. Sanger was herself a champion of female sexual pleasure, and a close friend of Ellis, and probably influenced Stopes' developing views on sexuality, as well as providing her with information on contraception.[5]

In 1918 she met, and married, her second husband, Humphrey Verdon Roe, who gave her £200 to finance the publication of *Married Love*. It was an immediate success and by the end of 1918 was already into its sixth edition. In Stopes' own words, it 'crashed into English society like a bombshell', its 'explosively contagious' main theme making Victorian husbands gasp. Between 1918 and 1928 Stopes published numerous books, pamphlets, and articles (including many in the popular press) on various aspects of sex, marriage, motherhood, and birth control. Throughout this period she was inundated with letters, initially from the middle classes, but later from all sections of society, asking for advice on sexual problems as well as birth control. Despite considerable opposition, especially from the Church and the medical profession, she was highly acclaimed by 'progressive' scientists, left-wing intellectuals, and especially by sexologists and sex reformers, for spreading a new 'gospel of hope'. Although a controversial figure she also enjoyed a high degree of respectability. She was appointed a member of the Birth Rate Commission, and also of the Cinema Commission of Enquiry, which had been set up by the National Council of Public Morals. She also found time to continue her scientific work, and in 1920 organized an unsuccessful campaign against the decision of the Rhondda Valley education authorities to sack all their married women teachers.

From this time onwards, however, her energies became increasingly consumed by the birth control campaign. At the end of 1920 she resigned her lectureship at University College, London, and three months later opened the Mothers' Clinic for Constructive Birth Control in the Holloway district of north London. The first birth control clinic in Britain, it was financed by herself and her husband, and offered free contraceptive advice. Cervical caps, her preferred method, were sold at cost price or supplied free to those who could not afford to pay. The opening of the clinic, and the accompanying propaganda campaign,[6] provoked the opponents of birth control, in particular the Catholic Church, into intensifying their campaign against her, and in 1922 this led to a famous libel case against Dr Halliday Sutherland, secretary of the League of National Life (a mainly Catholic anti-contraception organization), who implied that Stopes was experimenting on the poor by providing harmful means of contraception. Although Stopes eventually lost her case, public opinion was on her side and the resulting publicity produced such a boom in the sales of her books that her delighted publisher made a substantial contribution towards her costs. The trial also resulted in a vastly increased correspondence, which now contained a much greater proportion from the working classes, whom Stopes had long wanted to reach, for a mixture of humanitarian and eugenic reasons. Her series of articles in *John Bull* in 1926 had similar results, and the following year she instituted the world's first travelling birth control caravan. Meanwhile, in 1924, she had at last given birth to her only living child, a son, her first having been stillborn in 1919. In 1928 *Enduring Passion*, the sequel to *Married Love*, was published – at a time when, ironically, she and her second husband were already becoming estranged.

Stopes' Model of Sexuality

In some respects Stopes' two marriage manuals are typical of the genre of the period, with their emphasis on the importance of mutual sexual adjustment, not merely for its own sake, but in order to preserve the stability of marriage. At the same time, however, Stopes' writings are unique: not merely in terms of their romantic, semi-mystical style, but in terms of the deeply contradictory nature of her model of sexuality, which was, from a feminist perspective, both radical and reactionary. On the one hand, it combined a critique of the ideology and practice of male sexuality, which owed much to contemporary feminism, with a commitment to female sexual autonomy; on the other hand it remained ultimately rooted in the sexological, and hence patriarchal, model of sexuality – a model which assumed the biological necessity and inevitability of male dominance and female submission. Stopes' model thus had built into it fundamental patriarchal values and assumptions which undermined the female sexual autonomy she was asserting. The contradiction was reflected in her writing, which was an idiosyncratic blend of science, religion, mysticism, romanticism, and feminism.

Married Love

The 'explosively contagious' main theme of this book which, according to Stopes, made Victorian husbands gasp, was 'that woman like man had the same physiological reaction, a reciprocal need for enjoyment and benefit from union in marriage distinct from the exercise of maternal functions'. She dedicated it to young husbands and 'all those who are betrothed in love', and her aim was to increase the joys of marriage and show how much marital unhappiness might be avoided. Echoing Ellis, she emphasized that sexual love could not be safely left to instinct: 'The great majority of people in our country have no glimmering of the supreme human art, the art of love'.[7]

The central subject of the book was sexual incompatibility between husbands and wives, and how to overcome it. Stopes was extremely forthright in blaming men for women's apparent frigidity and revulsion for sexual intercourse, emphasizing the 'horrors' of the wedding night, from which many women never recovered. She also pointed to the masculine bias of most books, including scientific texts, on sex and marriage, which she linked to the politics of male sexuality:

> it has suited the general structure of society much better for men to shrug their shoulders and smile at women as irrational and capricious creatures, to be courted when it suited them, not to be studied. . . . Moreover, by attributing to mere caprice the coldness which at times comes over the most ardent woman, man was unconsciously justifying himself for at any time coercing her to suit himself.

Stopes had begun her research into sexuality in 1913, when the militant feminist campaign against the double standard was at its height. The previous year she had herself become a member of the Women's Social and Political Union, and the feminist influence in her early writing is strong. While she castigated the Church for promoting the notion that sex degrades women, she also blamed men for frequently using women as nothing but instruments of their own gratification: 'One result, apparently little suspected, of using the woman as a passive instrument for man's need has been, in effect, to make her that and nothing more'. Echoing the words of Forel, she maintained that the company of prostitutes often rendered men incapable of understanding feminine psychology, since prostitutes were hardly more than automata trained for the use of male sensuality. Any attempt to gain insight into the sexual psychology of women by analyzing prostitutes was therefore bound to fail, since men would find in them only their own sexuality reflected back at them.[8]

Stopes was adamant that if a husband insisted on his marital 'rights', regardless of his wife's wishes, this constituted rape. She argued that the married woman's body and soul should be essentially her own; that she needed spiritual, intellectual, and economic independence from her husband, and an 'inviolable retreat', in the form of a separate bedroom, or even a separate household. But above all, her demand for female sexual autonomy was based on the notion that female sexual desire was periodic in nature. As we have seen, Ellis had discussed this possibility in Volume I of his *Studies*, although Stopes gave the impression that it was she who first thought of it. Whatever the origins of the idea, however, Stopes was certainly the first to formulate what she called the 'Law of the Periodicity of Recurrence of Natural Desire in Healthy Women', based on her own and other women's personal observations. She argued that most women were at least dimly aware that their sexual desire waxed and waned according to a definite monthly rhythm, and that this was responsible for their apparent 'contrariness'. If a woman appeared 'cold', it was probably because her sexual tide was at the ebb; conversely, most men were blind to the signs of its welling up again, and failed to take the initiative. Further, the husband's regular habits of intercourse flattened out the curves of his wife's desire by claiming her, both when she would naturally enjoy it, and when it was repugnant to her. She believed that the women who were most aware of their sexual rhythm tended to be wives who were temporarily separated from their husbands for some months. She drew up a chart showing two peaks of female sexual desire, one a few days before menstruation, and the other approximately half way through the month.[9]

The roots of the problem of sexual adjustment in marriage lay, for Stopes, in the inherent difference between male and female sexual desire: while female sexual desire waxed and waned according to a recurring monthly rhythm, male sexual desire was always present. It was

> ever ready to awake at the lightest call, and often so spontaneously insistent as to require perpetual conscious repression. . . . It would go ill with the men of our race had women retained the wild animals' infrequent seasonal rhythm, and with it her inviolable rights in her own body save at the mating season. Woman, too, has acquired a much more frequent rhythm; but, as it does not equal man's, he has tended to ignore and override it, coercing her at all times and seasons, either by force, or by the even more compelling power of 'divine' authority and social tradition.

She recognized that, given this difference in male and female sexual desire, mutual sexual satisfaction might at first sight seem impossible. As one man had said frankly to her: '"As things are it is impossible for both sexes to get what they want. One must be sacrificed. And it is better for society that it should be the woman."' Stopes disagreed. She insisted that the solution to this problem was for the husband to adapt himself to his wife's sexual rhythm, a radical solution which may well have derived from Elizabeth Blackwell's generation of feminist sexual theorists. No other marriage manual in the inter-war period even hinted at the possibility that the husband could, let alone should, adapt to his wife's sexual needs. Indeed, not until the rise of radical feminism in the late 1960s was such an uncompromising stand against the tyranny of male sexual demands again to be taken.[10]

Stopes' attitude towards male sexuality was thus contradictory: on the one hand she accepted the dominant patriarchal and scientific view that the male sexual urge was 'spontaneously insistent', but on the other hand she shared with feminists the belief that this urge was amenable to rational control, that it could be adapted to suit the pattern of female sexual desire. In describing the penis and the process of male sexual arousal, for instance, she argued strongly that erection did not necessarily require relief through ejaculation, but that it could subside naturally and healthily 'when the nerves are soothed either physically or as a result of a sense of mental peace and exaltation'. She also maintained that it was mistaken to imagine that semen must be frequently discharged, arguing, like Frances Swiney, that the energy and chemical substances that went into its production could be better used by being transformed into other creative work. Moreover, the 'soothing of the nerves' necessary for erection to subside could be accomplished by 'a strong will' and the exercise of self-discipline and control. Furthermore, she added:

> It should never be forgotten that without the discipline of control there is no lasting delight in erotic feeling. The fullest delight, even in a purely physiological sense, can only be attained by those who curb and direct their natural impulses.

Thus the husband's adaptation to his wife's rhythm was seen as beneficial, not only to the wife, but to the husband himself. Assuming the wife to have a fortnightly potentiality of desire, Stopes' recommendation was for three or four days of repeated 'unions', followed by about ten days without any at all, unless 'some strong external stimulus has stirred a mutual desire'. She added that even if a woman had only one peak of desire per month, most men should still be able to adapt to this, though if a 'strongly sexed' man found this hard to endure he should 'set himself ardently to woo her' about a fortnight after her last peak, which would be when he had the best chance of succeeding.[11]

It is at this point that the contradictions in Stopes' model of sexuality begin to emerge much more sharply. The language of 'wooing and winning', directly echoing Ellis' analysis of courtship, begins to take over from the insistence on female sexual autonomy:

> The supreme law for husbands is: Remember that each act of union must be tenderly wooed for and won, and that no union should ever take place unless the woman also desires it and is made physically ready for it.

It did not occur to Stopes to wonder why, if the woman really did desire coitus, she needed to be *made* ready. Nor did she seem aware that the concept of courtship, based on the assumed biological necessity of the conquest of the female by the male, might undermine the notion of female sexual autonomy. She emphasized repeatedly that the husband must woo his wife before every separate act of coitus, 'for each act corresponds to a marriage as other creatures know it', adding that the man would also benefit from the increased intensity of pleasure when the woman was made 'ready'. She also emphasized that making a woman ready for coitus took time: 'So deep-seated, so profound are woman's complex sex-instincts as well as her organs, that in rousing them the man is rousing her whole body and soul. And this takes time'.[12]

The text abounds with references to 'man the hunter' and 'the thrills of the chase', and she even hinted that the wife should pretend to resist, lest 'by her very docility to his perpetual demands, she destroys for him the elation, the palpitating thrills and surprise, of the chase'. Although she had earlier blamed men for marital maladjustment, at this point in the book there was a subtle shift of sympathy in their direction. She accused women of neglecting their beauty, damaging their health through using corsets, and contributing to their husbands' disenchantment by allowing them to observe the 'unlovely' proceedings of the toilet:

> In this respect I am inclined to think that man suffers more than woman. For man is still essentially the hunter, the one who experiences the desires and thrills of the chase, and dreams ever of coming unawares upon Diana in the woodlands.

At times Stopes appeared much less concerned with female than with male sexual pleasure. She urged wives to participate actively in 'the chase', to 'be always escaping', in order to ensure their husbands were not deprived of their 'thrills'. She did, however, take husbands severely to task for neglecting their wives' sexual pleasure. She believed that the prevalent failure of most husbands to effect orgasms for their wives was a common cause of sleeplessness and the 'nervous diseases' of so many married women, and claimed that 'the modern civilised neurotic woman has become a by-word in the Western world'. Such neurosis, she argued, was caused by repeated sexual stimulation without 'normal satisfaction'. It made women feel they were merely passive instruments of their husbands' enjoyment, or even that they were actively abused, and led to bitterness and resentment at being sacrificed for their self-indulgence. Coitus interruptus, too, was bad for women's 'nerves', for similar reasons. But there was also another reason for condemning it: the physiological loss to the woman of the partial absorption of the man's secretions. She claimed that physiology had already 'proved' that the internal absorption of secretions from the sex organs played a large part in determining the health and character of remote parts of the body, and it was thus extremely likely that 'the highly stimulating secretions which accompany man's semen can and do penetrate and affect the woman's whole organism'. This was the initial statement, almost in passing, of an idea that was to become, ten years later, the major theoretical underpinning of her conception of both female and male sexuality.[13]

Enduring Passion

In this sequel to *Married Love*, subtitled 'further new contributions to the solution of sex difficulties', Stopes asserted that the countless expressions of gratitude she had received showed that her book had met a widespread need. It had been widely imitated, its ideas absorbed, and its phraseology had become part of the national vocabulary. Despite the opposition of some members of the medical profession, innumerable doctors had recommended it to their patients. But opposition there had certainly been, and not only from doctors. One 'Lord X' bitterly reproached her for having told women of the physical joys of marriage, and complained: ' "I cannot meet the demands of my wife now she knows. If you create these vampire women you will rear a race of effeminate men" '. Stopes' response to this shows that she still retained the sense of sex as political: 'did not this man . . . really reveal his own debased ideas of woman captive and enslaved in a home?' she asked. 'For him woman should be deprived not only of the enjoyment of true sex union, but of its health-giving balance, its vitalising power, and the very joyous sense of equality with her mate'. She reiterated her demand that husbands should not only woo their wives but give them sexual pleasure, claiming that this demand, which in 1918 had seemed so audacious, was now almost universally recognized as a woman's legitimate right.[14]

In *Enduring Passion* Stopes developed and expanded many of the themes of *Married Love*, but concentrated far more on specific sexual problems, especially male impotence and female frigidity. The same fundamental contradictions remained, but at the same time there was a definite shift of emphasis away from the concept of female sexual autonomy and the critique of male sexuality, towards a more 'scientific', physiological approach to sex. One of Stopes' major preoccupations at this time was sexual deprivation, particularly in women. She argued that there were many women whose sexual desire was stronger than their husbands', and that the resulting sexual 'starvation' was now being recognized as a cause of neurosis in women. She unequivocally condemned masturbation as a possible solution to the problem: it was *not* the proper remedy, she insisted, arguing that women's orgasms should always be given by their husbands. A far more dangerous solution to the problem, however, was lesbianism, which she alleged was 'much practised nowadays', particularly by the independent type of woman. She had discussed 'homosexual vice', as she preferred to call it, in *Sex and the Young*, a sex education book published two years earlier and intended for parents and teachers, in which she drew attention to the dangers of employing so many unmarried persons as teachers. Although she conceded that some would be perfectly 'normal' and worthy teachers, she believed that it was likely that some would be 'perverts' and have a corrupting influence on the young.[15]

There is evidence that Stopes had several passionate friendships with women, though whether she was aware of the possible sexual significance of these at the time is doubtful. The tirade against lesbianism that appeared in

Enduring Passion is certainly striking, and suggestive of some kind of emotional backlash. Stopes protested that lesbianism was unnatural, that it 'unfitted' women for 'real union' by accustoming the system to reactions 'which are arrived at by a different process from that for which the parts were naturally formed'. Moreover, a married woman who indulged in such practices would be likely to make her husband impotent. Following Ellis' distinction between 'real' lesbians and 'spurious imitations', she conceded that a very few women had strong inborn tendencies to lesbianism, but maintained that most drifted into it out of laziness or curiosity and allowed themselves to be corrupted. This kind of lesbianism was dangerous because it was contagious:

> No woman who values the peace of her home and the love of her husband should yield to the wiles of the Lesbian whatever the temptation to do so may be.... This corruption spreads as an underground fire spreads in the peaty soil of a dry moorland.[16]

Stopes considered that there were sound scientific arguments against lesbianism. The fundamental objection was that women could 'only play' with each other and could not

> in the very nature of things have natural union or supply each other with the seminal and prostatic secretions which they ought to have, and crave for unconsciously ... a woman's need and *hunger* for nourishment in sex union is a true physiological hunger to be satisfied only by the supplying of the actual molecular substances lacked by her system.

This was nothing more than a reiteration of the traditional patriarchal view that a woman without a man was sexually incomplete. For Stopes, women were inherently sexually deficient, and could only be made whole by physical union with a male. 'Sex starvation' was, for her, not a metaphor; she meant it quite literally. She stressed repeatedly that women had a real, physiological hunger for the chemical substances found in the accessory sex glands of the male, and that this accounted for the apparently excessive demands of some wives for coitus, as well as the neurosis of those women deprived of 'normal' sexual satisfaction. The only solution to sex starvation which could not be satisfied in the 'normal' way, i.e. by regular coitus, was to take daily capsules containing glandular, including prostatic, extracts. She recommended such treatment for married women temporarily separated from their husbands, for 'strongly sexed' women whose husbands could not satisfy them, and for unmarried women who wished to remain chaste. She did add that she still rated continence and self-control highly, but said that it was useless to preach this when there was a 'definite physiological deficit'. She acknowledged that her theory of the function of the prostatic fluid so far lacked empirical verification, but felt sufficient confidence in it to state: 'I have found out a law of love. I think it acts through mutual absorption. *I think* that the day will come when it will be scientifically proved'. She advised couples that after (preferably mutual) orgasm and ejaculation they should continue to lie in the coital embrace for at least an hour so that both were in a position to absorb and benefit from all ejaculated secretions. This 'law of union', if it were universally known and practised, would, she declared, almost revolutionize society by making the majority of marriages lastingly happy. At the same time, however, she emphasized that the theory of mutual absorption only applied to couples between whom there was mutual love and harmony; a man could not rape a woman and expect to get this result – though she did not explain why not.[17]

During the ten years following the publication of *Married Love* and *Wise Parenthood* Stopes had received a flood of letters from women and men of all classes of society, requesting further information and advice on contraception, abortion, and sexual problems. A selection of these was published in 1929 as *Mother England*, based on selected letters from one file in one year (1926), from women whose surnames began with the letters A–H. Many of these (and other letters published in the collection by Ruth Hall) contained complaints from women that their husbands' sexual demands upon them were excessive, even violent, and provided ample – and very moving – testimony that most women totally lacked any control, not only over their fertility, but over their sexuality. Some were explicitly critical of men's 'selfishness', though most appeared to accept that men were the victims of uncontrollable sexual urges and that husbands had a 'natural' right of access to their wives' bodies in order to gratify these urges, as the following examples show:

> I have a good husband and nature is nature

> since then we have never let Nature take her full swing . . . and I feel for his sake. It should not be so, it does not seem right to deprive him thus.

A few women wrote of their own desire for pleasure without risk of pregnancy, but whether they specifically desired coitus is far from clear; in most cases it seems that what they felt deprived of was love and affection and *any* form of sexual intimacy, because coitus was seen as the inevitable outcome:

> Dr Stopes, my husband tells me to control and hold myself in check, well I can, but we do without kisses, and oh, lots of other little things that help to make life pleasant, then I get depressed, my husband gets ill tempered, we quarrel, make it up and afterwards I am in torment.

For the overwhelming majority of women, however, the dominant feelings seem to have been guilt and fear: guilt at denying sexual pleasure to their husbands and depriving them of their 'rights'; and fear, not only of pregnancy, but that their husbands might gratify their sexual urges elsewhere. This was seen as a threat to the stability of the home, as well as carrying the risk of contracting venereal disease:

> I simply dread to see night time coming however tired I am because I am always dreading my husband wanting is [*sic*] wishes fulfilled and I am powerless to prevent him and above all things I don't want to drive him to go after other women which I am very sorry to say are plentifull [*sic*] enough worse luck around these parts yet how they manage to escape having children baffles me.[18]

Stopes' response to such testimony was ambivalent: on the one hand she remained critical of men's excessive sexual demands, maintaining that 'such demands, even if made by true love, generally result in the woman becoming the "slave of man", as it is rather luridly described by the feminists'. She continued to advocate that the best solution was for men to adapt themselves to woman's 'natural' (fortnightly) sexual rhythm. On the other hand she now seemed much less optimistic that such an adaptation could be achieved, for two reasons. First, because she now believed that it was impossible to define normality with regard to frequency of sexual desire; and second, because she now considered that 'insatiable' sexual desire in men was often the result of craving for nourishment similar to that of the sex-starved woman. Such men failed to achieve profound satisfaction from sexual intercourse because they merely 'snatch a mouthful of the feast each time'. Furthermore, in some men 'frantic need for coitus' was, she believed, caused by an enlarged prostate, which often led to the 'silly flirtations' of old men with young girls, to indecent exposure and other forms of sexual assault and abuse.[19]

This is a clear illustration of the increasing tendency during this period to redefine the problem of male sexual violence as a medical problem, a tendency which, as was pointed out in the previous chapter, may be attributed to the dominance of the sexological model. Stopes, in adopting this model, undermined her own critique of male sexuality, and her commitment to female sexual autonomy, by depicting men as victims of physiological forces beyond their control. Although she still believed that some 'excessively virile' men could overcome the problem by will-power, others needed help in the form of medical treatment in order to control their sexual desires. Stopes' sense of the sexual as political had by now all but given way to sympathy for such men: 'He is quite often a loving husband and father unaware what a lack of balance of his internal secretions is doing to him'.[20]

Stopes' change of attitude towards male sexuality was matched by a corresponding tendency to blame women for marital maladjustment and men's sexual problems. She blamed premature ejaculation, for example, on the refusal of some women to accede to their husbands' demands for coitus:

> The cooperation of the wife is often required, especially where she is the one who has led to an excessive tension of repression by that one-sided demand for very infrequent union made by some foolish women for various insufficient reasons.

Similarly, in a chapter on frigidity she attacked the 'prude', arguing that many 'advanced' married women who called for purity and 'union for pro-creation only' probably lacked 'normal clitoral development' and were there-fore incapable of experiencing or understanding a 'complete sex life'. These were the 'real prudes', as distinct from the 'hypocritical prude', whose clitoris was normal, but who pretended to be prudish, while being really lascivious-minded, merely using prudery as a cloak. She had warned of the dangers of abstinence in 1918, but by 1928 it had become a key element of her model of sexuality, underpinned by the theory of mutual absorption. It may prob-ably be laid down as a general rule, she claimed, 'that enforced and pro-tracted continence is almost always injurious to a less or greater extent, according to its duration'. It should be emphasized that continence or absti-nence meant abstaining from coitus. This was seen as the *only* legitimate and fulfilling form of sexual activity. While occasional masturbation, mutual or otherwise, was not seen as harmful, habitual or frequent masturbation was seen as unnatural and a threat to marital harmony, because it made it more difficult to achieve orgasm in coitus:

> I say emphatically that if there is the necessity to increase or to modify the type of stimulus, either manually or in any other way so as to depart from the natural mode of union or to intensify the stimulus so as to bring on the consequent orgasm, there will be an ever-recurring and accumulating strain both upon the nervous sys-tem and the ultimate health, but mainly upon the fundamental basis of the affection and harmony of the two.

She even coined a new verb, 'to defeminate', the equivalent of 'to emascu-late', to describe the woman who is deprived of sexual satisfaction from coitus. A woman, too, she wrote, 'is defeminated by protracted abstinence just as a man is emasculated by protracted abstinence'.[21]

Stopes remained optimistic that, in time, full sexual compatibility between most husbands and wives would be achieved. Nevertheless, the problem seemed to her much more intractable in 1928 than it had in 1918, perhaps due, in part, to the sexual disharmony in her own second marriage. She thought that only about 15 to 20 per cent of couples were mutually well adjusted, and estimated that about 30 per cent of couples were sexually in-compatible because of the husband's 'excess of potency', and 30 per cent

because of his 'lack of potency'. She conceded that if differences in physiological need were excessive, such couples would be unlikely to achieve
harmony. At the same time, she clung to the hope that eventually most
couples would become compatible, either as a result of individuals developing the ability to choose a mate with whom they were sexually in tune, or by
men evolving over time a fortnightly rhythm in harmony with their wives.
She considered the perfectly mated pair to be the highest social unit, the
perfect 'human duity', and that the path to Utopia was through the 'erogamic
life'. Mutual sexual adjustment was for her the bedrock of marriage; other
sources of disagreement or conflict had little significance as long as the sexual
aspect of marriage was harmonious. Sexual compatibility in marriage was
crucial, not only in terms of personal health and happiness, but in terms of
its social value in securing the stability of the state: 'I am convinced that the
more happy, child-bearing and enduringly passionate marriages there are in
a State, the more firmly established is that State'.[22]

The Unhappy Marriage of Feminism and Sexology

This analysis of Marie Stopes' popular marriage manuals highlights clearly
the anti-feminist implications of the sexological model, and the contradictions
which resulted from her attempt to 'marry' a feminist commitment to female
sexual autonomy with a fundamentally patriarchal, phallocentric model of
sexuality. Stopes shared with feminists such as Elizabeth Blackwell the belief
that women were independent sexual beings with their own needs and desires, to which male sexuality could and should be attuned. This implied a
potentially radical shift in the balance of power within marriage and heterosexual relationships. The implications of the sexological model, on the other
hand, were quite the reverse. Female sexual pleasure could only be achieved
by means of joyful submission to male sexual demands, and the eroticization
of the power relation which was seen as natural and intrinsic to heterosexual
sex. This was incompatible with the principle of female sexual autonomy, and
Stopes' inability to resolve the contradictions which resulted from the attempt to combine them became only too apparent, ironically, in *Enduring
Passion*. Female sexuality cannot be simultaneously autonomous *and* dependent on men for its expression and fulfilment. The 'laws of love' which
Stopes claimed to have discovered, and the sexual practices which she both
*pre*scribed and *pro*scribed, undermined her commitment to the sexual liberation of women.

Why was Stopes apparently so blinkered to the implications of the
sexological model? Why did she, a feminist, work so hard, not only to promote it, but to reinforce it with her own 'laws of love'? If it is true that she
read every book about sex that she could lay her hands on, why did she not
explore more fully the implications of the feminist challenge to male sexuality, to the centrality of coitus in heterosexual activity, and the emerging

feminist model of sexuality? Why did her solution to the problem of sexual 'maladjustment' in marriage embrace the kind of sexual practice which many feminists were rejecting? In order to throw some light on these questions it is necessary to take account of the political and historical context in which she lived and worked. There were three aspects of this that were important in shaping Stopes' thinking about sexuality. First, her socialization as a scientist, and her position as a female scientist in the early twentieth century; second, her relationship to feminism, and the change from the 'old feminism' to the 'new feminism' which was taking place during World War I and the inter-war period; and third, her involvement in the birth control movement. Each of these will be considered separately, though of course all three were closely interrelated.

Stopes as Scientist

As Stopes' contemporary critics never failed to point out, she was not a doctor of medicine. As a doctor of science, however, her credentials were impeccable. When she began her sex research in the British Museum she was in her early thirties and already had behind her more than sixteen years of scientific training. She had achieved distinction in what was then, and still is today, one of the most male-dominated fields of knowledge. She had many scientific publications to her credit, and was recognized within the scientific community as one of the leading palaeobotanists of her day. Her original research into the constituents of coal was sponsored by the Government, and she continued this work long after she had become famous as a sex reformer and birth controller. She was intensely proud of her reputation as a scientist and when in 1931 her success earned her a leader in *Nature* she wrote to a friend:

> As you are not a scientist you may not realise what a colossal honour this is. They generally only have three column leaders – it is the absolute blue ribbon of science to get a leader about you in 'Nature'. 'Nature' is the greatest scientific paper in the world, I am frightfully bucked.

She was also acutely aware of the legitimating power of science, and always ensured that her scientific qualifications and publications were prominently displayed on all her publicity material and publications relating to sex and birth control.[23]

Stopes did not simply use science to legitimate her views. She genuinely believed in the liberating potential of science and was totally committed to the search for 'truth' through the scientific method. There was at that time no recognized philosophy of science or sociology of knowledge, and conceptions of science were what we would now call crudely positivistic. Stopes shared with contemporary scientists and sexologists a completely apolitical view of science as essentially value-free and 'objective'. Although she pointed to examples of male bias in earlier scientific texts on sex and marriage, she appeared to believe that the elimination of such bias was a relatively straightforward matter. The increasing involvement of women in the production and dissemination of scientific knowledge would ensure that women's perspectives would be taken into account and male bias eliminated. The possibility that science as a practice and a method might be deeply saturated with patriarchal values and assumptions simply did not occur to her.[24]

For the positivist, scientific theories consist of sets of highly general universal statements, whose truth or falsity can be assessed by means of systematic observation and experiment. At its crudest, this approach may be characterized as a preoccupation with the accumulation of empirical 'facts' on the one hand, and the formulation of 'laws' on the other, both of which can be known with virtually absolute certainty. It was with this perspective that Stopes applied herself to the study of sex and birth control, and which led to her failure to challenge the sexological model and its scientific underpinnings. As a woman and a feminist she believed in female sexual autonomy, and the importance of the spiritual and emotional, as well as physical aspects of sex. As a scientist her increasing obsession with the search for the 'laws of love' led to the reduction of sexuality to a physiological need or drive; a drive which, like hunger, demanded physical satisfaction of a particular kind. This narrow, physiological definition of sex led inexorably to the view that heterosexual sex, and specifically coitus, was the only natural way to satisfy sexual desire, since only coitus ensured the mutual absorption of seminal and vaginal secretions which were allegedly essential to health. The everyday expression 'sex-starved', which we probably owe to Stopes, encapsulates perfectly this physiological model of sex.[25]

Methodologically her work could hardly be described as rigorous. She criticized other sexologists for failing to carry out original research, for instance into women's sexual rhythm, yet was herself only too ready to make sweeping generalizations and even formulate 'laws' on the basis of the most meagre and vague empirical evidence. Her 'Law of Periodicity of Recurrence of Desire in Women', which she illustrated with graphs, was, she claimed, based on the personal observations of an unspecified number of women, some of whom she asked to keep notes of dates. Her estimates (or guesses) as to the proportions of sexually incompatible couples, her theory of mutual absorption, her assertions about clitoral retardation and sexual deprivation were all totally unsupported by any evidence. At the same time, from a feminist perspective one would not wish her work to be judged by positivist criteria. On the contrary, the fact that she did consider her own and other women's experiences significant might, if these experiences had been properly documented, have provided a basis for feminist sex research.[26]

In short, Stopes' commitment to science undermined her feminism. The theory of mutual absorption illustrates this well. It was clearly Stopes' personal experience of heterosexual relationships and marriage which provided at least the initial impetus for her sex research. It has been suggested that Stopes herself was sexually 'deprived' as a result of the sexual impotence, not only of her first husband, but her second. Such a suggestion assumes, of course, the very model of sexuality that is the subject of this critique. There is certainly evidence that Stopes found heterosexual relationships problematic, including sexually. There is a letter from one of her doctors, for example, enquiring 'Can you tell me if there is any change in the disappointing nature of the orgasm as yet? I had hoped that was simply a passing phase due to all the nervous worry you had so recently passed through'.[27] Instead of applying a feminist perspective to the problem and seeking a *political* explanation of why sexual relationships with men were so unsatisfactory she searched for a scientific explanation. Having found in sexology and other scientific work 'evidence' which convinced her that she was sexually deprived (through lack of coitus) she invented a physiological 'law' of mutual absorption, based on a combination of a rather vague, mystical notion of Edward Carpenter's, her own interpretation of Starling's work on hormones, and other recent scientific discoveries regarding internal secretions and the function of 'ductless glands', or what we now refer to as the endocrine system.[28] Her socialization as a scientist blinkered her to the implications of the feminist critique of the patriarchal model of sexuality, with the result that she failed to explore and participate in the process of constructing a feminist model of sexuality. Her position as a woman scientist, and her determination to succeed as a woman on male terms in an almost exclusively male-dominated field, led to an uncritical adoption of the prevailing scientific values and methods, both positivist and patriarchal, and prevented her from exploring the implications of female sexual autonomy.

Stopes as Feminist

Stopes' relationship to feminism was, to say the least, ambivalent. She was an active supporter of women's suffrage, and a strong believer in economic independence for women, including married women. In many respects she epitomized the 'new feminism', with its glorification of marriage and motherhood as woman's primary source of fulfilment. She frequently contributed marital advice to women's magazines which would have horrified 'old feminists'. To quote one example: 'A woman's first baby should be her husband . . . he needs just the simple, loving petting that is demanded by a child'.[29] She considered the 'perfectly mated pair' to be the highest social unit, and despised not only lesbians but all 'anti-male spinsters'. When she was in Japan in 1908 she took part in a debate on the motion: 'That the unmarried life is the happier', and recorded in her journal:

> The people here are not in touch with all our modern types, and I did not need to speak against the ranting type, who rave against men and

marriage and prove themselves deformed. . . . The ranting type seems mercifully to be confined to big communities; I suppose it is an inevitable result of city life, where some must sterilise . . .[30]

She must have changed her views by 1912 because in that year she joined the Women's Social and Political Union, which was not only the most militant of all the women's suffrage organizations but probably contained by far the greatest proportion of 'anti-male spinsters' and 'ranting types'! It seems paradoxical that, disappointed though she was in both her marriages, and in all her relationships with men, she clung so resolutely to an absurdly idealistic and romantic view of marriage. On a number of occasions she complained bitterly of the constraints that marriage imposed on her independence, and once even wrote to *The Times* about it, yet the concluding lines of *Married Love* read:

> When knowledge and love together go to the making of each marriage, the joy of *that new unit, the pair*, will reach from the physical foundations of its bodies to the heavens where its head is crowned with stars.[31]

Her idealism and romanticism were also reflected in her public and private image, which she cultivated with great care. She loved to project a fragile femininity, accentuated by wearing soft fabrics and misty colours. She refused on health grounds to wear corsets, and usually did not wear a bra. She was especially fond of Isadora-Duncan-style floating, ethereal gowns, and had semi-erotic photographs taken of herself swathed in revealing chiffon.[32] She also wrote copious quantities of emotionally and sexually charged verse. Such a blend of feminism and femininity is not, of course, unusual in 'successful' women, either in Stopes' time or in the present day. Indeed, the accentuation of femininity is probably an essential ingredient for success as a woman in a male-dominated sphere. Women who become 'honorary men', in the sense of being accepted as 'doing a man's job as well as a man', enjoy a status that is always precarious and are particularly vulnerable to insinuations that they are deficient in womanliness. The implication is that if they succeed on male terms, and exhibit qualities such as strength, courage, intelligence, or determination, they cannot be 'real' women – they must either be asexual or 'masculine', which often carries connotations of lesbianism. It is hardly surprising, therefore, that some 'successful' women go to extreme lengths, consciously or unconsciously, to emphasize their femininity and attractiveness to men.

During the inter-war years, when the 'back-to-the-home movement' was in full swing, there was renewed stress on marriage, motherhood, and femininity, and the married woman's right to work was bitterly opposed and in many areas openly and officially denied. In some respects this was reinforced by the 'new feminists'' emphasis on the need for family endowments and their attitude towards protective legislation.[33] While most 'old feminists' believed that women should choose between marriage and motherhood on the one hand, and an independent career on the other, many 'new feminists', like Stopes, insisted that women could and should, if they wished, combine marriage and motherhood with work outside the home. Although this was in some respects a radical position, it was often combined, as it was in Stopes' case, with anti-spinster attitudes. Her campaign against the marriage bar on women teachers was based, not only on the right of married women to economic independence, but on the argument that spinster teachers were a dangerous influence on the young because they were sex-starved and sometimes had lesbian tendencies. A major problem with the 'new feminism' was that it was defined in terms of woman's freedom 'to follow her own nature', a 'nature' which was largely male-defined, and which, in the sexologists' version, substituted 'erotic rights' for equal rights. Stopes' model of sexuality was very much in tune with the 'new feminism', which derided spinsterhood and idealized heterosexual relationships. Although initially there were important elements of the 'old feminism' in her thinking, sexology, because of its scientific status, was a far more powerful force in shaping her ideas. *Married Love*, which was published in 1918 at a watershed between the 'old' and the 'new' feminisms, encapsulated the tension and struggle between the two, as well as celebrating and promoting the 'new feminism'.

Birth Control

The tensions between Stopes as a feminist and as a scientist, and her place in the 'new feminism', are highlighted by her involvement in the campaign for birth control. Although she became famous initially as a sex reformer, it is probably as a pioneer of birth control that she is best remembered. In fact she only became interested in the issue after she had almost completed writing *Married Love*, which deals only peripherally with questions of fertility and contraception. It appears that it was her meeting with Margaret Sanger in 1915 that prompted Stopes' interest, and resulted in the publication, shortly after *Married Love*, of *Wise Parenthood*. These two books paved the way for the setting up in 1921 of the Mothers' Clinic, the first birth control clinic in England. Five months later Stopes also founded the Society for Constructive Birth Control and Racial Progress (CBC), a separate organization whose function was to publicize the issue and support the work of the clinic. The CBC was established partly in opposition to the Malthusian League, which had been campaigning for birth control for many years, and opened its first clinic in the Walworth Road eight months after her own. Stopes had been a member of the League for about three years and her resignation marked the first of what were to be many bitter disagreements with other birth controllers, with Stopes becoming increasingly isolated from the rest of the movement, though she continued to regard herself as its leader.

The main ideological difference between the CBC and the Malthusian League is summed up in the word 'constructive'. The League's approach to birth control had always been, as Stopes perceived it, negative and repressive, whereas her own was positive and constructive. The main emphasis of the League had been on the bad economic effects of overpopulation, though later they used eugenic arguments as well. Stopes, however, stressed that there were three aspects of 'control', only the first of which was negative: (1) the provision of contraception on medical grounds, primarily to prevent congenital disease or abnormality; (2) advice on problems of infertility, which she always emphasized was an extremely important and positive function of her clinic; (3) advice on spacing births to ensure the health of both babies and mothers. Stopes argued that all three aspects of birth control were not only in the interests of 'the race' but also essential to the health and welfare of individual women and their children. It has been argued that it was precisely because Stopes approached population control via the health of the individual that her propaganda was more successful than that of the neo-Malthusians.[34] There was also a strong feminist strand to Stopes' thinking on birth control, which many commentators have tended to underplay. She believed passionately in a woman's right to control her own fertility, and directed most of her fury at the Catholic Church and the medical profession, whom she saw as the main obstacles to women's 'control of their own motherhood'. Furthermore, given her belief in a woman's right to sexual pleasure, and her commitment to the coital imperative, the two issues of sex reform and birth control were, for her as for other contemporary sex reformers, inextricably linked. Access to reliable methods of contraception was essential if women were to be able to enjoy the kind of regular sexual fulfilment she believed they needed, without fear of becoming pregnant.

Stopes' model of sexuality was not only heterosexist and phallocentric; it was, in essence, a reproductive model, in that it equated sexual desire with a biological urge to copulate and thus reproduce. In some respects Stopes was even more 'conservative' than the sexologists, many of whom, while adhering ultimately to this model, did at least give some credence to non-coital and non-heterosexual forms of sexual pleasure. Ellis, for instance, did acknowledge in later life that 'the act of intercourse, however essential to securing the propagation of the race, is only an incident, and not an essential to love'. For Stopes, however, the 'play function' of sex, as Ellis called it, was definitely secondary, and not to be encouraged at the expense of 'coital interlocking'. She remained adamant that orgasms should always come from this latter source, and her observation that lesbians could 'only play' with each other, together with her emphasis on the mutual absorption of vaginal and seminal secretions, make it clear that her model of sexuality was even more narrowly reproductive and physiological than the sexological model.[35]

It has already been noted that *Enduring Passion*, the sequel to *Married Love*, is characterized by a much more scientific, physiological approach to sex and a reduced emphasis on female sexual autonomy. It was during the ten years which elapsed between the publication of these two books that Stopes' preoccupation with the campaign for birth control was at its most intense, involving not only an enormous amount of work but bitter struggles with the opponents of birth control, both religious and medical. A common line of attack was to cast aspersions on her scientific credibility, implying that because she was not a doctor of medicine, which she never claimed to be, she had no right to meddle in matters of *human* reproduction. The leader of *The Practitioner* pointed out that 'medical men have found in popular handbooks, written by women with no medical qualification, practical information of which they had hitherto been ignorant and a great deal of which they might legitimately disapprove'. In the same issue Dr Norman Haire of the Malthusian League begged the medical profession to study contraception properly: 'Only thus may it be rescued from the hands of quacks and charlatans and non-medical "doctors" who write erotic treatises on birth control conveying misleading information in a highly stimulating form'.[36] Such vitriolic attacks made Stopes all the more determined to emphasize her impressive scientific reputation and to put her work as both sex reformer and birth controller on a sound scientific footing. The shift to a more 'scientific' view of sex, and a more narrowly reproductive, physiological model, may therefore be a result, both of her preoccupation with issues relating to reproduction, and of her determination to beat her opponents at their 'scientific' game. Thus what was offered in 1918 as a fairly tentative explanation, almost in passing, of why coitus interruptus might be bad for women's 'nerves', had by 1928 been elevated to the status of a 'law' of mutual absorption.

Stopes is widely regarded as a heroine, whose fight for birth control marked the real beginning of women's liberation, by enabling women to control their fertility and to separate sexual pleasure from reproduction. Such a view assumes a phallocentric, reproductive model of sexuality and ignores the contradictory implications of artificial means of contraception in a society in which heterosexuality and male-defined forms of heterosexual practice are central to the construction and maintenance of male power. Unless the use of contraception is combined with a feminist model of sexuality, based on the concept of female sexual autonomy, it tends inevitably to reinforce the phallocentric model of sexuality, and to facilitate male exploitation and control of women in and through heterosexual practices. Contraception has certain advantages for women, in that it gives them a degree of control over their own fertility, and enables them to enjoy coitus without pregnancy, *if that is what they wish*. At the same time, it makes it impossible to use the fear of pregnancy as a reason for *refusing* male sexual demands for coitus, and thus makes it *more* difficult for many women to resist those demands, and to define and control their own sexuality. This was precisely why the 'old feminists' were so wary of birth control. The 'new feminists', in contrast, embraced and promoted it to the extent that it became almost synonymous with feminism. In doing so they provided what has been termed 'sexual first aid', but at the cost of female sexual autonomy, in the sense of women's right *not* to engage in phallocentric, heterosexual sex.

Despite her criticisms of male sexuality, Stopes seemed unable to grasp this fundamental contradiction. She focused ever more narrowly on contraception as the *scientific* solution to women's sexual problems with men, problems which were essentially *political*, as the following extracts from women's letters to her show:

> I have never at any time had a desire to be with a man and even with my Husband I never get any sensation or feeling. My Husband on the other Hand is very lustfull [*sic*] and I think having no desires myself and keeping my Husband in check for long Periods before giving way to him has caused me to be Pregnant time after time.
>
> I would like my Husband to satisfy his Desires yet I am terrified at the thought anytime he comes near me and it causes unpleasant scenes in the Home.

> Another thing Doctor I very rarely get any desires and feel very repulsive [*sic*] to my husband who gets annoyed.

Other feminist birth control campaigners, too, seemed impervious to the political implications of providing sexual 'first aid' without demanding female sexual autonomy, despite the abundance of evidence contained in books such as Margaret Sanger's *Motherhood in Bondage*:

> I talked and pleaded with him and tried to show him where it was wrong to bring so many children in the world, but not one thing could I do with him. It looks as if he don't care just so he can get his wants filled. I tell him lots of times he has got me to the place where I wish I had never seen a man.

Stopes and Sanger were deluged with letters, not merely from women protesting against compulsory motherhood, but women who were forced to have intercourse with husbands infected with VD:

> But I would rather die than have another one, for my husband is a sufferer from gonorrhea [*sic*]. I have begged him to leave me. I would rather be separated than have any more. Please help me. I think the law is hideous. There ought to be a law against diseased men to marry pure, clean girls, to bring sickly children into the world to suffer, and oh! the suffering the poor women have to endure!

> My [diseased] husband has no desire for children but he takes the privilege of married life at will.

Other case studies were presented at the Sex Reform Congress which took place in London in 1929, and in which many 'new feminists', including Stella Browne, Dora Russell, Naomi Mitchison, Janet Chance, and Stopes herself participated. The following is a quotation from a paper by a Swedish participant, Elise Ottesen-Jensen, describing her birth control work among the poor. The speaker is a woman of about 50, who approached Ottesen-Jensen (referred to as 'the lady') crying:

> But I have such discharges as the lady spoke about. My vagina is like an open wound. But still my husband wishes that I shall do what he wants me to. If I don't do this he won't speak to me for a whole week: he slams the door and carries on like a wild man. He who otherwise is so good and we who have been so loving together.... But the lady understands it hurts so terribly, so that I must cry all night afterwards. Dear lady help me.[37]

It is difficult to see how contraception could possibly be perceived as a solution to such problems. There were some feminists who struggled against the promotion of birth control in the name of women's liberation. The feminist press, represented after World War I by *The Woman's Leader* and *The Vote*, were reluctant to address the question, and when they eventually did so, declined to take up a clear position, preferring to 'offer a platform for frank discussion of different aspects of this very complex subject'. One feminist who was prepared to challenge the ideology of birth control, and the model of sexuality which underpinned it, was Frances Prewett. She argued that the cause championed by birth controllers had nothing to do with women's liberty, but was essentially a masculine one: 'The truth is that Neo-Malthusianism is a man's solution for a man's problem'. She argued that compulsory motherhood was a consequence of male egoism and that it was hypocritical to declare that birth control gave woman 'the right to the control of her own body'. 'Woman is still bound', she asserted, '– bound by man's unrestrained exercise of his passions. It is man, not woman, who is set free by this mis-application of science'. She pointed out that those who claimed that conception could not be avoided by abstinence, because it was against human nature, 'identified human nature with masculinity'. The truths of woman's nature were obscured, 'because existing women are almost wholly the creatures of the civilization defined, moulded, and stamped by the energies, intellect, and passions of men'. Women today, she added, were 'so far hypnotized by the masculine reading of life that they applaud the use of contraceptives, and institute Mothers' Clinics to disseminate knowledge of such means'. She saw this as 'the negation of womanhood in woman, and the seal of her subordination to man'. Referring specifically to the work of Marie Stopes, she conceded that contraception was 'at best but an expedient', and added:

Let it be frankly admitted as such, and not glorified as the charter of woman's freedom. To prate of woman's liberty in such a connection is to say the thing that is not. *No man would submit himself to a similar abuse to suit another's gratification and consider himself still a free man.*[38]

The voices of 'old feminists' such as these were already rarely heard by the early 1920s, and were soon drowned by the rise of the 'new feminism' and the movement for sex reform. The promotion of birth control and the male-defined ideology of sexual liberation, masquerading as women's liberation, undermined the feminist demand for female sexual autonomy, and those who resisted the new sexual ideology were, as we shall see in the next chapter, increasingly dismissed as 'prudes' or as 'frigid'.

Stopes and Lesbianism

Further evidence of the power of patriarchal science to shape her thinking can be found in Stopes' attitude towards lesbianism. *Enduring Passion*, in which Stopes condemned lesbianism as unnatural, was published in 1928, the same year as Radclyffe Hall's *Well of Loneliness*. So great was her hostility towards lesbianism that she wrote to her publisher offering to write an attack on the novel, 'giving accurate, clear scientific reasons why, how and where the book is corrupt . . . it would, of course, make enemies of the homosexuals'.[39] Stopes' attitude towards lesbianism was consistent with her model of sexuality and the scientific 'laws' which underpinned it. Given the assumptions that 'sex' is ultimately reducible to coitus, and that woman's sexual physiology is inherently deficient until supplied with male secretions, homosexuality must necessarily be seen as an aberration, a violation of the laws of nature.

Nevertheless, the vehemence of Stopes' homophobia, and especially her anti-lesbianism, suggests that for her, this was more than a scientific matter, and it has been suggested that she herself had repressed lesbian tendencies. There is clear evidence that she had at least two emotionally intense relationships with women which, to judge from the correspondence between them, closely parallel the romantic friendships documented by feminist historians. One entry in her journal reads 'Why do I always fall in love with women?'; and she went on to extol the beauty of an American woman she had met in Tokyo: 'On her soft white neck were the loveliest little blue veins, I never saw anything so suggestive of living marble. She was like white marble, with an underflush of rose and violet. . . . She is the only woman in Tokyo who has bewitched me'. This was written in 1908, after her first heterosexual love affair, but before her first marriage, and before she had begun her scientific research into sexuality. It is interesting to wonder whether she would have included such an entry in a journal intended for publication *after* she had discovered the 'facts' about homosexuality from reading Ellis and other sexologists in the British Museum.

In 1926, two years before *Enduring Passion*, Stopes published a sex education book, *Sex and the Young*, in which she dealt at length with the dangers of homosexual practices which, she alleged, were at that time almost becoming a cult. Although she thought that problems were less likely to occur in girls' schools than in boys', she warned that a lesbian mistress might cause 'grave mental damage' to her pupils. She claimed to know of one teacher who had harmed a large number of adolescent girls, before eventually settling down to a stable relationship. She had been very popular with both the girls and the staff, and under the cloak of this general popularity had established relationships with a dozen or so adolescent girls, making each one separately think that she was her special favourite. She had vowed to each one, and persuaded each to vow in return, never to marry but always to remain loyal to herself. As a result:

> Each separately deluded girl felt herself pledged to remain all her life in a high faluting fantastic kind of secret Order based on a muddled mixture of mysticism, pseudo-theosophical fantasies of 'purity', and crude physical expressions of personal love and sex feeling.[40]

All this had allegedly gone on for years undetected, and the teacher had continued to hold a place in a school of high repute, while all the time being in reality 'a source of corruption and mental ill-health'. It was mainly for this reason that she considered the employment of unmarried teachers to be highly undesirable. If they were not actually 'perverts' they would probably be 'undersexed' or thwarted and embittered as a result of sexual 'deprivation'.

This account is probably based on her own personal experience while a pupil at the North London Collegiate School, where she developed a close relationship with one of the teachers, Clotilde van Wyss. The tone of their correspondence, which continued for some years after Stopes left the school, clearly betrays the emotional intensity characteristic of the romantic friendships described by feminist historians, as the following examples show:

> Psyche, my beloved . . . The picture that I send I chose a long time ago – when it seemed to me to put into form thoughts that were hovering in your mind – I would not choose it now. Accept it more as a memory of the past than as an expression of the present time. . . . And my love that I send always. Is it the same each time? I think not, grown a little wider, deeper, wiser, it loves you more and feels still more the impossibility of true expression. Marie.

This was written in 1899, when Stopes was 19, and still at school. Clotilde van Wyss replied:

> Mia Cara, I wonder if my thoughts reached you – even if I did not express them in a letter. I intended to reply to you straight off on my

birthday but my heart was too full for words and so I went for a walk through a ripe cornfield ablaze with dream-flowers and gave myself up to passionate thoughts.

In 1901, after Stopes had left school, Miss van Wyss invited her to spend a few days with her in Cambridge, and wrote to her, after she had returned to London: 'My Marie, my soul aches with the pain of having been torn away from all I love with a great deep still love'. Later the same year, when Stopes was a student at University College, London, she confided to her former teacher that she had a male admirer, a fellow student by the name of Guy Pilgrim. Even though she rejected his advances, the news clearly alarmed Miss van Wyss, who replied:

> Dear little one, I am sometimes filled with a vague dread that you are drifting beyond my reach. . . . As regards the subject of your last letter – a sickening dread came over me as I read. This thing ought not to have happened, Marie, I do not blame you for it, but it ought not to have happened. It is like a stain on your garment of purity.

By this time, Stopes knew that she had not been the only girl at school to be favoured with her teacher's affections, and probably also resented her attempts to control her. The tone of anger and disillusion with which she described the malign influence of the lesbian mistress in *Sex and the Young* is therefore hardly surprising. There is no evidence, however, that she regarded the feelings or the relationship between them as in any way unnatural at the time. Nor was it to be the last time she felt attracted towards women. At the age of 28 she formed another close friendship with an older woman, Dr Helen McMurchy. Few of Stopes' letters to her survive, which is odd, as she nearly always preserved copies or rough drafts of her correspondence, but Helen McMurchy's letters to her do survive, and are full of intimate endearments.

> In that moment I knew I loved you – when I found it in my heart to take you into my arms and kiss you. . . . You have 'got me' – dear – and what a sweet thing that you *knew* that you had got me and were a little glad about it.

Within two years Stopes was married. Helen McMurchy was one of the wedding guests, but as far as is known there was no further correspondence until sixteen years later, when Stopes wrote asking for statistical data in connection with birth control. She addressed Helen by the familiar 'Minky', but the latter replied formally 'My dear Doctor Stopes'.

When, on the breakdown of her first marriage, Stopes read about passionate friendships such as these in Ellis' *Studies* she may well have feared that she herself was a lesbian.[41] As Lillian Faderman has argued, Ellis' morbidification of love between women, and the horrific stereotypes of 'inverts' and 'pseudo-homosexuals' that he constructed, must have frightened many women away, both from feminism and from loving other women. Indeed, Ellis himself had included just such an example in his case studies of lesbians. 'Miss M.', whom Ellis defined as a true invert, even though she had never made love, in the physical sense, to other women, and preferred her relationships to remain on the level of 'exalted feelings', had come across a translation of Krafft-Ebing's *Psychopathia Sexualis*, in which he expounded his theory of homosexuality as a sign of degeneracy and hereditary taint. Before reading it she had no idea that her feelings for other women were in any way abnormal, but from the book she discovered that 'feelings like mine were "unnatural and depraved" and "under the ban of society"'. As Faderman points out, one wonders how many romantic friends, who had previously felt themselves to be perfectly healthy, suddenly saw themselves as perverted, even though their behaviour had in no way changed, as a result of the sexologists' formulations. Could Stopes' extreme condemnation of lesbianism have been a consequence of just such a process? It is not known how many letters Stopes received from lesbians, but given the negative attitude displayed in her books one assumes not many. Hall cites two: one from a woman who feared she had somehow transmitted her inversion to her former lover's son; and one from a woman who was worried about whether it was all right to live with her friend. Stopes replied to the latter that it was all right to live with her friend 'on rational, hygienic lines, without any hysterical excess', but that they must never go in for 'mutual self-abuse which often leads to very considerable nervous breakdown'.

Marie Stopes' attempt to 'marry' sexology and feminism was as unsuccessful, in terms of feminism, as her marriages were in real life. This analysis demonstrates clearly the anti-feminist implications of the sexological model, and its fundamental incompatibility with a feminist model of sexuality. The status of sexology as science, and Stopes' socialization as a scientist, resulted in her initial commitment to female sexual autonomy being undermined by an essentially phallocentric model of sexuality, in which sex was reduced to a coital imperative. Far from empowering women, which earlier feminist sexual theorists had sought to do, it reinforced male power in heterosexual relationships by eroticizing male dominance and female submission and underpinning them by so-called 'laws of love'. The emphasis on birth control, which was intended to give women control over their own bodies, made it more difficult for women to resist a sexual practice which many of them experienced as oppressive, and to define their own sexual needs and desires. Stopes' model of sexuality also undermined relationships between women, by defining them as unnatural and perverted, and helped to fuel the anti-spinster backlash.

Thus, although Stopes was in tune with the 'new feminism' of the interwar years, she was implicated in the decline of the 'old feminism', and the depoliticization of sexuality. Although further research would be necessary in order to establish to what extent her model of sexuality became part of 'common-sense' knowledge, her success in reaching a mass, popular audience, which sexologists such as Ellis never achieved directly, must make her a key figure in the dissemination of the sexological model. There were many others, however, who lacked her popular appeal, but as members of the medical profession had considerable power to educate and influence the behaviour of many 'ordinary' people. In the following chapter we shall examine the doctors' prescriptions about heterosexual relations.

Notes

1 These figures relate only to editions published in Britain. Other English language editions were also published in Australia, Canada, India, and the USA; an English edition was also published in Braille. The main sources of these and all subsequent bibliographical details are Hall (1978a) and Eaton and Warnick (1977).
2 I myself have clear memories of them being read and discussed by students when I was an undergraduate in the late 1950s.
3 Unless otherwise stated all biographical references in this chapter are to Hall (1978a).
4 Maude's biography of Stopes, published in 1924, was virtually dictated by Stopes herself (Hall, 1978a).
5 There are many similarities between Sanger's and Stopes' views on sexuality. (Sanger's own marriage manual will be discussed in the following chapter.) As far as birth control was concerned, however, the two women were soon to become and remain rivals.
6 This included the launching of the Society for Constructive Birth Control and Racial Progress, together with its journal, *Birth Control News*. There were also lecture tours, public meetings, and even a film, entitled *Maisie's Marriage*.
7 Stopes (1935), p. 44; Stopes (1918), p. xiii.
8 *Ibid.*, pp. 18–19; p. 28.
9 Olive Schreiner, with whose writings Stopes was familiar, also had this idea, which she discussed with Havelock Ellis. He corresponded with Stopes on the subject and conducted investigations of his own, which he published in an article (acknowledging his debt to Stopes), which was eventually incorporated into Volume II of the *Studies*. Stopes did not specifically link the second peak to ovulation. The relationship between ovulation and menstruation had not yet been demonstrated. She also argued that woman's rhythm was subject to considerable individual variation and could be depressed by factors such as overwork or fatigue.
10 Stopes (1918), pp. 38–9.
11 *Ibid.*, p. 41; p. 53; p. 43.
12 *Ibid.*, p. 45; p. 48; p. 50.
13 *Ibid.*, p. 68; p. 70; p. 64; p. 97. Together with most contemporary sexologists she also attributed the majority of uterine disorders to the lack of orgasm.
14 Stopes (1928), p. 6.
15 Stopes (1926).
16 Stopes (1928), p. 41.
17 *Ibid.*, pp. 42–44; p. 123, emphasis in original. She also advised strongly against coitus interruptus and the use of sheaths on the same grounds. She had hoped to

include a prescription for the prostatic extracts in the Appendix, but a 'distinguished doctor of medicine' who read the proofs advised against it, and Stopes could only suggest, in its place, that 'readers desirous of following the author's advice. . . . consult their physicians for details of treatment' (Stopes, 1928, p. 205). She did not actually recommend prostatic extracts as a cure for lesbianism, but this would be a logical inference from her argument.

18 Stopes (1929), p. 157; p. 41; p. 156; p. 145.
19 Stopes (1928), pp. 30–32.
20 *Ibid.*, p. 109.
21 *Ibid.*, p. 84; p. 91; p. 71; p. 67; p. 135. Stopes also wrote a play, *Vectia*, which tells the story of her sexual 'ignorance' and 'deprivation' and the nullity suit she brought against her first husband. It was denied a performing licence by the Lord Chancellor.
22 Stopes (1928), p. xi.
23 Lewis (1979).
24 Feminist critiques of science are now numerous. Those which I have found most useful include Bleier (1984) and Wallsgrove (1980).
25 Her frequent use of essentialist concepts such as 'strongly sexed', 'undersexed', and 'oversexed', which later became very common in sex manuals and in popular speech, is also a reflection of this kind of physiological reductionism.
26 She did claim that she possessed such information and that it would be published elsewhere, but I have been unable to track it down.
27 Hall (1978a), p. 154.
28 Carpenter's version of this idea is contained in a short pamphlet, *Sex-Love, and its place in a free society* (1894) and was subsequently published in *Love's Coming-of-Age* (1896). It would be interesting to discover how Carpenter came to develop this idea, and what his interest was, as a homosexual man, in theorizing in this way about heterosexual sex. It would also be interesting to know why Stopes was so impressed by Carpenter, given her strong aversion to homosexuality. She sent him her manuscript of *Married Love*, which he pronounced 'excellent and most enlightening', and invited her to his home, where they went through it together page by page (Hall, 1978a, p. 12). Later, he was to become one of the patrons of her clinic.
29 *Woman's Pictorial*, 11 March 1922.
30 Hall (1978a). The quotation is taken from Stopes' *A Journal from Japan* (1910), entry dated 24 October 1908.
31 Stopes (1918), p. 187, emphasis in original.
32 Examples of these photographs can be seen in Hall (1978), and one of them has been used as the cover illustration of that book.
33 The most recent and comprehensive study of the 'back-to-the-home-movement' during this period is Beddoe (1989). The 'new feminism' and its implications have been discussed by Jane Lewis (1975); for a different interpretation which focuses on the sexual aspects of the 'new feminism', see Jeffreys (1985), especially Chapters 7 and 8.
34 In common with most of her contemporary birth controllers, Stopes believed in the sterilisation of the unfit, but did not publicise this in the early days as she thought the public was not yet ready for it.
35 Ellis (1921). *Coital Interlocking: a physiological discovery* is the title of an article by Stopes, originally published in the CBC Bulletin no. 2, 1930. It was reprinted in *Clinical Medicine and Surgery*, vol. 38, no. 3, March 1931, pp. 179–180. It was also reprinted as a Mothers' Clinic pamphlet in 1952. In *Married Love* there was a very veiled suggestion that mutual masturbation between married couples might be advisable during pregnancy; usually, however, masturbation was mentioned by Stopes only with disapproval.

36 *The Practitioner*, July 1923.
37 Stopes (1929), p. 11; p. 5. Sanger (1928), p. 18; p. 126; p. 132. Haire (1930), p. 175. For further discussion of the Sex Reform Congress of 1929, see Jeffreys (1985), from where the term 'Sexual First Aid' has been borrowed.
38 *The Woman's Leader*, 12 May 1921, my emphasis.
39 Hall (1978a), p. 187; all subsequent biographical details and quotations are from this source unless otherwise stated.
40 Stopes (1926), p. 55.
41 Ellis (1915) vol, II, p. 137; Faderman (1981). In late Victorian and Edwardian England many women might have preferred non-genital expressions of love, whether or not they consciously identified themselves as lesbians. The campaigns against the double standard and the feminist critiques of male sexuality may well have led many women to view physical sexual activity, even between women, as male-defined and therefore inappropriate to the expression of their feelings of tenderness and mutual trust and respect. Ellis' 'Miss M.' may perhaps have exemplified such an attitude. Ellis and other sexologists had by this time formally redefined homosexuality as *in*version rather than *per*version (the latter referring to phenomena such as sado-masochism, urolagnia etc.). They nevertheless continued to refer to it frequently as a perversion, and Stopes herself never ceased to refer to it as such, except when she called it simply 'homosexual vice'. Despite her avowed aversion to homosexuality, female and male, she developed close friendships with one or two male homosexuals, notably Edward Carpenter and Lord Alfred Douglas.

Chapter 7

Teaching What Comes Naturally?
The Politics of Desire in the Marriage Manuals of the '20s and '30s

> The wife must be *taught*, not only how to behave in coitus, but above all, how and what to feel in this unique act!, *Van de Velde (1928), p. 232.*

The inter-war period witnessed the birth of the modern sex manual, written with the explicit aim of teaching the 'facts of life' to 'ordinary' people. It was chiefly by this means that the ideas of Havelock Ellis and other sexologists were disseminated, and the sexological model became part of the popular consciousness. Very few members of the general public had direct access to sexological literature at this time, since both sales and borrowing from libraries were restricted to people such as doctors, lawyers, and scientific researchers. Some feminists were able to obtain them through the Cavendish-Bentinck Library, which was housed in the International Women's Suffrage Club.[1] Others would have had access to sexological literature through membership of organizations such as the Association of Moral and Social Hygiene, which had its origins in the campaign to repeal the Contagious Diseases Acts, and continued throughout this period to campaign against state regulation of prostitution and to raise the age of consent. Most 'ordinary' people, however, were denied access to sexological literature, and the authors of marriage manuals saw themselves as radical in breaking what they called this 'conspiracy of silence'. It is probably no accident that they chose to adopt the same phrase which feminists had used in their campaigns against the double standard, but the 'facts' which the marriage manuals purveyed were very different from what feminists had called 'the *real* facts of life'.

Sexologists and sex reformers regarded 'ordinary' people as generally ignorant and in need of sexual enlightenment. They believed it was important to popularize the new science, but that the only people with the necessary credentials to teach it and give practical advice were doctors. Marie Stopes, despite her excellent scientific credentials, was regarded with hostility and suspicion by the medical profession, who considered her unqualified to meddle in what they defined as essentially medical matters. The role of the medical profession in the social control of women in the nineteenth century has been well documented.[2] This intervention of the medical profession into the field of sexual relations can also be seen as an extension of the medicalization of reproduction and motherhood which had already been established by the early twentieth century, and which extended the degree of patriarchal control over women's lives in these traditionally female spheres. Some of those who assumed the mantle of 'sex expert' specialized in gynaecology, and were also involved in the birth control movement, though many were general practitioners, sometimes with an interest in the relatively new fields of psychology and psychoanalysis. They included a small but significant number of women doctors, to whom the expanding birth control movement offered an opportunity of making their mark in an overwhelmingly male-dominated profession. All the doctors claimed to be 'in touch' with ordinary men and women and to understand their sexual problems. They frequently claimed that many of the women presenting themselves in their surgeries and clinics with a variety of physical and 'nervous' disorders were, usually without knowing it, 'really' suffering from sexual deprivation. The marriage manuals ostensibly represented a form of 'treatment' for such problems, and a means of promoting sexual health.[3]

Marital Maladjustment: Teaching Women what to Feel

The explicit rationale of the inter-war marriage manual, and of sex education literature in general, was the prevention and cure of sexual 'maladjustment' in marriage. This was seen not only as the primary cause of marital unhappiness and instability, but as a threat to the institution of marriage, and thus to the social order itself. The rising divorce rate, following the Divorce Act of 1923, was a cause of considerable concern, and during the early 1930s there was something of a 'moral panic' about an alleged increase in juvenile delinquency, which was attributed to 'broken homes', as the following letter to *The Times* indicates:

> Experience is teaching us more and more the importance of matrimonial discord, not only in the health and happiness of the parents, but in the well-being of the children. In a large proportion of 'difficult' children in our clinics their delinquencies and abnormalities of character and conduct are found to be due in part to conditions of disharmony between the parents. . . . Medical science gives ample and increasing evidence of the importance of sexual discord as a factor in matrimonial disputes.[4]

The writers went on to suggest that 'more scientific handling of the factor of matrimonial discord would very considerably strengthen our attack on the kindred social problems of divorce and child delinquency', and there is evidence that at least one London magistrates' court regularly referred the parents of juvenile offenders for sexual counselling. The new sex experts were convinced that the cause of marital disharmony was almost invariably sexual discontent, and they saw it as their task to teach husbands and wives the sexual techniques which would promote mutual sexual adjustment, thereby restoring stability to marriage and thus to the social order:

> Marriage being the mainstay of modern society, its widespread disruption involves not only individual happiness but also the security of our social order.... If we succeed through practical advice in increasing marital happiness ... we shall feel that we have fulfilled our mission, namely, to tighten dangerously relaxed conjugal ties.[5]

Many sex experts harnessed religion to legitimate the new doctrine of sexual enlightenment. Marriage manuals usually had a strongly evangelical tone, often referring to heterosexual intercourse as a 'sacrament', and there would often be a preface written by a clergyman. Although the Church, like the medical profession, was by no means unanimous in its attitudes towards sex and birth control, the impression given was that 'progressive' doctors and clergy were united in preaching a new gospel of hope, of personal happiness and fulfilment through the achievement of mutual sexual harmony in marriage.[6]

The main cause of marital discord was defined as sexual 'ignorance', though often this was a euphemism for women's dislike of sexual intercourse. As one minister of religion expressed it:

> Very often wives remain sexually unawakened, and therefore inclined to dislike sexual intercourse. When that happens husbands do not experience what they long for, and are apt to be sexually starved.... Being strained, repressed and strung-up, they [husbands and wives] find that little things irritate them to an absurd degree.

He warned wives that it was not enough for them to submit to their husbands out of duty or simply in order to have children. It was their duty to consent to their husbands' arousal of their sexual feelings. He implied that since God had ordained that husband and wife should be one flesh, prudery was contrary to God's law. He assured them that sex intimacy was a 'natural, clean and right thing', and insisted, with an insidious mixture of threat and emotional manipulation:

> you *must* be willing to be awakened, and must let yourself go till you are carried away by spontaneous desire.... If you do not consent to be awakened your husband will be deeply disappointed and feel hurt. He will not call it purity, he will call it prudery; and he will be right.

He also warned husbands to be patient and considerate, for it was a 'fact' that only a small minority of women were capable of feeling spontaneous sexual desire. In the vast majority of cases that capacity had to be awakened in them by their husbands: 'They can feel, but they have to be made to feel'.[7]

The assumption that sexual disharmony was the root cause of all marital discord made it possible to deflect criticisms of marriage as an institution and to side-step questions of the power relations between the sexes. Indeed most of the 'experts' assumed that women's emancipation had already been achieved, and occasionally suggested that it might even have gone too far. Some who claimed to be in favour of the increasing social and economic independence of women described the 'new woman' in terms which betrayed an underlying anti-feminism:

> The feminine type which still prevailed as late as 1900 has now fast disappeared. We are all aware of the outward signs of this radical change; women are becoming 'masculinized'; cropped hair, smoking, thinning cures, hectic flirting, sports, and the resulting angularity of hitherto rounded contours, are so many symptoms which cannot pass unnoticed.[8]

The only remaining obstacle to sexual equality lay, apparently, in the sphere of sexual fulfilment. This was the *only* aspect of 'women's rights' which the experts unanimously endorsed and which they set out wholeheartedly to promote. As Kenneth Walker pointed out, however, the fact that the husband often failed to satisfy his wife's sexual 'needs' was not invariably his fault. It was not easy to be the husband of an emancipated woman. Feminism had upset the balance of power between the sexes, and especially in marriage:

> what is found in the greater world outside is sometimes only too apparent in the miniature world of the home. Woman has gained her independence but the nature of sexual love remains the same. In the act of physical union the male must still play the dominant part, and if he has sunk to second place in the home, he is likely to be unsuccessful in the sphere of love.[9]

This suggests that the 'problem' with which marriage manuals were really grappling was not so much sexual maladjustment as feminism, and the threat, or in some cases perhaps the reality, of men's loss of power in heterosexual relationships. The sexological model provided a means of restructuring the hetero-relations which feminism had disturbed, and restoring the balance of power in men's favour. As we have seen, Ellis' concept of women's 'erotic rights' was based on a complete denial of female sexual autonomy. For him the 'art of love' meant orchestrating female sexual pleasure in such a way as to transform submission to the male into an 'erotic' experience for women, as it already was for men. Ellis himself, however, gave very little in the way of explicit advice on sexual technique. It was left to the doctors to translate the basic principles established by Ellis into practice, and to teach women – more precisely, to teach *men* how to teach their wives – how to participate actively and enthusiastically in their own sexual slavery. The 'Bible' of marriage manuals expressed it emphatically: 'The wife must be *taught*, not only how to behave in coitus, but above all, how and what to feel in this unique act!'[10]

Marriage manuals were extremely didactic and prescriptive, and reflected the hierarchical relationship between doctor and patient, and the attitude that 'doctor knows best'. They insisted that the education and practical advice they offered was grounded in scientific facts and laws, the implication being that no sane or rational person would challenge or contradict it. Sexual relationships and practices were expressed not only in terms of what was 'natural' or 'normal', but in terms of health and sickness. The primary prescription was that 'sex is good for you', and especially for women: 'Sexual activity, *in itself*, has *an extremely favourable influence on a woman's mind and body*'. Women were assured that regular and frequent coitus would cure a wide variety of ills, from fatigue and nervous tension to menstrual irregularity and pain. Psychologically, coitus was claimed to be 'a real psychic panacea', which developed 'all the latent strength and sweetness' of a woman's character and gave her 'serenity and poise'.[11]

'Sex' was of course shorthand, not merely for heterosexual intercourse, but for a particular form of heterosexual intercourse. Ellis' concept of courtship was accepted and taught as axiomatic, and encapsulated in the imagery of 'The Chase' and 'Man the Hunter', which meant that in every act of sexual intercourse the woman needed to be 'wooed and won', as decreed by nature. Leonora Eyles, for instance, declared: 'Every woman likes a man to be, at times, something of a caveman; she likes surprise; she likes to run away and be captured and made love to'. Courtenay Beale wrote that 'it is of nature's own decree and contrivance that man should be the pursuer, woman the pursued, in the great drama of sex; that her coyness should increase and stimulate his eagerness', and that this coyness 'forms an integral part of woman's original endowment'. Estelle Cole, who also ran sex education classes for young girls, urged women to remember

> that man is a hunter by nature. He likes to chase his game. His pleasure lies in the pursuit. With capture and possession there often comes loss of interest; so that the wise woman restrains herself at such passionate moments, in order that he may be kept eager in his pursuit.

Margaret Sanger, the well-known American feminist birth control campaigner, who had a close relationship with Havelock Ellis, also asserted that 'nature and tradition have decreed that man shall be the wooer, the pursuer, the huntsman. Man is the aggressor . . . adventurous, primitive man does not value highly an easy capture'.[12]

Most of the marriage manuals were obviously written with a predominantly male readership in mind, and some were explicitly addressed to husbands, since it was they whom the experts charged with the responsibility for initiating and directing their wives' sexual education. The relationship between husband and wife was usually conceptualized in terms of a teacher-pupil relationship, with the medical expert hovering in the background, guiding the teacher. The newly married woman was often referred to as a 'novice', sometimes even a 'child', and the early months of married life were an 'apprenticeship', or 'school' in which the wife received her 'elementary education'.[13] Husbands were exhorted to be patient and considerate, and assured that the long-term rewards would be far greater than any pleasure they might gain from selfish and clumsy attempts at immediate gratification. Women were 'slow' to arouse and needed to be made 'ready' for coitus; considerable time and, above all, regular practice would be needed in order to establish mutual, and preferably simultaneous, orgasm, which was the marriage manuals' 'Holy Grail'. The strong prevalence of musical imagery tended to cast husbands in the role of conductors, or as orchestrating their wives' sexual pleasure. The pages of Van de Velde's *Ideal Marriage* are littered with words like 'prelude' and 'leitmotiv', and husbands were actually instructed how to stimulate their wives to 'concert pitch' by playing on the clitoris! While the clumsy, inept husband was symbolized by an orang-utan trying to play the violin, woman was variously described as a harp or other delicate instrument who, provided that her husband conscientiously studied the book of rules, would eventually reward him with melodious tunes:

'woman is a harp who only yields her secrets of melody to the master who knows how to handle her' . . . the husband must study the harp and the art of music . . . this is the book of rules for his earnest and reverent study . . . his reward comes when the harp itself is transformed into an artist in melody, entrancing the initiator.[14]

Van de Velde's *Ideal Marriage* was extremely influential. It was translated into English by Stella Browne and soon after publication in 1928 it rapidly became regarded as the 'Bible' of sex manuals, a status which it continued to enjoy right up to the 1970s.[15] Van de Velde was a Dutch gynaecologist who was hailed by a historian of sex research as the man who 'taught a generation how to copulate'. Of all the texts of the inter-war period *Ideal Marriage* is the most thoroughly medical and clinical in its approach and most other writers used it as their principal source after Ellis, Bloch, and Forel. One of its major themes is the relationship between sexuality, power, and violence. While Van de Velde warned husbands of the need to be considerate and sensitive to their wives, especially in the early days of marriage, he was adamant that pain and violence were inherent in sexual intercourse. He included a lengthy discussion of Ellis' concept of courtship and the biologically inevitable association between love and pain, concluding:

> What both man and woman, driven by obscure primitive urges, wish to feel in the sexual act, is the essential force of *maleness* which expresses itself in a sort of violent and absolute *possession* of the woman. And so both of them can and do exult in a certain degree of male aggression and dominance – whether actual or apparent – which proclaims this essential force.[16]

He admitted that the infliction of pain on a woman, as a prelude to or as part of coitus, reflected the man's pleasure in manifesting power over her, but argued that since this was an outcome and survival of the primitive process of courtship, it must be 'an almost or quite normal constituent of the sexual impulse in man'. Other texts, too, underlined the inherently violent nature of the sexual act, and stressed that most women wanted to be deeply, even 'savagely' penetrated, 'even if that penetration should imply suffering'. Some women, they claimed, were incapable of having orgasms unless they were beaten and brutalized.[17]

The experts conceded that, for most women, this 'natural' association between sex and violence was not, at first, acceptable. The first experience of coitus was often painful and traumatic, and could lead to permanent aversion. Margaret Sanger wrote that some women never got over the shock of discovering that all men want is 'perfunctory sex gratification', and Estelle Cole quoted a recently married woman who said that if she had known what 'wifely duty' meant she would never have married. According to Beale, most brides never suspected such 'male brutality' as was revealed on the wedding night: 'she has not been won but "humbled", to use an expressive archaism, and a permanent, insuperable repugnance to conjugal relations may have been set up'. Husbands were given advice on how to overcome the problem with a minimum of pain, such as by gradual dilation of the hymen, and urged to seek medical advice in cases of unusual difficulty. But ultimately, women had to be *taught* how and what to feel, because they themselves did not really know what they wanted: 'A woman . . . may be quite unaware of just what she does want and courtship and preliminary love-making by the male are necessary to focus her feelings and make her aware of the real presence of sex desire'.[18]

For Van de Velde, the process of 'genital initiation' was crucial, and conceptualized, significantly, in terms of a power struggle. However intensely the couple loved each other, he wrote, it would be necessary to overcome the bride's 'spiritual and bodily resistance' to sexual intercourse by 'wooing her into compliance'. He believed that in the case of 'novices' the resistance was real, and not, according to Ellis' model, pretence. This did not mean, however, that they did not desire sexual intercourse, merely that they were in the grip of a struggle between their instinctive dread and the equally instinctive desire to yield: 'their movements and expressions betray a profound struggle between the elemental urge to yield and a sort of shyness, and instinctive dread; and the victory of desire over dread is often very slow and difficult'. The bride's 'dread' was not primarily a fear of physical pain, but had 'far deeper origins and significance', and masked an 'unconscious resistance'. Many experts acknowledged this problem of the bride's aversion or resistance to coitus. Isabel Hutton, for example, wrote that 'the idea that they are beginning the sex life creates a feeling almost of repulsion', and admitted that in some women the sexual instinct did not develop until after years of marriage. Some women never experienced a desire for sexual intercourse; nevertheless, however distasteful it was to them, they were urged to engage in coitus in the hope that the desire would develop, for 'they must realise that in wedlock it is natural and proper to develop such feelings and that such emotions will gradually come to them'. Precisely what 'such feelings' were was not always made explicit, but some experts stated unequivocally that a woman must learn to desire actual penetration: 'if the bride's modesty and instinctive resistance raise obstacles that are too great for him to seduce her, consummation of the marriage is better postponed ... until she has accustomed herself to physical contact and learned to desire actual penetration'. Hutton's comment on those who never developed such feelings was chilling: 'If after a year or so the woman does not begin to take part with her husband in the unions, then she is probably an abnormal person and it would have been better for her to remain a spinster'.[19]

Most experts were prepared to accept that women's sexual feelings, once awakened, fluctuated to some extent during the monthly cycle, and advised husbands to be sensitive to this. None of them, however, went as far as Marie Stopes in suggesting that coitus should be restricted as far as possible to the wife's periods of maximum sexual desire. Van de Velde was extremely critical of Stopes and devoted several pages to a refutation of her 'law of periodicity', arguing that recurrent ten days' abstentions from sexual intercourse would be harmful. He considered the theory of 'the famous biologist' (whom he refused to call 'Dr', on the grounds that she was not medically qualified) to be extremely risky. He thought she would have a very bad influence on women, especially anyone who was 'somewhat tepid and deficient in sexuality', and would undermine the husband in his role as erotic educator: 'Mrs Stopes' view might influence her to such an extent, that her husband's attempts at a cure by skilled erotic education, would be counteracted, and *both* partners harmed thereby'. He considered that the demand that the woman's wishes should be paramount was 'both unjust and, what is practically more important, incorrect', and that it offended against the 'fundamental principle of sexual altruism', according to which husbands and wives had equal rights and equal duties. In his sequel to *Ideal Marriage*, which was devoted to the subject of frigidity, he made it clear that no *real* man could possibly tolerate such a degree of female sexual autonomy as implied by Stopes:

I most emphatically advise both [husbands and wives] *not* to let themselves be deceived by such theories as those of *Marie Stopes*. . . . The consequences of such theories lead to heräism of the most dangerous sort, which will, sooner or later, drive a *real man* into the arms of another, owing to his sexual dissatisfaction and to involuntary feelings of revolt.[20]

Educating the Vagina

The same concern to preserve male dominance and female submission is evident in the marriage manuals' discussion of the female orgasm and the role of the clitoris. Although some acknowledged the existence of clitoral orgasms, most regarded the clitoris merely as an especially sensitive erogenous zone, to be 'used' to make a woman 'ready' for coitus, or to speed up her orgasm so that it coincided with her husband's ejaculation. Some also recommended clitoral manipulation as a last resort when ejaculation occurred too soon, but 'autotherapeutic measures' were definitely not encouraged. The clitoris was seen essentially as a tool which men could use to control female sexual response, rather than as evidence that women possessed the capability of controlling it themselves. Van de Velde argued that the clitoris was intended by nature to be stimulated in coitus. This was 'proved' by the fact that when excited it protruded downwards, 'seeming to urge and press towards the phallos [*sic*]'. He admitted, however, that this rarely happened in 'women of our race', for the extraordinary reason that most Western women suffered from a degree of 'arrested development' or 'genital infantilism', and the clitoris was placed too high! Overcoming this deficiency, he warned, would demand all the husband's knowledge and skill, but it was worth persevering, because it was possible that after years of active sex life the 'infantile type' would grow larger! 'In this respect, as in many others', added Van de Velde, 'practice makes perfect'. Detailed advice was given on the sexual techniques most likely to produce clitoral and vaginal stimulation during coitus. 'Perfect and natural coitus', wrote Van de Velde, would give woman 'a blend of both types of stimulation', resulting in 'supreme pleasure' and very rapid orgasm: 'in ideal communion the stimulation will generally be focussed on and in the vagina, including introitus and portio. And this will be fully adequate for such a variety and intensity of sensation as will culminate in the orgasm'. In the event of failure, clitoral manipulation was preferable to leaving the woman unsatisfied.[21]

The experts found themselves in a dilemma concerning which positions to recommend during coitus: on the one hand logic seemed to demand that they recommend those positions which afforded women most pleasure, since one of the main motivations for writing marriage manuals at all was to enable women to achieve orgasms from coitus; on the other hand they felt unable to recommend those positions because they were precisely the ones in which the 'natural' roles of the sexes were reversed, i.e. positions which rendered the man relatively passive, with the woman active and in control. Both Van de Velde and Haire, for instance, acknowledged that women were now recognized as active sexual beings and were entitled to take the sexual initiative occasionally. But they strongly advised that the only positions which should be regularly adopted were those which enabled the man 'to entirely play the active part allotted to him'. They warned that too great a degree of female activity and male passivity was 'directly contrary to the natural relationship of the sexes, and must bring unfavourable consequences if it becomes habitual'. They argued that what became known later as the 'missionary position' *must* be more natural because it allowed 'the two primitive instincts, the woman's desire to surrender herself and the man's desire to possess her', to be 'completely satisfied'.[22]

Of all the authors of marriage manuals during this period, the one who paid most attention to the role of the clitoris and the nature of the female orgasm was Helena Wright, who to some extent anticipated the clitoral *versus* vaginal orgasm debate within feminism in the late 1960s and early 1970s. For this reason there has been in recent years a renewal of feminist interest in her work and ideas, and it has been suggested that her recognition of the location of the female orgasm in the clitoris led her to reject penile penetration as the best sexual practice for women. In order to examine this claim I undertook a detailed investigation of her work and background, which included interviews with her authorized biographer, Barbara Evans, and with Helena Wright herself, shortly before her death in 1982. These interviews enabled me to explore some of the ambiguities I discovered in her two marriage manuals, *The Sex Factor in Marriage* and *More About the Sex Factor in Marriage*. They also gave me an insight into the role of women doctors in promoting the sexological model of sexuality.[23]

Helena Wright

Like Marie Stopes, Helena Wright was both a pioneer of birth control and a sex reformer. Though not as well known as Stopes she was probably at least as influential, owing to her much longer involvement in the birth control movement, as well as the fact that she was a practising gynaecologist. She was an extremely assertive woman, who believed in women's right to economic independence from men and in 'open' marriages, but she never defined herself as a feminist. Born in 1887, Wright trained as a doctor and gynaecologist and in the late 1920s became involved in the birth control movement. At the invitation of Margery Spring Rice she joined the staff of the clinic in Telford Road, North Kensington, the third to be established in London, after the Mothers' Clinic (founded by Marie Stopes) and the Walworth Road Clinic (founded by the Malthusian League). She first met Stopes in 1918, shortly after she had read the recently published *Married Love*, and commented:

We discussed it a lot. I remember Marie flouncing all over those rocks in long white lace dresses. It was quite comical. She asked me to read the text of her next book 'Wise Parenthood'. I agreed – on condition that she let me take out all the nonsense. The fact that that book has no nonsense in it was due to me.[24]

In 1930 she was invited by Margaret Pyke to help form the National Birth Control Association, an umbrella organization uniting all the birth control clinics in the country, and later to be renamed the Family Planning Association. In the same year she was also invited to address the Lambeth Conference of bishops of the Church of England on the subject of birth control, and claimed that it was her speech which finally succeeded in persuading them to vote that sexual intercourse in marriage could allowably occur when no reproduction was intended. She was also instrumental in securing the provision of training in methods of birth control in medical schools, and after the second world war became a prime mover in the formation of the International Planned Parenthood Federation. She continued to work at the Telford Road clinic for thirty years, retiring at the age of 70, but continuing in her private practice, her international work, and the training of doctors, especially from overseas.

Like Stopes, Wright's work as a sex reformer appears to have originated in her own disappointment in heterosexual activity. As a young married woman she found sex 'boring', and although she did not say so to her husband, she thought to herself 'there must be more to it than this'. She too read the works of Havelock Ellis and other sexologists, as well as *Married Love*, and her first book, *The Sex Factor in Marriage*, was a simple and concise distillation of her research into the subject. A close examination of the text suggests that the most formative influence on her thinking at this time was Van de Velde, whose *Ideal Marriage* had been published in English two years earlier. Her book's main theme was the familiar one of sexual maladjustment in marriage, and its aim was to teach couples how to achieve the 'perfect sex-act'. Sexual maladjustment was seen as the result of ignorance about the differences between female sexuality and male sexuality. Wright argued that male sexuality was aroused spontaneously and quickly satisfied, whereas women were not only slow to respond sexually – their sexuality needed to be awakened by their husbands: 'his is the magic touch that will awaken his wife's physical nature'. She believed that the mechanism of physical satisfaction was different in the two sexes: 'She needs arousing; he needs relief'. Repeating the familiar musical refrain, 'a woman's body can be regarded as a musical instrument awaiting the hand of an artist', she insisted that, however willing a woman was to be aroused – and it was her *duty* to be willing – it was not something she could do for herself:

If a wife remains cold and unresponsive, it may be the husband's fault; however willing she is, she cannot arouse her own feelings. On the other hand, no amount of skill and tenderness on the husband's part can be successful unless the wife *is* willing to be roused.[25]

In most respects Helena Wright's first marriage manual differed little from other contemporary texts, with one major exception: she paid more attention than most to the role of the clitoris in female sexual satisfaction, and it is this aspect of her writing that has attracted the attention of some feminists interested in the clitoral *versus* vaginal orgasm controversy, and its implications for heterosexual relations. Beatrix Campbell has claimed that Wright believed that penile penetration was not essential to female sexual pleasure, and that she challenged the 'penis-vagina fixation'. Campbell also claims that in the sequel, *More About the Sex Factor in Marriage*, Wright rejected the idea that female orgasms are located in the vagina, thus anticipating the critique of dominant heterosexual ideology which feminists were not to launch until the 1970s. A close reading of both texts does not, however, support such an interpretation. My own reading and my interview with Helena Wright, shortly before her death in 1982, suggest that not only did she regard coitus as the most natural and best means to achieve sexual pleasure, but that she considered the vagina to have *greater* potential than the clitoris for female sexual pleasure.[26]

In her first book Wright argued that the sensations provided by clitoris and vagina were different in kind, but that the vagina was 'capable of an almost equal acuteness'. Vaginal sensation had to be awakened by love-play, and the establishing of acute pleasure by stimulation of the vaginal walls was sometimes only accomplished after months of marriage. In her discussion of the 'perfect sex-act' she elaborated the point: 'Sensation in the clitoris seems to be natural to every normal woman, but it often takes considerable time and patience to establish a vivid degree of sensitiveness in the vagina'. She stressed that there was considerable variation between women, and within women according to mood, but asserted that the clitoris was essentially the gateway to the more 'mature' vaginal sensation:

> Theoretically it might be said that the ideal type of feminine sensation is concerned with the vagina alone, but that ideal is seldom realised. As a general rule it is true to say that a woman has not attained a full sex maturity until she is able to feel pleasure as acutely in the vagina as in the region of the clitoris. ... Nearly all women find vaginal sensation through, as it were, the gateway of clitoris sensation. ... For the full experience of the orgasm or sexual climax, intense feeling must be generally present in both places.

In her discussion of masturbation, which she argued was at best a substitute for coitus, she warned that if practised to excess before marriage it could make adjustment difficult: 'Especially can this occur in women, because the stimulation most generally used before marriage is purely of the clitoris, *whereas in perfect marital stimulation the vaginal sensation predominates'*. Her views were thus entirely consistent with those expressed by other sexologists and sex reformers on the dangers of clitoral fixation.[27]

As a result of her work in the birth control clinic and in her private practice it gradually began to dawn on Wright that not only did most women not enjoy sexual intercourse, they did not even *expect* to enjoy it. She recalled the precise occasion on which the penny finally dropped. She asked a working-class woman at the clinic: 'Do you enjoy having intercourse with your husband, as you should do?' At first the woman looked blank; even when the question was repeated she did not reply immediately but appeared (according to Wright) to be thinking: 'I trust my doctor – she must mean something'. Eventually she said 'But doctor, what is there to enjoy?' It was this and many similar experiences during the 1930s that provided the impetus to publish the second book, *More About the Sex Factor in Marriage*, which was designed to amplify 'certain fundamentals' essential to the understanding of heterosexual relations, which were more subtle and complicated that she had originally thought.[28]

According to Wright, the most common misunderstandings were:

1   failure to grasp the difference between orgasm and sexual response in the erogenous zones;
2   failure to understand the unique role played by the clitoris;
3   unconscious adherence to preconceived notions of what women ought to experience during intercourse, based on the male rather than the female pattern.

Essentially the problem was that men, on the basis of their own experience, expected women to be quickly and easily aroused and to have an orgasm as quickly and easily as they did, induced by the movements of the penis in the vagina – and most women expected the same. 'So strongly held and widespread is this expectation', she wrote,

> that it can be said to amount to a penis-vagina fixation in the mind of the public as far as orgasm is concerned. I have tested the truth of this observation hundreds of times, and when asked the question 'Where do you expect to feel an orgasm?' my patients always reply, 'In the vagina, of course, where else could I expect it?'

Wright believed that lack of vaginal orgasm made women feel that they were failures, and that it was necessary to question the assumption that the vagina is 'the natural place where a woman should feel an orgasm *at the beginning of her sexual experience*'. The last part of the sentence is crucial because it indicates that her thinking on this matter had remained basically unchanged. She still thought it was mainly a question of *time* before vaginal sensation was achieved.[29]

There was, however, some ambiguity in her argument. In Chapter 5 of the later book she discussed the female orgasm as though it were purely clitoral. In order to clarify the distinction between feeling pleasurably aroused and having an actual orgasm, she used the analogy of the sneeze: a build-up of tension, a short explosion, followed by relief. A sneeze, she wrote, 'occurs in the nose, and only in the nose'. This clearly implied that an orgasm occurs in the clitoris, and only in the clitoris, an impression strengthened by the fact that the remainder of the chapter was devoted to a detailed description of the clitoris, how to find it and how to discover its sensation. Wives were advised to discover for themselves the specific pattern of rhythmic friction their clitoris needed and to teach this to their husbands by moving their fingers for them. Wright conceded that this was something no man could do properly on his own, and that it meant that, temporarily, the wife had to take an active and the husband a passive role. But she emphasised that it was *only* for this specific purpose and only *after* the husband had awakened his wife's physical sensitivity by caressing her erogenous zones. In the following chapter Wright admitted that it was difficult to account for the apparent contradiction that the vagina, which functioned to produce orgasm in the penis, was relatively insensitive from the point of view of female sexual pleasure. She did attempt an explanation, however, but it was an explanation which was essentially no more than an elaboration of her original statement that clitoral sensation was the gateway to vaginal sensation:

> it looks as the sensory nerve endings [in the vagina] need practice and experience before they acquire full sensitivity ... the vagina appears to learn best and most quickly after successful experience with the clitoris has been established. The clitoris can, therefore, be regarded as a kind of teacher for the vagina.

She believed that, while all women had the capacity for clitoral orgasm, provided that the right kind of rhythmic friction was applied, most women had to *learn* how to achieve vaginal orgasm. While clitoral orgasm could be regarded as an end in itself in the early days, or months, of marriage, in the long term it was only to be regarded as a means to an end: 'If sensitive response can be induced to begin [in the vagina], sooner or later it will develop into orgasm capacity'. She emphasized that 'every wife should maintain an optimistic attitude and never give up hope', if necessary seeking expert help.[30]

The implication was that a wife who lacked vaginal orgasm was at best missing something or at worst a failure. It is hard to see how the women who wrote to Wright complaining that they 'only' had clitoral orgasms would be reassured by such advice. I took up this matter with her during the interview and received a somewhat defensive response. Why, I asked, had she placed so much emphasis on vaginal orgasm, when failure to achieve it clearly made so many women feel inadequate? Furthermore, she herself had told me that many women either did not enjoy penile penetration or positively disliked it. The example which she was fond of quoting was as follows: 'Doctor, have I got to put up with this? I can't bear it [the penis] pumping in and out!' Wright's response to my question was stern and unequivocal: she insisted that the vagina had *greater* capacity for sexual sensation than the clitoris and that coitus was the 'ultimate ideal' for maximum pleasure for the heterosexual couple. Moreover, it was 'unfair' to deny penetration to men. She reiterated the need to 'educate the vagina to experience sexual sensation', emphasizing that 'the clitoris should be fully used', but that 'vaginal friction could be just as pleasurable to the woman as to the man'. She insisted repeatedly that sexual intercourse 'uses the physiological potential of both sexes to the maximum', and argued that the reason that penetration *must* be ultimately pleasurable (to both sexes) lay in the reproductive significance of the sex act. If it were *not* pleasurable there would be no motivation to procreate and thus to maintain the species. Asked to explain why some women apparently never achieve vaginal orgasms she replied that in some women the vagina is 'dead'.[31]

This model of female sexual pleasure could hardly be said to constitute a challenge to the penis-vagina fixation. On the contrary, if anything it reinforced it. Helena Wright's interpretation of the role of the clitoris in female orgasm was no more than an elaboration of the general view of the clitoris as a tool which could be used to make women ready for coitus and to help them achieve orgasm from coitus. Although Wright gave women a slightly more active role in heterosexual intercourse, they were still represented as essentially dependent on men for sexual fulfilment. Her attitude towards lesbianism also supports this interpretation. As she had made no reference to lesbianism in either of her marriage manuals, I asked her whether it had been discussed among her contemporaries during the 1930s. She replied that it had not: that 'the most important issue at that time was reproduction', and that lesbianism was therefore seen as 'not relevant'. This lends support to my argument that the preoccupation with birth control during the inter-war period was significant in reinforcing the sexological model of sexuality along rigidly heterosexist and reproductive lines. It also helps to account for the enthusiasm of women doctors in teaching the 'facts of life' and promoting an essentially patriarchal model of sexuality. As doctors, these women were thoroughly socialized into the values and assumptions of the patriarchal medical profession, which made it difficult for them to appreciate the anti-feminist and anti-woman implications of the sexological model of sexuality. As women, they felt it was in the interests of women to be able to control their fertility, and as doctors they felt they had a special responsibility to enable them to do so. Thus their energies were channelled into providing 'sexual first aid', which in turn made it even more difficult for them to question a phallocentric model of sexuality, based on the coital imperative. Despite ample evidence that many women did not desire coitus, Wright, Stopes, and their co-workers in the birth control movement assumed that by making contraception available to women they were enabling them to control not only their fertility but also their sexuality. In fact, they were in many respects undermining their sexual autonomy even further.

The Politics of Frigidity: Resisting Nature or Male Power?

Despite the tremendous efforts expended by the experts, the vast majority of whom, it must be remembered, were male, to educate women and their vaginas, many women obstinately refused to be 'wooed into compliance'. The 'problem' of frigidity, which the 'art of love' had been designed to overcome, appeared to become more and more intractable as the 1920s wore on. Marriage manuals and sex reformers devoted more and more space to it, and whole volumes were written about the subject, giving the reader the impression that female sexual 'anaesthesia' was reaching epidemic proportions.

Although frigidity was usually defined simply as aversion to coitus, or failure to achieve orgasm from coitus, most experts believed that the problem was far more deep-rooted than such simple definitions implied. Woman was considered to be essentially frigid or 'cold': although she was biologically endowed with a sexual instinct, it did not emerge spontaneously but had to be 'awakened'. This could only be done by a man. Van de Velde made a double analogy between woman and ovum, man and sperm: just as the ovum could not develop without the sperm, he argued, so woman's sexual feelings could not develop without the active stimulation of the man. He also linked this with the theory of seminal absorption: he described woman's whole body as being 'saturated' by masculine materials, a process which he compared to the effects of the injection of serum. Unlike Stopes, he saw this as entirely a one-way process; nothing comparable was done to the man by the woman. Husbands were repeatedly warned that if they did not exercise great skill in the art of love-making they risked creating a permanently frigid wife. Nevertheless, the awakening of a woman's sexual instinct did not depend solely on her husband's skill and patience: she had to be *willing* to have it awakened. If she were not, no amount of artistry on the part of the husband, with the guiding hand of the expert, could succeed. Women were warned that they *must* be willing to have their sexual instinct awakened, or risk condemnation as prudes. Refusal to do so was seen as insubordination, an attempt by woman to assert her will in deliberate defiance of both men and nature: 'A woman does herself and her husband a great wrong when, for any reason, she exercises such cerebral control of her own sex desires that she will not let herself respond fully and eagerly to his advances'. Such a woman also ran the risk that her husband would 'naturally' seek consolation elsewhere:

> Let the plain truth be plainly and warningly stated. It is the man who has what he calls a frigid wife at home, with no ardour answering his ardour, suffering his caresses without returning them – palpably, unconcealedly apathetic – who will sooner or later be tempted to

seek consolation elsewhere; and while such a course must evoke the reprobation of the moralist, it will hardly excite the surprise of the student of human nature.[32]

The notion of a woman exercising control over her own sexuality was clearly deeply threatening to male power. Wilhelm Stekel, the recognized psychoanalytic authority on frigidity, who was frequently cited in the marriage manuals, expressed succinctly how he viewed the relationship between sexuality and male power: 'To be aroused by a man means acknowledging oneself as conquered'. Quoting approvingly from Stekel, Walter Gallichan agreed that 'the cold woman suffers from an inhibitory force, which is hidden, and expresses itself as "*I will not*"'. It is significant that most of the experts explained frigidity in terms of a power struggle between women and men, on both personal and societal levels. According to Norman Haire, there was a constant struggle between man and woman within marriage which was ceaselessly being renewed, because the woman refused to submit. In essence, the reason why the frigid woman could not have an orgasm was because she rebelled against being conquered:

The woman knows that with the orgasm her resistance melts, her last defence is gone, she surrenders, she forgoes her personality, 'the man can do as he likes with her'. And this is precisely the cause of her rebellion; she is willing to give herself, but not to lose herself, and therefore wants to avoid the orgasm. Her instinct to dominate is stronger than her sex hunger; she wants, while being subjected, to remain unconquered.

Haire did not explain how one could be subjected without being conquered; and he seemed astonished that the woman should insist on 'keeping her individuality even in bed'. 'Poor woman!' he said, 'She does not know that it is precisely by renouncing the strongest element of her personality that she preserves the essence of her femininity'.[33]

For Van de Velde, it was a double power struggle: between woman and man, and between the woman's desire to submit, which was the essence of her sexuality, and her 'will to power'. Biologically, woman was sexually dependent on man, and consequently female sexual desire was synonymous with the desire to submit to the male. Such was his determination to get this point across that one whole page of his argument was printed in capital letters. The following is a short extract:

SHE NOT ONLY ACCEPTS BUT DESIRES THIS DEPENDENCE, BECAUSE HER HIGHLY DEVELOPED INTUITIVE FEELING TELLS HER THE REASONS FOR THIS DEPENDENCE ARE BASED ON NATURAL (BIOLOGICAL) CAUSES.

DEPENDENCE IS ALWAYS CONNECTED WITH SUBMISSION, AND THE DESIRE FOR THE ONE INVOLVES THE OTHER. IN ADDITION TO THIS, NUMEROUS

POWERFUL INFLUENCES MAKING FOR SUBMISSION TO THE MALE ARE PRESENT IN SEXUAL CONNECTION, AS FAR AS THE WOMAN IS CONCERNED, SO THAT THE DESIRE FOR THIS CONNECTION, THE SEXUAL IMPULSE, IS ASSOCIATED IN THE WOMAN WITH A TENDENCY TO SUBMIT HERSELF.

He argued that in woman, the desire to submit was a kind of reversal of the will to power, which he believed was one of the strongest human impulses: 'FROM THIS COMES THE DESIRE FOR SUBORDINATION, PARTICULARLY FOR SUBMISSION TO THE MAN'. The 'psychological tragedy of woman' was that she desired submission with her whole soul but sought to gain power. If she won the struggle for power she lost the very thing she needed most, the protection and support of man. If, however, the man had enough strength of mind to oppose her struggle for power successfully, and wits enough to see behind 'the usually unpleasant glamour of modern slogans', and was able 'to understand the real nature of woman'; if he was capable of persuading his wife of 'the fruitlessness of further attempts to gain dominance', he would be able to arrest the course of the tragedy. 'If not', warned Van de Velde, 'it will take its course, to the injury of both'. He explained, with peculiar logic, that it was like a game in which the winner loses and the loser wins. '*Here*, likewise', he wrote,

> 'the woman who wins the game of the struggle for power, loses. Only if the man carries off the prize can both husband and wife win. If the woman wins, then both lose. The man loses much, but his work remains to him and he can make this a substitute. But the woman loses *everything* in her victory'.[34]

Frigidity, then, was seen as a form of *resistance*, a refusal not merely to comply with male sexual demands, but to accept the 'facts of life'. Frigidity was dangerous because it was *political*, an 'unconscious protest against man's supremacy'. All the male experts claimed to agree that the oppression of women by men must cease, and unjust laws be repealed, but they continued to maintain that ultimately male supremacy was a biological fact of life. In Van de Velde's words:

> The dependence of the woman on the man, and, in consequence, his supremacy in marriage and in Society, is based on biological and natural facts . . . [and] it is ridiculous to try, as is being done increasingly by certain people, to reverse the parts played in life by man and woman.

If 'certain people' persisted in trying to change the natural order in this way, he added, society would be bound to suffer, and, in the end, women most of all: 'If the primary processes of life, which are based on biological facts, are ignored, time will have its revenge. One cannot assault Nature with impunity'.

Walter Gallichan was even more explicit in connecting the alleged increase in frigidity with feminism, and especially the campaigns against the double standard:

> the cold natured woman is often an active supporter of reformative organisations, female emancipation crusades, purity campaigns, and societies for the suppression of vice . . . [she is] lacking understanding of the fundamental facts of life.

He believed that the increasing incidence of frigidity in modern times was 'distinctly a social manifestation', specifically 'a phase in woman's struggle for equal rights'. According to Van de Velde, however, the double standard had nothing to do with women's rights. 'But it is not *I*', he protested, 'who judge man and woman by a different standard; it is nature herself who has made the sexual act of far greater importance, both mentally and physically, to the woman'. It was nature, and not men, who had endowed men with sexual autonomy, and withheld it from women:

> only unbounded ignorance and superficiality or short-sighted pedantry could attribute 'double sexual morality' to the so-called domination of the woman by the man . . . nature gives man the greatest possible sexual freedom, while the woman has to bear the results of her sexual act for a relatively long time, in some cases, throughout her whole life.

Gallichan maintained that the 'prude' and the 'frigide' – the terms were more or less interchangeable – were a danger to society, especially to the young. Although he saw their resistance as political, he also defined them as degenerate and diseased:

> The erotically impotent women have an enormous influence upon the young, the conventions and regulations of society, and even upon sex legislation. These degenerate women are a menace to civilisation. They provoke sex misunderstanding and antagonism; they wreck conjugal happiness, and pose as superior moral beings when they are really victims of disease.

He thought it was absolutely vital that their 'sexophobia' be overcome: 'The hysterical frigide must be taught to face the realities of Nature, and to abandon the false perceptions of the "horridness", of sexuality'. Unfortunately, however, such women were 'extremely resistant' to such teaching: 'Their resistance to the acceptance of the facts of the love of the sexes is frequently so stubborn that no kind of instruction appears possible in their case'. He divided feminists into those who proclaimed the joys of heterosexual sex and were therefore 'truly' emancipated, and those who refused to do so. He praised feminists such as Olive Schreiner and Edith Lees, who were 'well-balanced' and understood the 'beauty and sacredness of sex'. The rest were dismissed as frigid and prudish man-haters, who were not only sexually anaesthetic, but neurotic and hysterical. Although they regarded themselves as a superior order of womanhood they were often, he alleged, 'secretly obsessed' with sex. Van de Velde also maintained that 'man-haters' were a product of lack of sexual satisfaction, and that their contempt for men was a 'reversal of the characteristic feminine desire to be dominated'.[35]

Given that frigidity was perceived as fundamentally a political problem, it is easy to see how sex reformers fuelled·the anti-spinster backlash which has already been discussed. The 'old maid' was in a sense the archetypal frigide, whose sexual 'starvation' was the inevitable consequence of her absolute resistance to the eroticization of her oppression. During the 1920s and 1930s spinsters who did not have sexual relationships with men came to be regarded, not merely as 'incomplete', but as ill: 'A realization of the results of thwarted sexual needs makes it possible to see that the typical "old maid", pictured as a cross, irritable being, is really ill, a true psychoneurotic, the result of an unfortunate psychological past'. This morbidification of the spinster paralleled the morbidification of love between women by sexologists, and reinforced the tendency to impute lesbian tendencies to any spinster who was not actively involved in heterosexual relationships. This was a pervasive feature, not merely of marriage manuals, but of more general tracts on marriage and sex education, written with the intention of preventing marital maladjustment and frigidity. Maud Churton Braby, for instance, in a book entitled *Modern Marriage and How to Bear It*, proposed the establishment of a state-run Institution for Encouraging Marriage, and insisted that all girls should be taught that [hetero]sex is the pivot on which the world turns', and that 'the natural companion of woman is man'. The need for such teaching was usually coupled with strong advocacy for coeducation. Estelle Cole argued that training for marriage should begin in the nursery, and that boy–girl friendships during puberty were essential in order to encourage the sexes towards heterosexuality. Recent research by Annabel Faraday has revealed the implicit, and sometimes explicit, anti-lesbianism in the arguments for coeducational schools put forward during this period by progressive educators such as A.S. Neill, who wrote: 'If a woman is unconsciously seeking love from a schoolmistress, she cannot be much of a wife or mistress to a mere man'.[36]

These, then, were the 'facts of life' which were taught to generations of women and men, based on the scientific model of sexuality constructed by the sexologists. The effect of the intervention of the medical profession was not merely to popularize and promote the model, but to add its own legitimating power to that of science, thus cementing the model more securely and rendering it even more immune to feminist challenge. To teach, not only that heterosexuality is natural, but that a particular form of heterosexual practice which institutionalizes male domination and female submission is natural, cannot but have adverse implications for female sexual autonomy, especially when presented in the guise of sexual 'liberation'. Although women were now permitted to have sexual feelings and to experience sexual pleasure, it was to be strictly on male terms. The 'experts' attempted to define and control female sexuality in such a way as to destroy any potential autonomy and to harness it in the service of men. Female sexuality was seen as having no independent existence of its own. A woman's sexual instinct could only be awakened by, and satisfied by, a man, thus rendering women sexually dependent on men at precisely that point in history when they were achieving a significant degree of political, economic, and sexual independence.

Exactly why female sexuality needed to be awakened by a man, while male sexuality was 'ever-ready', was never explained. The notion of an instinct which has to be awakened is very puzzling, if not paradoxical. A more glaring contradiction, however, lies in the notion of an instinct which has to be *learned*; yet all the experts were agreed that women had to learn, not merely to *enjoy* coitus, but to *desire* it. Nobody seems to have asked: if the desire for coitus is natural and instinctive, why does it need to be taught? The concept of frigidity was a convenient label with which to pathologize those women who resisted the attempt to eroticize their oppression. Their refusal to accept the 'facts of life' and to learn what was supposed to be natural was a threat to the sexual basis of male power. Defining them as 'frigid' was an attempt to remove from wives the right to refuse sexual intercourse, to deny them sexual autonomy. 'Frigidity' was to the twentieth-century medical profession what 'hysteria' was to that of the nineteenth century: it justified the intervention of the doctor, whose 'prescription' was essentially an attempt to force the wife to do what the husband had been unable to make her do – to submit.

The blurring of the distinction between the 'frigide', the spinster, the lesbian, and the 'prude' can be seen as a strategy for depoliticizing all forms of resistance to both the hetero-relational imperative and the coital imperative. By pathologizing that resistance, it represented in effect an attempt to pathologize feminism itself, especially those forms of feminism which challenged the male sexual exploitation and control of women, and the patriarchal model of sexuality.

Notes

1 The Cavendish-Bentinck Library had been founded by Ruth Cavendish-Bentinck in order to supply suffragists with books they could not procure in the ordinary way. Margaret Thomas, later Viscountess Rhondda, recalled borrowing Ellis' *Studies* from this library, and admitted to feeling very pleased that she had had no difficulty in obtaining it, while her much more eminent father, a Liberal MP, had been told, on trying to buy a copy, that he must first obtain a doctor's authorization (Rhondda, 1933).

2 See, for example Ehrenreich and English (1973; 1979); Oakley (1976).

3   The marriage manuals analyzed in this chapter came from three main sources: (1) the Fawcett Library, which incorporates the Cavendish-Bentinck Library and the Josephine Butler collection, which is the name now given to the former library of the Association for Moral and Social Hygiene; (2) a random 'trawl' of second-hand bookshops, mainly in London; (3) the British Library, where I followed up references cited in books from the first two sources. I have also included a few books which were not strictly marriage manuals but which dealt with sex and marriage from an educational perspective. A brief, preliminary survey of the material was published in Jackson (1987).

4   *The Times*, 13 December 1934, quoted in Griffith (1937). This letter, which had five signatories, including the Director of the Institute of Medical Psychology and the Director of the London Child Guidance Clinic, indicates current thinking about the link between juvenile delinquency and marital sexual discord. The Divorce Act of 1923 went some way to removing the double standard in the divorce laws by enabling women as well as men to sue for divorce on the grounds of adultery alone, without having also to prove other bad behaviour such as incest or bestiality.

5   Haire (1934), pp. 179–80; see also Beale (1926).

6   'A New Gospel' was in fact the title of a pamphlet which Marie Stopes addressed to the Anglican bishops, in which she claimed that God had spoken personally to her as his prophet, commanding her to pass on his revelation of the divine nature of sexual union between man and woman as an end in itself and not merely as a means to procreation (Hall, 1978a).

7   Wright (1930), pp. 10–11; pp. 14–17. This marriage manual also included a quotation from a speech by the Archbishop of Canterbury, in which he said: 'We want to liberate the sex impulse from the impression that it is always to be surrounded by negative warnings and restraints, and to place it in its rightful place among the great creative and formative things' (*ibid.*, p. 8).

8   Haire (1934), p. 179.

9   Walker (1935), p. 95. He also maintained that having obtained equality and power 'by hunger-striking and making life impossible for the pre-war politician', woman had not yet learned to use her power well. Shrewishness and tyranny, he asserted, were more likely to be found in an office run by a female manager than in one in which a male was in charge, and matrons and hospital sisters were often much harsher than men.

10   Van de Velde (1928), p. 232, emphasis in original.

11   *Ibid.*, p. 234. There must still be many women alive today who have been told at some time by their doctor that their menstrual problems would disappear 'when you get married', i.e. begin having regular coitus.

12   Eyles (1923), p. 96; Beale (1926), p. 68; Cole (1938), p. 53; Sanger (1926), p. 61. Margaret Sanger was one of the few authors of marriage manuals who was not a doctor. She was, however, a trained nurse and midwife. On her relationship with Havelock Ellis, see Grossskurth (1980).

13   See, for example, Clark (1937), p. 108; Griffith (1937), p. 128.

14   Van de Velde (1928), p. 214.

15   The 1977 paperback edition informs us that the book has been reprinted, with revisions, thirty-eight times. The cover proclaims that over 1,000,000 copies have been sold, and that it is still 'the book doctors recommend'.

16   Van de Velde (1928), pp. 138–9.

17   Haire (1934), p. 379.

18   Beale (1926), p. 69; Clark (1937), p. 32.

19   Van de Velde (1928), pp. 227–8; Hutton (1923), p. 32; p. 54; Haire (1934), p. 196.

20   Van de Velde (1928), p. 202; (1931), p. 275, emphasis in original.

21   Van de Velde (1928), pp. 156–7.

22 *Ibid.*, p. 198; Haire (1934), pp. 186–7.
23 Wright (1930; 1947). See also Campbell (1980); Ruehl (1983).
24 *Sunday Times*, 11 September 1977.
25 Wright (1930), p. 32; p. 58; p. 68.
26 Campbell (1980). See also Koedt (1970).
27 Wright (1930), p. 51; p. 57; pp. 71–2; p. 93, my emphasis.
28 Interview with Helena Wright, 5 January 1982. Although Wright's second book was not published until 1947, which is outside the period under discussion, it is included here because it is impossible to understand Wright's position fully without reference to it.
29 Wright (1947), pp. 48–9, my emphasis.
30 *Ibid.*, p. 54; pp. 71–2; p. 77.
31 Interview with Helena Wright, 5 January 1982.
32 Clark (1937), p. 97; Beale (1926), p. 82. See the introduction to Wright (1930), especially pp. 14–16.
33 Stekel (1926), p. 1; Gallichan (1927), p. 185; Haire (1934), pp. 318–19.
34 Van de Velde (1931), pp. 65–6. The concept 'will to power' seems to have been borrowed from the psychoanalyst Alfred Adler. It was also popular with Stekel and Gallichan.
35 Haire (1934), p. 319; Van de Velde (1931), p. 67; p. 274; p. 91; p. 17. Gallichan (1927), pp. 1–2; (1929), p. 184. As we have seen in Chapter 1, Gallichan was married to the well-known feminist who usually wrote under the name of Mrs Gasquoigne-Hartley. Both were extremely hostile to militant feminism and also expressed strongly anti-spinster attitudes. Edith Lees was married to Havelock Ellis, and reputedly was a lesbian. One wonders whether Gallichan knew she was a lesbian; certainly there is no indication that he did in his writings. Havelock Ellis had himself used the term 'resistance' in connection with frigidity; it is also important to remember that according to Ellis the function of 'courtship' was to overcome female resistance.
36 See Clark (1937), p. 50; Braby (1918); Cole (1938); Neill (1945), p. 78. For a discussion of the links between coeducation and anti-lesbianism between the wars, see Faraday (1989).

Conclusion

Feminism and the Power to Define our own Sexuality

The struggles of Victorian and Edwardian feminists to politicize sexuality, and to theorize the links between the sexual, political, and economic aspects of women's subordination, deserve to be much more widely known and understood. Too many people, including many scholars, still characterize these feminists as sexual puritans who either ignored sexual issues or demanded 'equal sexual repression'. There is ample evidence, much of which I have had no space to discuss, that the sexual economics of male power was of central concern to feminists at this time. They sought to challenge it in three main ways: by campaigning against marriage as a form of institutionalized female sexual slavery; by asserting spinsterhood as a positive choice and a form of resistance to male power; and by breaking the conspiracy of silence which obscured male violence and the sexual exploitation and abuse of women and children. I have argued that this challenge threatened to undermine, not only the institution of marriage, but the structure of hetero-relations fundamental to male power. At the height of the suffrage campaign and during the phase of militant feminism all these struggles were given added coherence by a concerted campaign against the double standard of sexual morality. The demand for an equal moral standard encapsulated the feminists' aim to emancipate women from all forms of female sexual slavery, inside and outside marriage; in other words, it represented a demand for female sexual autonomy. Their insistence that 'the *real* facts of life' be revealed indicated their refusal to be silenced and their determination to expose the realities of male violence and sexual exploitation, and the use of male sexuality as a weapon of male power. They aimed to expose not only the facts but the ideology which legitimated the double standard: the myth that male sexual needs are 'natural' and beyond their control.

The campaign for an equal moral standard was informed by and in turn stimulated a feminist analysis of sexuality which developed into a radical redefinition of the 'natural' as political. The main focus of feminist critique was the patriarchal model of sexuality, according to which sex was defined in masculine, phallocentric terms as a biological urge for heterosexual intercourse which men had a right – and women a duty – to satisfy. Feminists argued not only that men had no such right but that sexuality was just as amenable to rational control as any other human faculty. In other words they argued that sexuality was socially constructed and an integral part of the way male power was constituted and maintained. The demand for female sexual autonomy implied not only a change in the power relations between the sexes and a redistribution of power within heterosexual relationships, but a radical redefinition of the nature of sexuality itself. Some feminists attempted to move beyond a critique of the patriarchal model towards a feminist model of sexuality; to explore ways of thinking about sexuality which would empower women and enable them to retain their autonomy both within and outside heterosexual relationships. Emphasis on the unity of the emotional, spiritual, and physical aspects of sexuality – what we might now call a 'holistic' approach – was a crucial element in this process, together with the displacing of heterosexual intercourse as *the* goal of sexual expression, and a positive attitude towards celibacy.

In teasing out the complexities, ambiguities, and ambivalences of feminist ideas about sexuality I have tried to point out what was common to almost all strands of feminism at that time: an absolute insistence on the right to refuse compulsory heterosexuality and compulsory motherhood, and a shared commitment to female sexual autonomy. But it is clear that the concept of female sexual autonomy to some extent had different meanings for different groups and individuals, and I have suggested that these differences, though not unconnected to broader political differences, may have been rooted in a fundamental difference in their respective concepts of sexuality. The 'new moralists'' concept of sexual freedom betrayed an uncritical acceptance of the patriarchal model of sexuality, while the advocates of an equal moral standard were striving for a fundamental change in the way sexuality itself was conceptualized. These divisions were exacerbated and fuelled by the intervention of sexology, the anti-feminist implications of which are still rarely recognized. I have argued that sexology represented the appropriation of the sexual by male scientific 'experts', who overturned more than half a century of feminist struggle to politicize sexuality and promote female sexual autonomy. What feminists had defined as political, the experts redefined as 'natural'. The reassertion of sex as basically a coital imperative, an uncontrollable biological urge, provided 'scientific' legitimation of male sexual violence and exploitation and undermined both the campaign for an equal moral standard and the construction of a feminist model of sexuality. The sexological model was essentially the patriarchal model of sexuality repackaged in scientific form. After the vote was won the popular purveyors of the new 'facts of life' promoted, in the guise of sexual 'liberation', a form of heterosexuality and sexual pleasure which eroticized male dominance and female submission, and pathologized all manifestations of female sexual autonomy or resistance, including spinsterhood, lesbianism, and 'frigidity'.

Nowhere are the anti-feminist implications of the sexological model seen more clearly than in the work of Marie Stopes, whose attempts to marry sexology and feminism highlighted the problems and contradictions experienced by many feminists who tried to adopt scientific modes of thought for feminist purposes. Ironically, the emphasis on a rationalist approach to sexuality, which characterized feminist thought and action from the very beginning of the century, may to some extent have contributed to the relatively uncritical acceptance by some feminists of scientific theories and methods. The patriarchal values and assumptions with which science was (and still is) saturated constrained their thinking and subverted their feminism. It led to the construction of 'laws of love' which negated the concept of sexuality as socially constructed and therefore open to challenge and change. Sexuality was once again consigned to the sphere of the 'natural' where, guarded and protected by science, it remained virtually immune from challenge until the rise of the Women's Liberation Movement in the 1960s. When we did at last begin to analyze once again the relationship between sexuality and male power, most of us were completely unaware that it had all been done before, albeit in different ways. The fact that the history of women's struggles for female sexual autonomy had been virtually erased is in itself an indication of the strength of the patriarchal model of sexuality and the ideology of sexual 'liberation' which it underpins.

No-one who has been involved during the last twenty-five years in feminist campaigns around sexuality needs reminding that the goal of female sexual autonomy is still a long way from being achieved. Despite the very real progress which feminists have made, the patriarchal model of sexuality has lost none of its resilience and continues to permeate the whole of Western culture. During the second half of the twentieth century it has received further reinforcement from a variety of scientific sources, including the sexological work of the Kinsey Institute and Masters and Johnson, psychoanalytic theories, and sociobiology, all of which have been widely popularized by such means as sex manuals, magazines, and videos, with their theories and assumptions represented as 'facts'. I have argued in detail elsewhere that although women are now encouraged to be active rather than passive sexual beings, what constitutes being active – what constitutes being *sexual* – is still defined in masculine terms. In other words, male sexuality has been universalized and the coital imperative reigns supreme.[1] What is particularly disturbing is the influence of the patriarchal model of sexuality within feminism itself, which is as divided now over sexuality as were our Victorian and Edwardian foresisters. While we would probably all endorse the demand for female sexual autonomy, or the right to define and control our own sexuality, this still appears to have different meanings for different groups, and there are fierce disagreements about strategies for achieving it, as well as about what constitutes feminist sexual practice.

Without attempting to discuss all the arguments here it seems clear to me that some feminists still interpret female sexual autonomy in terms of extending to women sexual freedom as defined and enjoyed by men, without challenging the patriarchal model of sexuality on which it is based. Some feminists go so far as to claim that the eroticization of power is both desirable and natural, and not only defend but advocate pornography and the actual enactment of dominant and submissive sexual 'scripts', whether by hetero-sexuals, lesbians, or gay men. To quote just one example:

> The suburban woman who gets her thrills from watching male strippers is paying, with her admission price, to invert the usual relationship between men and women, consumer and object. At a different end of the cultural spectrum, a practitioner of ritualistic sadomasochism confronts social inequality by encapsulating it in a drama of domin-ation and submission.[2]

The moral justification for this position is usually expressed in the liberal or libertarian rhetoric of 'freedom of speech', or 'freedom of choice', with the caveat of 'consent'. Anything goes, it seems, even if it causes pain, injury, or other harm, as long as it is 'consensual'. I find it extraordinary that feminists, many of whom have been involved in various forms of politics for a very long time, appear to find the notion of consent so unproblematic. Wherever there is an imbalance of power consent can never be taken for granted; and those with power, whether they be individuals, groups, institutions, or other social structures, invariably use their power to secure consent in more or less subtle ways. That is what ideologies are all about. That is what I have argued the 'art of love' was about: securing the consent of women to male dominance and female submission by eroticizing it and defining it as 'natural'. We need to ask how it is that experiencing arousal and orgasm in the course of acting out dominance and submission comes to be *perceived* by some women as liberating, or as defining our own sexuality. To account for this in terms of an essentialist notion of 'desire' assumes what has to be explained. It implicitly accepts as natural what is in fact a social and political construct. We need to explain how it is that women come to desire and choose what men *want* us to choose. As Susanne Kappeler has pointed out, it seems that the greater sexual 'freedom' which is being demanded is in fact 'the licence to continue to regard the other as sexual object, a vehicle for his – or her – pleasure'.[3]

The power to define what is 'natural' remains crucial to the maintenance of male power and the structure of hetero-relations. Whenever there is a threat to any system of power, theories and ideologies are constructed and promoted which legitimate that power and attempt, either to show that change is not possible, or to direct change in such a way that the fundamental power structure is maintained. Challenging patriarchal definitions of the 'natural' is in many ways as difficult and dangerous now as it was in the nineteenth cen-tury, as the current anti-feminist backlash shows, with the forceful reassertion by successive Conservative governments and their right-wing ideologues of the naturalness of heterosexuality and the patriarchal family.[4] Despite our persistent attempts to deconstruct the patriarchal model of sexuality, it con-tinues to dominate, operating through subversion and division to obscure the link between sexuality, male power and hetero-relations, and to obstruct the exploration of possible ways forward in the struggle for female sexual and reproductive autonomy. Nevertheless many women, and especially feminist lesbians, are demonstrating in their lives that we do have the power both to imagine a feminist model of sexuality and to construct it, even though we may find difficulty in creating a language in which to express it. Feminist sexual practice requires both a radical critique of sex as it is defined and constructed within a patriarchal society, and a commitment to working out our own model based on mutual interchange between equals and on pleasure without objectification. A deeper understanding of the political processes by which definitions of the 'natural' are constructed may help in this continuing struggle.

Notes

1 For an analysis of the work of the Kinsey Institute, and of Masters and Johnson, see: Jackson (1984; also in Coveney *et al.*, 1984). See also rhodes and McNeill (1985) and Jeffreys (1990). For a critique of sociobiology see Bland (1981).
2 Ehrenreich *et al.* (1987). For other examples see various articles in Vance (1984), Snitow *et al.* (1984), and Rodgerson and Wilson (1991). For more detailed critiques of this position see Linden *et al.* (1982); Jeffreys (1990); Leidholt and Raymond (1990).
3 Kappeler (1990), in Leidholt and Raymond (1990).
4 For further discussions of this point see Jackson (1989) and other articles in the collection by Jones and Mahony (1989); as well as articles by Lynn Alderson and Harriet Wistrich in *Trouble and Strife* 13, Spring 1988.

Bibliography

ACTON, WILLIAM (1857) *Prostitution Considered in its Social and Sanitary Aspects*, London: John Churchill.

ACTON, WILLIAM (1870) *The Contagious Diseases Act. Shall the Contagious Diseases Act be Applied to the Civil Population?*, London: John Churchill and Sons.

ACTON, WILLIAM (1875) *The Functions and Disorders of the Reproductive Organs*, London: J. and A. Churchill.

ADDAMS, JANE (1912) *A New Conscience and an Ancient Evil*, New York: The Macmillan Co.

AUCHMUTY, ROSEMARY (1975) *Victorian Spinsters*, unpublished PhD thesis, Australian National University.

BANKS, OLIVE (1981) *Faces of Feminism*, Oxford: Martin Robertson.

BAUER, CAROL and RITT, LAWRENCE (Eds) (1979) *Free and Ennobled: Source Readings in the Development of Victorian Feminism*, Oxford: Pergamon Press.

BEALE, G. COURTENAY (1926) *Wise Wedlock*, London: Health Promotion Ltd.

BEDDOE, DEIRDRE (1989) *Back to Home and Duty: Women Between the Wars 1918–1939*, London: Pandora Press.

BESANT, ANNIE (1876) 'The Legalisation of Female Slavery in England', reprinted in JEFFREYS (1987).

BESANT, ANNIE (1882) 'Marriage: As It Was, As It Is, and As It Should Be', reprinted in JEFFREYS (1987).

BESANT, ANNIE (1893) *An Autobiography*, London: T. Fisher Unwin.

BESANT, ANNIE (1901) *Theosophy and The Law of Population*, London: Theosophical Publishing.

BILLINGTON-GREIG, TERESA (1913) 'The Truth About White Slavery', *The English Review*, June.

BLACKWELL, ELIZABETH (1879) *Counsel to Parents on the Moral Education of the Young in Relation to Sex*, London: Hatchards.

BLACKWELL, ELIZABETH (1881) *Rescue Work in Relation to Prostitution and Disease*, London: T. Danks.

BLACKWELL, ELIZABETH (1883) *Wrong and Right Methods of Dealing with Social Evil: As Shewn by Lately-Published Parliamentary Evidence*, Hastings, Sussex: D. Williams.

BLACKWELL, ELIZABETH (1894 [1880]) *The Human Element in Sex: Being a Medical Inquiry into the Relation of Sexual Physiology to Christian Morality*, London: J. and A. Churchill.

BLACKWELL, ELIZABETH (1902/1916 [1885]) *Purchase of Women: The Great Economic Blunder* (foreword by Mrs Fawcett to 1916 edition), London: G. Bell and Sons; also reprinted in BLACKWELL, ELIZABETH (1902) *Essays in Medical Sociology*, Vol. 1, London: Ernest Bell.

BLACKWELL, ELIZABETH (1889) *The Religion of Health*, London: Moral Reform Union.

Bibliography

BLACKWELL, ELIZABETH (1891) *Christian Duty in Regard to Vice: A Letter Addressed to the Brussels International Congress, against State Regulation of Vice, with the Hearty Sympathy of Dr Elizabeth Blackwell*, London: Moral Reform Union.

BLACKWELL, ELIZABETH (1895) *Pioneer Work in Opening the Medical Profession to Women. Autobiographical Sketches*, London and New York: Longmans Green.

BLACKWELL, ELIZABETH (1902) *Essays in Medical Sociology*, Ernest Bell, London.

BLAND, LUCY (1981) 'It's Only Human Nature?: Sociobiology and Sex Differences', *Schooling and Culture*, 10, pp. 6–10.

BLAND, LUCY (1985) 'In the Name of Protection: The Policing of Women in the First World War', in BROPHY and SMART (1985).

BLAND, LUCY (1986) 'Marriage Laid Bare: Middle-Class Women and Marital Sex c. 1880–1914', in LEWIS (1986).

BLEIER, RUTH (1984) *Science and Gender*, London: Pergamon Press.

BLOCH, IWAN (1909) *The Sexual Life of Our Time*, London: Heinemann.

BODICHON, BARBARA LEIGH SMITH (1857) *Women and Work*, New York: C.S. Francis.

BOUCHERETT, JESSIE (1869) 'How To Provide For Superfluous Women', in BUTLER (1869).

BOYLE, NINA (1912) *The Traffic in Women*, London: Minerva Publishing Co.

BRABY, MAUD CHURTON (1918) *Modern Marriage and How to Bear It*, London: T. Werner Laurie.

BRAKE, MIKE (Ed.) (1982) *Human Sexual Relations: A Reader*, Harmondsworth: Penguin.

BRECHER, EDWARD M. (1970) *The Sex Researchers*, London: Andre Deutsch.

BRIGHTON WOMEN AND SCIENCE GROUP (1980) *Alice Through the Microscope*, London: Virago.

BRISTOW, E. (1977) *Vice and Vigilance: Purity Movements in Britain since 1700*, Dublin: Gill and Macmillan.

BRITTAIN, VERA (1933) *Testament of Youth*, London: Victor Gollancz.

BRODY, MIRIAM (1983) 'Mary Wollstonecraft: Sexuality and Women's Rights', in SPENDER (1983).

BROPHY, JULIA and SMART, CAROL (Eds) (1985) *Women-In-Law*, London: Routledge and Kegan Paul.

BROWNE, F.W. STELLA (1917) *Sexual Variety and Variability Among Women and their Bearing upon Social Reconstruction*, London: British Society for the study of Sex Psychology.

BROWNE, F.W. STELLA (1923) 'Studies in Feminine Inversion', reprinted in ROWBOTHAM (1977).

BURMAN, SANDRA (Ed.) (1979) *Fit Work For Women*, Oxford: Oxford University Press.

BURT, CYRIL (1925) *The Young Delinquent*, London: University of London Press.

BUTLER, JOSEPHINE (Ed.) (1869) *Woman's Work and Woman's Culture*, London: Macmillan.

BUTLER, JOSEPHINE (1898) *Personal Reminiscences of a Great Crusade*, London: H. Marshall and Son.

CAIRD, MONA (1888) 'Marriage', *Westminster Review*, 130 (2), pp. 186–201.

CAMPBELL, BEATRIX (1980) 'Feminist Sexual Politics', *Feminist Review*, 5, pp. 1–18.

CAPLAN, PAT (Ed.) (1987) *The Cultural Construction of Sexuality*, London: Tavistock.

CARPENTER, EDWARD (1894) *Sex-Love, and its Place in a Free Society*, Manchester: The Labour Press.

CARPENTER, EDWARD (1896) *Love's Coming-of-Age*, Manchester: The Labour Press.

CHAPMAN, MARIA WESTON (Ed.) (1877) *Harriet Martineau's Autobiography and Memorials of Harriet Martineau*, Boston.

CLARK, LE MON (1937) *Emotional Adjustment in Marriage*, London: Henry Kimpton.

COBBE, FRANCES POWER (1862a) 'Celibacy vs. Marriage', *Fraser's Magazine*, LXV, pp. 228–35.

COBBE, FRANCES POWER (1862b) 'What Shall We Do With Our Old Maids?', *Fraser's Magazine*, LXVI, pp. 594–610.

COBBE, FRANCES POWER (1868) 'Criminals, Idiots, Women and Minors', *Fraser's Magazine*, LXXVIII, pp. 777–94.

COBBE, FRANCES POWER (1878) 'Wife Torture in England', *Contemporary Review*, 32, pp. 55–87.

COBBE, FRANCES POWER (1894) *The Life of Frances Power Cobbe*, Boston and New York: Houghton Mifflin.

COLE, ESTELLE (1938) *Education for Marriage*, London: Duckworth.

COLLET, CLARA (1902) 'Women's Work', in BOOTH, CHARLES *Life and Labour of The People in London (1902–1904)*.

COOTE, ANNA and CAMPBELL, BEATRIX (1982) *Sweet Freedom: The Struggle for Women's Liberation*, London: Pan Books.

COTT, NANCY F. (1978/9) 'Passionlessness: An Interpretation of Victorian Sexual Ideology, 1790–1850', *Signs*, 4, pp. 219–36.

COVENEY, LAL, JACKSON, MARGARET, JEFFREYS, SHEILA, KAYE, LESLIE, and MAHONY, PAT (1984) *The Sexuality Papers: Male Sexuality and the Social Control of Women*, London: Hutchinson.

COWARD, ROSALIND (1978) 'Sexual Liberation and the Family'.

COWARD, ROSALIND (1983) *Patriarchal Precedents: Sexuality and Social Relations*, London: Routledge and Kegan Paul.

COWARD, ROSALIND (1984) Preface to the British edition of SNITOW, STANSELL and THOMPSON.

DAVIN, ANNA (1978) 'Imperialism and Motherhood', *History Workshop*, 5, pp. 9–65.

DEGLER, CARL (1974) 'What Ought to Be and What Was: Women's Sexuality in the Nineteenth Century, *American Historical Review*, 79, pp. 1467–90.

DELAMONT, SARA and DUFFIN, LORNA (1978) *The Nineteenth Century Woman: Her Cultural and Physical World*, London: Croom Helm.

DWORKIN, ANDREA (1981) *Pornography: Men Possessing Women*, The Women's Press.

DYHOUSE, CAROL (1976) 'Social Darwinistic Ideas and the Development of Women's Education in England, 1880–1920', *History of Education*, 5, pp. 41–58.

DYHOUSE, CAROL (1978) 'Towards a "Feminine" Curriculum for English Schoolgirls: The Demands of Ideology, 1870–1963', *Women's Studies International Quarterly*, 1 (4), pp. 297–330.

DYHOUSE, CAROL (1989) *Feminism and the Family in England, 1880–1939*, Oxford: Basil Blackwell.

EASLEA, BRIAN (1981) *Science and Sexual Oppression*, London: Weidenfeld and Nicholson.

EATON, PETER and WARNICK, MARILYN (1977) *Marie Stopes: A Preliminary Checklist of her Writings Together with some Biographical Notes*, London: Croom Helm.

EGERTON, GEORGE (1983 [1894]) *Keynotes and Discords*, London: Virago.

EGERTON, JAYNE (1981) 'The Goal of a Feminist Politics . . . The Destruction of Male Supremacy or the Pursuit of Pleasure?', *Revolutionary and Radical Feminist Newsletter*, 8.

EHRENREICH, BARBARA and ENGLISH, DEIRDRE (1973) *Complaints and Disorders*, New York: The Feminist Press.

EHRENREICH, BARBARA and ENGLISH, DEIRDRE (1979) *For Her Own Good: 150 Years of the Experts' Advice to Women*, London: Pluto Press.

EHRENREICH, B., HESS, E. and JACOBS, G. (1987) *Remaking Love: the feminization of sex*, Garden City, New York: Anchor Books.

ELLIS, H. HAVELOCK (1934 [1894]) *Man and Woman: a Study of Secondary and Tertiary Sexual Characteristics*, London: Heinemann.

ELLIS, H. HAVELOCK (1913a) *Studies in the Psychology of Sex*, Vols. I–VI, Philadelphia: F.A. Davis.

ELLIS, H. HAVELOCK (1913b) *The Task of Social Hygiene*, London: Constable.
ELLIS, H. HAVELOCK (1917) *The Erotic Rights of Women*, London: British Society for the Study of Sex Psychology.
ELLIS, H. HAVELOCK (1921) *The Play-Function of Sex*, London: British Society for the Study of Sex Psychology.
ELLIS, H. HAVELOCK (1946) Studies in The Psychology of Sex, *Sex in Relation to Society*, Vol. VI, Heinemann.
EXNER, M. (1932) *The Sexual Side of Marriage*, London: G. Allen and Unwin.
EYLES, LEONORA (1923) *Family Love*, London: Andrew Melrose.
FADERMAN, LILLIAN (1981) *Surpassing the Love of Men: Romantic Friendship and Love Between Women from the Renaissance to the Present*, New York: William Morrow.
FARADAY, ANNABEL (1989) 'Lessoning Lesbians: Girls' Schools, Coeducation and Anti-Lesbianism Between the Wars', in JONES and MAHONY (1989).
FAWCETT, MILLICENT (1885) 'Speech or Silence?', *The Contemporary Review*, September.
FAWCETT, MILLICENT (1891) Introduction to reprint of WOLLSTONECRAFT (1792).
FAWCETT, MILLICENT (1916) Introduction to reprint of BLACKWELL (1885).
FEE, ELIZABETH (1978) 'Psychology, Sexuality, and Social Control in Victorian England', *Social Science Quarterly*, 58.
FEMINIST ANTHOLOGY COLLECTIVE (Ed.) (1981) *No Turning Back: Writings from the Women's Liberation Movement 1975–80*, London: The Women's Press.
FERGUSON, ANN (1981) 'Patriarchy, Sexual Identity and the Sexual Revolution', *Signs*, 7, 1.
FIRST, RUTH and SCOTT, ANN (1980) *Olive Schreiner: A Biography*, London: Andre Deutsch.
FOREL, AUGUST (1908) *The Sexual Question*, London: Rebman.
FORSTER, MARGARET (1984) *Significant Sisters: The Grassroots of Active Feminism 1839–1939*, Harmondsworth: Penguin.
GALLICHAN, WALTER (1909) *Modern Woman and How to Manage Her*, London: T. Werner Laurie.
GALLICHAN, WALTER (1927) *Sexual Apathy and Coldness in Women*, London: T. Werner Laurie.
GALLICHAN, WALTER (1929) *The Poison of Prudery*, London: T. Werner Laurie.
GASQUOIGNE-HARTLEY, C. (1913) *The Truth About Woman*, London: Eveleigh Nash.
GILLIS, JOHN P. (1979) 'Servants, Sexual Relations, and the Risks of Illegitimacy in London, 1801–1900', *Feminist Studies*, 5.
GILMAN, CHARLOTTE PERKINS (1966 [1899]) *Women and Economics: The Economic Factor between Men and Women as a Factor in Social Revolution*, New York: Harper and Row.
GORDON, LINDA (1977) *Woman's Body, Woman's Right*, New York: Penguin.
GORDON, LINDA and DUBOIS, ELLEN (1984) 'Seeking Ecstasy on the Battlefield: danger and pleasure in nineteenth century feminist sexual thought', in VANCE CAROLE, S. (Ed.) *Pleasure and Danger*, Routledge and Kegan Paul.
GORDON, MICHAEL (1978) 'From an Unfortunate Necessity to a Cult of Mutual Orgasm: Sex in Americal Marital Education Literature, 1830–1940', in HENSLIN and SAGARIN (1978).
GORHAM, DEBORAH (1978) 'The "Maiden Tribute of Modern Babylon" Re-Examined', *Victorian Studies*, 21 (3) (Spring).
GREG, WILLIAM R. (1850) 'Prostitution', *Westminster Review*, LIII; pp. 448–506.
GREG, WILLIAM R. (1862) 'Why Are Women Redundant?', *National Review*, April.
GREY, MARIA (1875) 'Old Maids' (a lecture), reprinted in MURRAY (1984).
GRIFFITH, EDWARD F. (1937) *Modern Marriage and Birth Control*, London: Gollancz.
GROSSKURTH, PHYLLIS (1980) *Havelock Ellis: A Biography*, London: Quartet Books.

HAIRE, NORMAN (Ed.) (1930) *The Sex Reform Congress*, London: Kegan Paul, Trench, Trubner.

HAIRE, NORMAN (Ed.) (1934) *Encyclopaedia of Sexual Knowledge*, London: Encyclopaedia Press.

HALL, CATHERINE (1979) 'The Early Formation of Victorian Domestic Ideology', in BURMAN (1979).

HALL, RUTH (1978a) *Marie Stopes: A Biography*, London: Virago.

HALL, RUTH (Ed.) (1978b) *Dear Dr Stopes: Sex in the 1920s*, London: Andre Deutsch.

HAMILTON, CICELY (1981 [1909]) *Marriage as a Trade*, London: The Women's Press.

HEAPE, WALTER (1913) *Sex Antagonism*, London: Constable.

HELLERSTEIN, ERNA O., HUME, LESLIE P., and OFFEN, KAREN M. (Eds) (1981) *Victorian Women: A Documentary Account of Women's Lives in Nineteenth-Century England, France, and the United States*, Brighton: Harvester Press.

HENSLIN, JAMES M. and SAGARIN, EDWARD (Eds) (1978) *The Sociology of Sex: An Introductory Reader*, New York: Schocken Books.

HOLCOMBE, LEE (1973) *Victorian Women at Work*, London: David and Charles.

HOLCOMBE, LEE (1977) 'Victorian Wives and Property: Reform of the Married Women's Property Law', in VICINUS (1977).

HOPKINS, ELLICE J. (1899) *The Power of Womanhood: Or Mothers and Sons*, London: Wells Gardner.

HUTTON, ISABEL (1923) *The Hygiene of Marriage*, London: Heinemann.

JACKSON, MARGARET (1981) 'Sex and the Experts', *Scarlet Women*, no. 13.

JACKSON, MARGARET (1983) 'Sexual Liberation or Social Control?', *Women's Studies International Forum*, 6 (1), pp. 1–17; reprinted in COVENEY *et al.* (1984).

JACKSON, MARGARET (1984) 'Sex Research and the Construction of Sexuality: A Tool of male supremacy?', *Women's Studies International Forum*, 7 (1), pp. 43–51; reprinted in COVENEY *et al.* (1984).

JACKSON, MARGARET (1985) 'Sexual Pleasure and Women's Liberation', in RHODES and MCNEILL (1985).

JACKSON, MARGARET (1987) 'Facts of Life or the Eroticisation of Women's Oppression?: Sexology and the Social Construction of Heterosexuality', in CAPLAN (1987).

JACKSON, MARGARET (1989) 'Sexuality and Struggle: Feminism, Sexology and the Social Construction of Sexuality', in JONES and MAHONY (1989).

JACKSON, MARGARET (1990) *The Political Versus The Natural: Case Studies in The Struggle for Female Sexual Autonomy, 1800–1940*, PhD Thesis, University of Birmingham.

JALLAND, PATRICIA (1986) *Women, Marriage and Politics*, Oxford: Basil Blackwell.

JEFFREYS, SHEILA (1982) 'Free from All Uninvited Touch of Man: Women's Campaigns Around Sexuality 1880–1914', *Women's Studies International Forum*, 5 (6), pp. 629–45.

JEFFREYS, SHEILA (1983) 'Sex and Anti-Feminism in the 1920s', in LONDON FEMINIST HISTORY GROUP (1983).

JEFFREYS, SHEILA (1984) 'Does it matter if they did it? Lillian Faderman and Lesbian History', *Trouble and Strife*, 3, Summer.

JEFFREYS, SHEILA (1985) *The Spinster and Her Enemies: Feminism and Sexuality 1880–1930*, London: Pandora Press.

JEFFREYS, SHEILA (Ed.) (1987) *The Sexuality Debates*, London: Routledge.

JEFFREYS, SHEILA (1990) *Anticlimax: a feminist perspective on the sexual revolution*, The Women's Press.

JONES, CAROL and MAHONY, PAT (Eds) (1989) *Learning Our Lines: Sexuality and Social Control in Education*, London: The Women's Press.

KAMM, JOSEPHINE (1966) *Rapiers and Battleaxes: The Women's Movement and its Aftermath*, London: George Allen and Unwin.

KAPPELER, SUSANNE (1990) 'Liberals, Libertarianism and the Liberal Arts Establishment', in LEIDHOLT and RAYMOND (1990).

KLEIN, VIOLA (1946) *The Feminine Character: History of an Ideology*, London: Kegan Paul, Trench, Trubner and Co.

KOEDT, ANNE (1970) 'The Myth of the Vaginal Orgasm', reprinted in KOEDT, LEVINE and RAPONE (1973).

KOEDT, ANNE, LEVINE, ELLEN, and RAPONE, ANITA (Eds) (1973) *Radical Feminism*, New York: Times Books.

LANE, ANN J. (Ed.) (1981) *The Charlotte Perkins Gilman Reader*, London: The Women's Press.

LANE, ANN J. (1983) 'Charlotte Perkins Gilman: The Personal is Political', in SPENDER (1983).

LEIDHOLT, DORCHEN and RAYMOND, JANICE, G. (Eds) (1990) *The Sexual Liberals and The Attack on Feminism*, The Athene Series, Pergamon Press.

LESBIAN HISTORY GROUP (1989) *Not a Passing Phase: Reclaiming Lesbians in History 1840–1985*, London: The Women's Press.

LEVINE, PHILIPPA (1989) ' "So Few Prizes and So Many Blanks": Marriage and Feminism in Later Nineteenth-Century England', *Journal of British Studies*, 28, pp. 150–74.

LEWIS, JANE (1975) 'Beyond Suffrage: English Feminism in the 1920s', *Maryland Historian*, VI, pp. 1–17.

LEWIS, JANE (1979) 'The Ideology and Politics of Birth Control in Inter-War England', *Women's Studies International Quarterly*, 2 (1), pp. 33–48.

LEWIS, JANE (1981) Introduction to HAMILTON (1981 [1909]).

LEWIS, JANE (1984) *Women in England, 1870–1950*, Brighton: Wheatsheaf.

LEWIS, JANE (Ed.) (1986) *Labour and Love: Women's Experience of Home and Family, 1850–1940*, Oxford: Basil Blackwell.

LIDDERDALE, J. and NICHOLSON, M. (1970) *Harriet Shaw Weaver, 1876–1961*, London: Faber and Faber.

LINDEN, R.R., PAGANO, D.R., RUSSELL, D.H. and STAR, S.L. (Eds) (1982) *Against Sadomasochism: A Radical Feminist Analysis*, California: Frog in the Well.

LOCK, JOAN (1979) *The British Policewoman: Her Story*, London: Hale.

LONDON FEMINIST HISTORY GROUP (1983) *The Sexual Dynamics of History*, London: Pluto Press.

MARTINDALE, LOUISA (1910) *Under The Surface*, Brighton, The Southern Publishing Company.

McLAREN, ANGUS (1978) *Birth Control in Nineteenth-Century England*, London: Croom Helm.

MENDUS, SUSAN (1989) 'The Marriage of True Minds: The Ideal of Marriage in the Philosophy of John Stuart Mill', in MENDUS and RENDALL (1989).

MENDUS, SUSAN and RENDALL, JANE (Eds) (1989) *Sexuality and Subordination*, London: Routledge.

MILL, JOHN STUART (1832) 'Essay on Marriage and Divorce', in ROSSI (1970).

MILL, JOHN STUART (1974 [1869]), *The Subjection of Women*, Oxford: Oxford University Press.

MITCHELL, DAVID (1966) *Women on the Warpath*, London: Cape.

MITCHELL, DAVID (1967) *The Fighting Pankhursts: A Study in Tenacity*, London: Cape.

MITCHELL, DAVID (1977) *Queen Christabel: A Biography of Christabel Pankhurst*, London: McDonald and Jane.

MITCHELL, JULIET and OAKLEY, ANN (Eds) (1976) *The Rights and Wrongs of Women*, Harmondsworth: Penguin.

MOHIN, LILIAN and WILSON, ANNA (1983) *Past Participants: A Lesbian History Diary for 1984*, Onlywomen Press.

MORRELL, CAROLINE (1981) *'Black Friday' and Violence Against Women in the Suffragette Movement*, London: Women's Research and Resources Centre.

MORT, FRANK (1987) *Dangerous Sexualities: Medico-Moral Politics in England since 1830*, London: Routledge and Kegan Paul.

MULLINS, CLAUD (1935) *Wife v. Husband in the Courts*, London: George Allen and Unwin.

MURRAY, JANET HOROWITZ (Ed.) (1984) *Strong-Minded Women and Other Lost Voices from Nineteenth-Century England*, Harmondsworth: Penguin.

MYRON, NANCY and BUNCH, CHARLOTTE (Eds) (1975) *Lesbianism and the Women's Movement*, Baltimore: Diana Press.

NEILANS, ALISON (1936) 'Changes in Sex Morality', in STRACHEY (1936).

NEILL, A.S. (1945) *Hearts Not Heads in The School*, Herbert Jenkins.

NEVINSON, MARGARET WYNNE (1926) *Life's Fitful Fever*, London: A. and C. Black.

NORTON, CAROLINE (1854) 'English Laws for Women in the Nineteenth Century', reprinted in MURRAY (1984).

OAKLEY, ANN (1976) 'Wisewoman and Medicine Man: Changes in the Management of Childbirth', in MITCHELL and OAKLEY (1976).

PANKHURST, CHRISTABEL (1913) *The Great Scourge and How to End It*, London: E. Pankhurst.

PANKHURST, SYLVIA (1977 [1931]) *The Suffragette Movement*, London: Virago.

PARKES, BESSIE RAYNER (1865) *Essays on Woman's Work*, London: Alexander Strahan.

PETHICK LAWRENCE, FREDERICK (1943) *Fate Has Been Kind*, Hutchinson.

RAEBURN, ANNA (1973) *The Militant Suffragettes*, London: Michael Joseph.

RAYMOND, JANICE (1986) *A Passion for Friends*, London: The Women's Press.

RE-BARTLETT, LUCY (1912) *Sex and Sanctity*, London: Longmans.

RHODES, DUSTY and McNEILL, SANDRA (Eds) (1985) *Women Against Violence Against Women*, London: Onlywomen Press.

RHONDDA, MARGARET HAIG, VISCOUNTESS (1933) *This was my World*, London: Macmillan.

RICH, ADRIENNE (1981) *Compulsory Heterosexuality and Lesbian Existence*, London: Onlywomen Press.

RIEMER, ELEANOR S. and FOUT, JOHN C. (Eds) (1983) *European Women: A Documentary History 1789–1945*, Brighton: Harvester.

ROBINSON, PAUL (1976) *The Modernization of Sex*, New York: Harper and Row.

RODGERSON, GILLIAN and WILSON, ELIZABETH (Eds) (1991) *Pornography and Feminism: The Case Against Censorship by Feminists Against Censorship*, Lawrence and Wishart.

ROSEN, ANDREW (1974) *Rise Up Women! The Militant Campaign of the Women's Social and Political Union 1903–1914*, London: Routledge and Kegan Paul.

ROSSI, ALICE (Ed.) (1970) *Essays on Sex Equality*, Chicago: University of Chicago Press.

ROSSI, ALICE S. (Ed.) (1974) *The Feminist Papers: From Adams to De Beauvoir*, New York: Bantam Books.

ROVER, CONSTANCE (1970) *Love, Morals and the Feminists*, London: Routledge and Kegan Paul.

ROWBOTHAM, SHEILA (1977) *A New World for Women: Stella Browne – Socialist Feminist*, London: Pluto Press.

ROWBOTHAM, SHEILA and WEEKS, JEFFREY (1977) *Socialism and the New Life: The Personal and Sexual Politics of Edward Carpenter and Havelock Ellis*, London: Pluto Press.

RUEHL, SONJA (1983) *The Changing Experience of Women: Unit 4: Sexuality*, Milton Keynes: Open University Press.

SAHLI, NANCY (1979) 'Smashing: Women's Relationships Before the Fall', *Chrysalis*, 8.

SANGER, MARGARET (1926) *Happiness in Marriage*, New York: Brentano.

SARAH, ELIZABETH (1983) 'Christabel Pankhurst: Reclaiming her Power', in SPENDER (1983).

SCHREINER, OLIVE (1978 [1911]) *Woman and Labour*, London: Virago.

SHOWALTER, ELAINE (1978) *A Literature of Their Own*, London: Virago.

SHULMAN, ALIX KATES (1980) 'Sex and Power: Sexual Bases of Radical Feminism', *Signs*, 5 (4).

SMITH-ROSENBERG, CARROLL (1975) 'The Female World of Love and Ritual: Relations Between Women in 19th Century America', *Signs*, 1 (1).

SNITOW, ANN, STANSELL, CHRISTINE, and THOMPSON, SHARON (Eds) (1984) *Desire: The Politics of Sexuality*, London: Virago.

SNOWDEN, ETHEL (1911) *The Feminist Movement*, London: Collins.

SPENDER, DALE (1982) *Women of Ideas and What Men have Done to them: From Aphra Behn to Adrienne Rich*, London: Routledge and Kegan Paul.

SPENDER, DALE (Ed.) (1983) *Feminist Theorists: Three Centuries of Women's Intellectual Traditions*, London: The Women's Press.

STEKEL, WILHELM (1926) *Frigidity in Woman in Relation to her Love Life*, New York: Livewright.

STOPES, MARIE C. (1918a) *Married Love: A New Contribution to the Solution of Sex Difficulties*, London: A.C. Fifield.

STOPES, MARIE C. (1918b) *Wise Parenthood*, London: A.C. Fifield.

STOPES, MARIE C. (1926) *Sex and the Young*, London: Gill Publishing Co.

STOPES, MARIE C. (1928) *Enduring Passion: Further New Contributions to the Solution of Sex Difficulties*, London: Putnam.

STOPES, MARIE C. (Ed.) (1929) *Mother England*, London: John Bale and Danielson.

STOPES, MARIE C. (1935) *Marriage in My Time*, London: Rich and Cowan.

STOPES, MARIE C. (1939) 'Havelock Ellis', *Literary Guide*, September.

STRACHEY, RAY (1978 [1928]) *The Cause: A Short History of the Women's Movement in Great Britain*, London: Virago.

STRACHEY, RAY (Ed.) (1936) *Our Freedom and Its Results by Five Women*, London: Hogarth Press.

SWANWICK, HELENA M. (1918) 'Committee of Inquiry into Sexual Morality', reprinted in JEFFREYS (1987).

SWINEY, FRANCES (1908) *The Mystery of the Circle and the Cross Or The Interpretation of Sex*, London: Open Road Publishing.

SWINEY, FRANCES (n.d). 'Man's Necessity', *Racial Problems*, no. 2.

SWINEY, FRANCES (1912 [1907]) *The Bar of Isis or The Law of the Mother*, London: C.W. Daniel.

SWINEY, FRANCES (1912) *Woman and Natural Law*, London: C.W. Daniel.

TAYLOR, BARBARA (1983) *Eve and the New Jerusalem: Socialism and Feminism in the Nineteenth Century*, London: Virago.

TAYLOR, HARRIET (1851) 'The Emancipation of Women', *Westminster Review*, LX, pp. 150–61 (published anonymously).

TAYLOR, MARY (1870) 'Redundant Women', *Victoria Magazine*, June.

UGLOW, JENNY (1983) 'Josephine Butler: From Sympathy to Theory', in SPENDER (1983).

VANCE, CAROLE S. (Ed.) (1984) *Pleasure and Danger: Exploring Female Sexuality*, London: Routledge and Kegan Paul.

VAN DE VELDE, THEODOOR (1928) *Ideal Marriage: Its Physiology and Technique*, London: Heinemann.

VAN DE VELDE, THEODOOR (1931) *Sex Hostility in Marriage*, London: Heinemann.

VICINUS, MARTHA (Ed.) (1972) *Suffer and Be Still: Women in the Victorian Age*, Bloomington: Indiana University Press.

VICINUS, MARTHA (Ed.) (1977) *A Widening Sphere: Changing Roles of Victorian Women*, Bloomington: Indiana University Press.

WALKER, KENNETH (1935) *Sex and a Changing Civilization*, London: John Lane, Th. Bodley Head.

WALKOWITZ, JUDITH (1980) *Prostitution and Victorian Society: Women, Class and the State*, Cambridge: Cambridge University Press.

WALKOWITZ, JUDITH (1982) 'Male Vice and Feminist Virtue: Feminism and the Politics of Prostitution in Nineteenth-Century Britain', *History Workshop*, 13, pp. 79–93.

WALKOWITZ, JUDITH (1986) 'Science, Feminism and Romance: The Men and Women's Club 1885–1889', *History Workshop*, 21, pp. 36–59.

WALLSGROVE, RUTH (1980) 'The Masculine Face of Science', in BRIGHTON WOMEN AND SCIENCE GROUP (1980).

WALTERS, MARGARET (1976) 'The Rights and Wrongs of Women: Mary Wollstonecraft, Harriet Martineau and Simone de Beauvoir', in MITCHELL and OAKLEY (1976).

WEEKS, JEFFREY (1977) *Coming Out: Homosexual Politics in Britain from the Nineteenth Century to the Present*, London: Quartet.

WEEKS, JEFFREY (1981) *Sex, Politics and Society: The Regulation of Sexuality since 1800*, London: Longmans.

WEEKS, JEFFREY (1982) 'The Development of Sexual Theory and Sexual Politics', in BRAKE (1982).

WEEKS, JEFFREY (1985) *Sexuality and its Discontents: Meanings, Myths and Modern Sexualities*, London: Routledge.

WHITELAW, LIS (1990) *The Life and Rebellious Times of Cicely Hamilton: Actress, Writer, Suffragist*, London: The Women's Press.

WOLLSTONECRAFT, MARY (1967 [1792]) *A Vindication of the Rights of Woman*, New York: Norton.

WOLSTENHOLME ELMY, ELIZABETH C. [Ellis Ethelmer] (1892) *The Human Flower*, Congleton: Women's Emancipation Union.

WOLSTENHOLME ELMY, ELIZABETH C. [Ellis Ethelmer] (1893) *Woman Free*, Congleton: Women's Emancipation Union.

WOLSTENHOLME ELMY, ELIZABETH C. (1897) *Phases of Love*, Congleton: Women's Emancipation Union.

WOLSTENHOLME ELMY, ELIZABETH C. [Ignota] (1898) 'Judicial Sex Bias', *Westminster Review*.

WRIGHT, ALMOTH E. (1913) *The Unexpurgated Case Against Woman Suffrage*, London: Constable.

WRIGHT, HELENA (1930) *The Sex Factor in Marriage*, London: Williams and Northgate.

WRIGHT, HELENA (1947) *More About the Sex Factor in Marriage*, London: Williams and Northgate.

Index